Cambridge, Massachusetts

Monica Sullivan

Contents

References

Overview of Cambridge, MA

Cambridge, Massachusetts

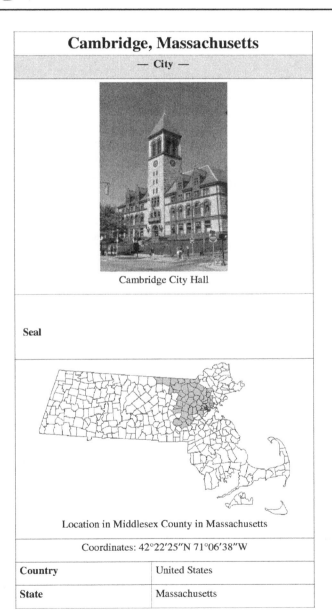

Cambridge, Massachusetts	
— City —	
Cambridge City Hall	
Seal	
Location in Middlesex County in Massachusetts	
Coordinates: 42°22′25″N 71°06′38″W	
Country	United States
State	Massachusetts

County	Middlesex
Settled	1630
Incorporated	1636
Government	
- Type	Council-City Manager
- Mayor	David P. Maher
- City Manager	Robert W. Healy
Area	
- Total	7.13 sq mi (18.47 km^2)
- Land	6.43 sq mi (16.65 km^2)
- Water	0.70 sq mi (1.81 km^2)
Elevation	40 ft (12 m)
Population (2008)	
- Total	105,594 (est'd.)
- Density	16,422.08/sq mi (6,341.98/km^2)
- Demonym	Cantabrigian
Time zone	Eastern (UTC-5)
- Summer (DST)	Eastern (UTC-4)
ZIP code	02138, 02139, 02140, 02141, 02142
Area code(s)	617 / 857
FIPS code	25-11000
GNIS feature ID	0617365
Website	www.cambridgema.gov [1]

Cambridge is a city in Middlesex County, Massachusetts, United States, in the Greater Boston area. It was named in honor of the University of Cambridge in England, a nexus of the Puritan theology embraced by the town's founders. Cambridge is home to two internationally prominent universities, Harvard University and the Massachusetts Institute of Technology. According to a 2008 census estimate the city population was 105,594. It is the fourth most populous city in the state, behind Boston, Worcester, and Springfield. Cambridge is one of the two county seats of Middlesex County (Lowell is the other).

A resident of Cambridge is known as a *Cantabrigian*.

History

The site for what would become Cambridge was chosen in December 1630, because it was located safely up river from Boston Harbor, which made it easily defensible from attacks by enemy ships. Also, the water from the local spring was so good that the local Natives believed it had medicinal properties.[citation needed] The first houses were built in the spring of 1631. The settlement was initially referred to as "the newe towne". Official Massachusetts records show the name capitalized as **Newe Towne** by 1632. Located at the first convenient Charles River crossing west of Boston, Newe Towne was one of a number of towns (including Boston, Dorchester, Watertown, and Weymouth) founded by the 700 original Puritan colonists of the Massachusetts Bay Colony under governor John Winthrop. The original village site is in the heart of today's Harvard Square. The marketplace where farmers brought in crops from surrounding towns to sell survives today as the small park at the corner of John F. Kennedy (J.F.K.) and Winthrop Streets, then at the edge of a salt marsh, since filled. The town included a much larger area than the present city, with various outlying parts becoming independent towns over the years: Newton (originally Cambridge Village, then Newtown) in 1688, Lexington (Cambridge Farms) in 1712, and both West Cambridge (originally Menotomy) and Brighton (Little Cambridge) in 1807. West Cambridge was later renamed Arlington, in 1867, and Brighton was later annexed by Boston, in 1874. In the late 19th century, various schemes for annexing Cambridge itself to the City of Boston were pursued and rejected.

In 1636 Harvard College was founded by the colony to train ministers and the new town was chosen for its site by Thomas Dudley. By 1638 the name "Newe Towne" had "compacted by usage into 'Newtowne'." In May 1638 the name was changed to **Cambridge** in honor of the university in Cambridge, England. The first president (Henry Dunster), the first benefactor (John Harvard), and the first schoolmaster (Nathaniel Eaton) of Harvard were all Cambridge University alumni, as was the then ruling (and first) governor of the Massachusetts Bay Colony, John Winthrop. In 1629, Winthrop had led the signing of the founding document of the city of Boston, which was known as the Cambridge Agreement, after the university. It was Governor Thomas Dudley who in 1650 signed the charter creating the corporation which still governs Harvard College.

Cambridge grew slowly as an agricultural village eight miles (13 km) by road from Boston, the capital of the colony. By the American Revolution, most residents lived near the Common and Harvard College, with farms and estates comprising most of the town. Most of the inhabitants were descendants of the original Puritan colonists, but there was also a small elite of Anglican "worthies" who were not involved in village life, who made their livings from estates, investments, and trade, and lived in mansions along "the Road to Watertown" (today's Brattle Street, still known as Tory Row). In 1775, George Washington came up from Virginia to take command of fledgling volunteer American soldiers camped on the Cambridge Common — today called the birthplace of the U.S. Army. (The name of today's nearby Sheraton Commander Hotel refers to that event.) Most of the Tory estates were confiscated after the Revolution. On January 24, 1776, Henry Knox arrived with artillery captured from

Fort Ticonderoga, which enabled Washington to drive the British army out of Boston.

Between 1790 and 1840, Cambridge began to grow rapidly, with the construction of the West Boston Bridge in 1792, that connected Cambridge directly to Boston, making it no longer necessary to travel eight miles (13 km) through the Boston Neck, Roxbury, and Brookline to cross the Charles River. A second bridge, the Canal Bridge, opened in 1809 alongside the new Middlesex Canal. The new bridges and roads made what were formerly estates and marshland into prime industrial and residential districts.

In the mid-19th century, Cambridge was the center of a literary revolution when it gave the country a new identity through poetry and literature. Cambridge was home to the famous Fireside Poets—so called because their poems would often be read aloud by families in front of their evening fires. In their day, the Fireside Poets—Henry Wadsworth Longfellow, James Russell Lowell, and Oliver Wendell Holmes—were as popular and influential as rock stars are today.[citation needed]

Soon after, turnpikes were built: the Cambridge and Concord Turnpike (today's Broadway and Concord Ave.), the Middlesex Turnpike (Hampshire St. and Massachusetts Ave. northwest of Porter Square), and what are today's Cambridge, Main, and Harvard Streets were roads to connect various areas of Cambridge to the bridges. In addition, railroads crisscrossed the town during the same era, leading to the development of Porter Square as well as the creation of neighboring town Somerville from the formerly rural parts of Charlestown.

Cambridge was incorporated as a city in 1846. Its commercial center also began to shift from Harvard Square to Central Square, which became the downtown of the city. Between 1850 and 1900, Cambridge took on much of its present character — streetcar suburban development along the turnpikes, with working-class and industrial neighborhoods focused on East Cambridge, comfortable middle-class housing being built on old estates in Cambridgeport and Mid-Cambridge, and upper-class enclaves near Harvard University and on the minor hills of the city. The coming of the railroad to North Cambridge and Northwest Cambridge then led to three major changes in the city: the development of massive brickyards and brickworks between Massachusetts Ave., Concord Ave. and Alewife Brook; the ice-cutting industry launched by Frederic Tudor on Fresh Pond; and the carving up of the last estates into

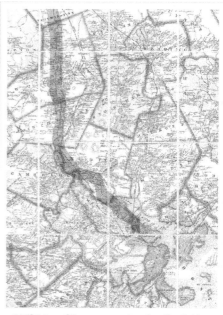

1852 Map of Boston area showing Cambridge and rail lines.

residential subdivisions to provide housing to the thousands of immigrants that arrived to work in the new industries.

For many years, the city's largest employer was the New England Glass Company, founded in 1818. By the middle of the 19th century it was the largest and most modern glassworks in the world. In 1888, all production was moved, by Edmund Drummond Libbey, to Toledo, Ohio, where it continues today under the name Owens Illinois. Flint glassware with heavy lead content, produced by that company, is prized by antique glass collectors. There is none on public display in Cambridge, but there is a large collection in the Toledo Museum of Art.

Among the largest businesses located in Cambridge was the firm of Carter's Ink Company, whose neon sign long adorned the Charles River and which was for many years the largest manufacturer of ink in the world.

By 1920, Cambridge was one of the main industrial cities of New England, with nearly 120,000 residents. As industry in New England began to decline during the Great Depression and after World War II, Cambridge lost much of its industrial base. It also began the transition to being an intellectual, rather than an industrial, center. Harvard University had always been important in the city (both as a landowner and as an institution), but it began to play a more dominant role in the city's life and culture. Also, the move of the Massachusetts Institute of Technology from Boston in 1912 ensured Cambridge's status as an intellectual center of the United States.

After the 1950s, the city's population began to decline slowly, as families tended to be replaced by single people and young couples. The 1980s brought a wave of high technology start-ups, creating software such as Visicalc and Lotus 1-2-3, and advanced computers, but many of these companies fell into decline with the fall of the minicomputer and DOS-based systems. However, the city continues to be home to many startups as well as a thriving biotech industry. By the end of the 20th century, Cambridge had one of the most expensive housing markets in the Northeastern United States.

While maintaining much diversity in class, race, and age, it became harder and harder for those who grew up in the city to be able to afford to stay. The end of rent control in 1994 prompted many Cambridge renters to move to housing that was more affordable, in Somerville and other communities. In 2005, a reassessment of residential property values resulted in a disproportionate number of houses owned by non-affluent people jumping in value relative to other houses, with hundreds having their property tax increased by over 100%; this forced many homeowners in Cambridge to move elsewhere.

As of 2006, Cambridge's mix of amenities and proximity to Boston has kept housing prices relatively stable.

Geography

Cambridge is located at 42°22′25″N 71°6′38″W.

According to the United States Census Bureau, the city has a total area of 7.1 square miles (18.5 km²), of which 6.4 square miles (16.7 km²) of it is land and 0.7 square miles (1.8 km²) of it (9.82%) is water.

Adjacent towns

Cambridge is located in eastern Massachusetts, bordered by:

- the city of Boston to the south (across the Charles River) and east
- the city of Somerville to the north
- the town of Arlington to the northwest
- the town of Belmont and
- the city of Watertown to the west

A view from Boston of Harvard's Weld Boathouse and Cambridge in winter. The Charles River is in the foreground.

The border between Cambridge and the neighboring city of Somerville passes through densely populated neighborhoods which are connected by the MBTA Red Line. Some of the main squares, Inman, Porter, and to a lesser extent, Harvard, are very close to the city line, as are Somerville's Union and Davis Squares.

Neighborhoods

Squares

Cambridge has been called the "City of Squares" by some,Wikipedia:Avoid weasel words as most of its commercial districts are major street intersections known as squares. Each of the squares acts as something of a neighborhood center. These include:

- Kendall Square, formed by the junction of Broadway, Main Street, and Third Street, is also known as "Technology Square," a name shared with an office and laboratory building cluster in the neighborhood. Just over the Longfellow Bridge from Boston, at the eastern end of

Central Square

the MIT campus, it is served by an MBTA Red Line
station. Most of Cambridge's large office towers are
located here, giving the area somewhat of an office park
feel. A flourishing biotech industry has grown up around
this area. The "One Kendall Square" complex is nearby,
but—confusingly—not actually in Kendall Square.

Harvard Square

- Central Square, formed by the junction of Massachusetts
  Avenue, Prospect Street, and Western Avenue and is
  well-known for its wide variety of ethnic restaurants. Even
  as recently as the late 1990s it was rather run-down; it
  underwent a controversial gentrification in recent years (in
  conjunction with the development of the nearby University
  Park at MIT), and continues to grow more expensive. It is
  served by a Red Line station. *Lafayette Square*, formed by
  the junction of Massachusetts Avenue, Columbia Street,
  Sidney Street, and Main Street, is considered a part of the

Inman Square

Central Square area. Cambridgeport is south of Central Square along Magazine Street and Brookline
Street.

- Harvard Square, formed by the junction of Massachusetts Avenue, Brattle Street, and JFK Street.
  This is the primary site of Harvard University, and is a major Cambridge shopping area (although
  not as exclusively so as in years past). It is served by a Red Line station. Harvard Square was
  originally the northwestern terminus of the Red Line and a major transfer point to streetcars that also
  operated in a short tunnel – which is still a major bus terminal, although the area under the Square
  was reconfigured dramatically in the 1980s when the Red Line was extended. The Harvard Square
  area includes Brattle Square and Eliot Square. A short distance away from the square lies the
  Cambridge Common, while the neighborhood north of Harvard and east of Massachusetts Avenue is
  known as Agassiz in honor of the famed scientist Louis Agassiz.
- Porter Square, about a mile north on Massachusetts Avenue from Harvard Square, is formed by the
  junction of Massachusetts and Somerville Avenues, and includes part of the city of Somerville. It is
  served by the Porter Square station, a complex housing a Red Line stop and a Fitchburg Line
  commuter rail stop. Lesley University's University Hall and Porter campus are located at Porter
  Square.
- Inman Square, at the junction of Cambridge and Hampshire streets in Mid-Cambridge. Inman
  Square is home to many diverse restaurants, bars and boutiques. The funky street scene still holds
  some urban flair, but was dressed up recently with Victorian streetlights, benches and bus stops. A
  new community park was installed and is a favorite place to enjoy some takeout food from the
  nearby restaurants and ice cream parlor.

- Lechmere Square, at the junction of Cambridge and First streets, adjacent to the CambridgeSide Galleria shopping mall. Perhaps best known as the northern terminus of the MBTA Green Line subway.

Other neighborhoods

The residential neighborhoods (map [2]) in Cambridge border, but are not defined by the squares. These include:

- East Cambridge (Area 1) is bordered on the north by the Somerville border, on the east by the Charles River, on the south by Broadway and Main Street, and on the west by the Grand Junction Railroad tracks. It includes the NorthPoint development.
- MIT Campus (Area 2) is bordered on the north by Broadway, on the south and east by the Charles River, and on the west by the Grand Junction Railroad tracks.
- Wellington-Harrington (Area 3) is bordered on the north by the Somerville border, on the south and west by Hampshire Street, and on the east by the Grand Junction Railroad tracks.
- Area 4 is bordered on the north by Hampshire Street, on the south by Massachusetts Avenue, on the west by Prospect Street, and on the east by the Grand Junction Railroad tracks. Residents of Area 4 often refer to their neighborhood simply as "The Port", and refer to the area of Cambridgeport and Riverside as "The Coast".
- Cambridgeport (Area 5) is bordered on the north by Massachusetts Avenue, on the south by the Charles River, on the west by River Street, and on the east by the Grand Junction Railroad tracks.
- Mid-Cambridge (Area 6) is bordered on the north by Kirkland and Hampshire Streets and the Somerville border, on the south by Massachusetts Avenue, on the west by Peabody Street, and on the east by Prospect Street.
- Riverside (Area 7), an area sometimes referred to as "The Coast", is bordered on the north by Massachusetts Avenue, on the south by the Charles River, on the west by JFK Street, and on the east by River Street.
- Agassiz (Harvard North) (Area 8) is bordered on the north by the Somerville border, on the south and east by Kirkland Street, and on the west by Massachusetts Avenue.
- Peabody (Area 9) is bordered on the north by railroad tracks, on the south by Concord Avenue, on the west by railroad tracks, and on the east by Massachusetts Avenue. The Avon Hill sub-neighborhood consists of the higher elevations bounded by Upland Road, Raymond Street, Linnaean Street and Massachusetts Avenue.
- Brattle area/West Cambridge (Area 10) is bordered on the north by Concord Avenue and Garden Street, on the south by the Charles River and the Watertown border, on the west by Fresh Pond and the Collins Branch Library, and on the east by JFK Street. It includes the sub-neighborhoods of Brattle Street and Huron Village.
- North Cambridge (Area 11) is bordered on the north by the Arlington and Somerville borders, on the south by railroad tracks, on the west by the Belmont border, and on the east by the Somerville

border.

- Cambridge Highlands (Area 12) is bordered on the north and east by railroad tracks, on the south by Fresh Pond, and on the west by the Belmont border.
- Strawberry Hill, also known as West Cambridge (Area 13), is bordered on the north by Fresh Pond, on the south by the Watertown border, on the west by the Belmont border, and on the east by railroad tracks.

Parks and outdoors

Consisting largely of densely built residential space, Cambridge lacks significant tracts of public parkland. This is partly compensated for, however, by the presence of easily accessible open space on the university campuses, including Harvard Yard and MIT's Great Lawn, as well as the considerable open space of Mount Auburn Cemetery. At the western edge of Cambridge, the cemetery is well known as the first garden cemetery, for its distinguished inhabitants, for its superb landscaping (the oldest planned landscape in the

Alewife Brook

country), and as a first-rate arboretum. Although known as a Cambridge landmark, much of the cemetery lies within the bounds of Watertown. It is also a significant Important Bird Area (IBA) in the Greater Boston area.

Public parkland includes the esplanade along the Charles River, which mirrors its Boston counterpart, Cambridge Common, a busy and historic public park immediately adjacent to the Harvard campus, and the Alewife Brook Reservation and Fresh Pond in the western part of the city.

Demographics

Census	Pop.	%±
1790	2115	—
1800	2453	16.0%
1810	2323	−5.3%
1820	3295	41.8%
1830	6072	84.3%
1840	8409	38.5%
1850	15215	80.9%
1860	26060	71.3%

1870	39634	52.1%
1880	52669	32.9%
1890	70028	33.0%
1900	91886	31.2%
1910	104839	14.1%
1920	109694	4.6%
1930	113643	3.6%
1940	110879	−2.4%
1950	120740	8.9%
1960	107716	−10.8%
1970	100361	−6.8%
1980	95322	−5.0%
1990	95802	0.5%
2000	101355	5.8%
Est. 2008	105594	4.2%

As of the census of 2000, there were 101,355 people, 42,615 households, and 17,599 families residing in the city. The population density was 15,766.1 people per square mile (6,086.1/km²), making Cambridge the fifth most densely populated city in the U.S. and the second most densely populated city in Massachusetts behind neighboring Somerville. There were 44,725 housing units at an average density of 6,957.1/sq mi (2,685.6/km²). The racial makeup of the city was 68.10% White, 11.92% Black or African American, 0.29% Native American, 11.88% Asian, 0.08% Pacific Islander, 3.19% from other races, and 4.56% from two or more races. 7.36% of the population were Hispanic or Latino of any race. This rather closely parallels the average racial demographics of the United States as a whole, although Cambridge has significantly more Asians than the average, and fewer Hispanics and Caucasians. 11.0% were of Irish, 7.2% English, 6.9% Italian, 5.5% West Indian and 5.3% German ancestry according to Census 2000. 69.4% spoke English, 6.9% Spanish, 3.2% Chinese or Mandarin, 3.0% Portuguese, 2.9% French Creole, 2.3% French, 1.5% Korean and 1.0% Italian as their first language.

There were 42,615 households out of which 17.6% had children under the age of 18 living with them, 29.1% were married couples living together, 9.7% had a female householder with no husband present, and 58.7% were non-families. 41.4% of all households were made up of individuals and 9.2% had someone living alone who was 65 years of age or older. The average household size was 2.03 and the average family size was 2.83.

In the city the population was spread out with 13.3% under the age of 18, 21.2% from 18 to 24, 38.6% from 25 to 44, 17.8% from 45 to 64, and 9.2% who were 65 years of age or older. The median age was 30 years. For every 100 females there were 96.1 males. For every 100 females age 18 and over, there were 94.7 males.

The median income for a household in the city was $47,979, and the median income for a family was $59,423 (these figures had risen to $58,457 and $79,533 respectively as of a 2007 estimate). Males had a median income of $43,825 versus $38,489 for females. The per capita income for the city was $31,156. About 8.7% of families and 12.9% of the population were below the poverty line, including 15.1% of those under age 18 and 12.9% of those age 65 or over.

Cambridge was ranked as one of the most liberal cities in America. Its residents jokingly refer to it as "The People's Republic of Cambridge." Its FY 2007 residential property tax rate, $7.48 per $1000 of assessed valuation, is one of the lowest in Massachusetts. Cambridge enjoys the highest possible bond credit rating, AAA, with all three Wall Street rating agencies.

Cambridge is noted for its diverse population, both racially and economically. Residents, known as *Cantabrigians*, range from affluent MIT and Harvard professors to working-class families to immigrants. The first legal applications in America for same-sex marriage licenses were issued at Cambridge's City Hall.

Cambridge is also the birthplace of Thai king Bhumibol Adulyadej (Rama IX), who is the world's longest reigning monarch at age 82 (2010) as well as the longest reigning monarch in Thai history. He is also the first king of a foreign country to be born in the United States.

Government

State and federal representation

Voter Registration and Party Enrollment as of October 15, 2008		
Party	Number of Voters	Percentage
Democratic	37,822	58.43%
Republican	3,280	5.07%
Unaffiliated	22,935	35.43%
Minor Parties	690	1.07%
Total	64,727	100%

Federally, Cambridge is part of Massachusetts's 8th congressional district, represented by Democrat Mike Capuano, elected in 1998.

The state's senior member of the United States Senate is Democrat John Kerry, elected in 1984. The state's junior member of the United States Senate is Republican Scott Brown, elected in 2010 to fill the vacancy caused by the death of long-time Democratic Senator Ted Kennedy. The Governor of Massachusetts is Democrat Deval Patrick, elected in 2006; he is up for re-election in 2010.

On the state level, Cambridge is represented in six districts in the Massachusetts House of Representatives: the Twenty-fourth Middlesex (which includes parts of Belmont and Arlington), the Twenty-fifth and Twenty-sixth Middlesex (the latter which includes a portion of Somerville), the Twenty-ninth Middlesex (which includes a small part of Watertown), and the Eighth and Ninth Suffolk (both including parts of the City of Boston). The city is represented in the Massachusetts Senate as a part of the "First Suffolk and Middlesex" district (this contains parts of Boston, Revere and Winthrop each in Suffolk County); the "Middlesex, Suffolk and Essex" district, which includes Everett and Somerville, with Boston, Chelsea, and Revere of Suffolk, and Saugus in Essex; and the "Second Suffolk and Middlesex" district, containing parts of the City of Boston in Suffolk county, and Cambridge, Belmont and Watertown in Middlesex county. In addition to the Cambridge Police Department the city is patrolled by the Fifth (Brighton) Barracks of Troop H of the Massachusetts State Police Due however to close proximity, the city also practices functional cooperation with the Fourth (Boston) Barracks of Troop H also.

City government

Cambridge has a city government led by a Mayor and nine-member City Council. There is also a six-member School Committee which functions along side the Superintendent of public schools. The councilors and school committee members are elected every two years using the single transferable vote (STV) system. Since the disbanding of the New York City Community School Boards in 2002, Cambridge's Council is now unusual in being the only governing body in the United States to still use STV. Once a laborious process that took several days to complete by hand, ballot sorting and calculations to determine the outcome of elections are now quickly performed by computer, after the ballots have been optically scanned.

The mayor is elected by the city councilors from amongst themselves, and serves as the chair of City Council meetings. The mayor also sits on the School Committee. However, the Mayor is not the Chief Executive of the City. Rather, the City Manager, who is appointed by the City Council, serves in that capacity.

Under the City's Plan E form of government the city council does not have the power to appoint or remove city officials who are under direction of the city manager. The city council and its individual members are also forbidden from giving orders to any subordinate of the city manager.

Currently, Robert W. Healy is the City Manager; he has served in the position since 1981. The city council consists of:

City Council
• Leland Cheung
• Henrietta Davis
• Marjorie C. Decker
• Craig A. Kelley
• David Maher
• Kenneth Reeves
• Sam Seidel
• E. Denise Simmons
• Timothy J. Toomey, Jr.

Fire Department

Gerald R. Reardon is the chief of the Cambridge Fire Department. John J. Gelinas, the chief of operations, is in charge of day to day operation of the department. The Cambridge Fire Department is rated as a class 1 fire department by the Insurance Services Office (ISO), and is one of only 32 fire departments so rated, out of 37,000 departments in the United States. The other class 1 departments in New England are in Hartford, Connecticut and Milford, Connecticut. Class 1 signifies the highest level of fire protection according to various criteria.

The Cambridge Fire Department is a professional fire department which protects the city of Cambridge 24 hours a day, 7 days a week. It operates out of eight city-wide firehouses in two divisions (downtown and uptown), and has a frontline fire apparatus fleet of 11 engine companies (two of which are reserve engines), five ladder companies (one of which is a reserve ladder), a tactical rescue unit, a "hazmat" unit, a dive rescue unit, two marine units, and two non-transporting paramedic ambulances.

Water Department

Cambridge is unusual among cities inside Route 128 in having a non-MWRA water supply. City water is obtained from Hobbs Brook (in Lincoln and Waltham), Stony Brook (Waltham and Weston), and Fresh Pond (Cambridge). Water is treated at Fresh Pond, then pumped uphill to an elevation of 176 feet above sea level at the Payson Park Reservoir (Belmont); From there, the water is redistributed downhill via gravity to individual users in the city.

County government

Cambridge is a county seat of Middlesex County, Massachusetts, along with Lowell. Though the county government was abolished in 1997, the county still exists as a geographical and political region. The employees of Middlesex County courts, jails, registries, and other county agencies now work directly for the state. At present the county's registrars of Deeds and Probate remain in Cambridge, however the Superior Court and District Attorney have had their base of operations transferred to Woburn. Third District court has shifted operations to Medford, and the Sheriff's office for the county is still awaiting a near-term relocation.

Education

Higher education

Cambridge is perhaps best known as an academic and intellectual center, owing to its colleges and universities, which include:

Aerial view of part of MIT's main campus

- Cambridge College
- Cambridge School of Culinary Arts
- Episcopal Divinity School
- Harvard University
- Hult International Business School
- Lesley University
- Longy School of Music
- Massachusetts Institute of Technology
- Le Cordon Bleu College of Culinary Arts in Boston

At least 129 of the world's total 780 Nobel Prize winners have been, at some point in their careers, affiliated with universities in Cambridge.

The American Academy of Arts and Sciences is also based in Cambridge.

Primary and secondary public education

The Cambridge Public School District encompasses twelve elementary schools that follow a variety of different educational systems and philosophies. All but one of the elementary schools extend up to the junior high school grades as well. The twelve elementary schools are:

Dunster House, Harvard

- Amigos School
- Baldwin School
- Cambridgeport School
- Fletcher-Maynard Academy

- Graham and Parks Alternative School
- Haggerty School
- Kennedy-Longfellow School
- King Open School
- Martin Luther King, Jr. School
- Morse School (a Core Knowledge school)
- Peabody School
- Tobin School (a Montessori school)

The sole public high school in the Cambridge Public School District is the Cambridge Rindge and Latin School.

In recent years the school system has struggled to increase its performance. In 2003 the high school came close to losing its educational accreditation when it was placed on probation by the New England Association of Schools and Colleges.

Then in 2005, the public school system's then Superintendent Thomas Fowler-Finn stated that the Cambridge school system ranked 311th out of the 373 Massachusetts school districts, on the statewide MCAS exams required for high school student graduation. Despite these setbacks the high school was taken off academic probation.

Outside of the main public schools are charter schools including: Benjamin Banneker Charter School, the Community Charter School of Cambridge, located in East Cambridge, and Prospect Hill Academy, a charter school whose upper school is in Central Square, though it is not a part of the Cambridge Public School District.

Primary and secondary private education

There are also many private schools in the city including:

- Boston Archdiocesan Choir School (BACS)
- Buckingham Browne & Nichols (BB&N)
- Cambridge Montessori School
- Cambridge Friends School. Thomas Waring served as the founding headmaster of the school.
- Fayerweather Street School [3] (FSS)

Cambridge Public Library

- International School of Boston (ISB, formerly École Bilingue)
- Matignon High School
- North Cambridge Catholic High School
- Shady Hill School
- St. Peter School

Economy

Manufacturing was an important part of the economy in the late 19th and early 20th century, but educational institutions are the city's biggest employers today. Both Harvard and MIT together employ about 20,000. As a cradle of technological innovation, Cambridge was home to such legendary technology firms as Analog Devices, Akamai, Bolt, Beranek, and Newman (BBN Technologies) (now part of Raytheon), General Radio (later GenRad), Lotus Development Corporation (now part of IBM), Polaroid, Symbolics, Thinking Machines, and VMware.[citation needed]

Buildings of Kendall Square, center of Cambridge's biotech economy, seen from the Charles River

Over the years, most of these tech companies either have grown and moved away or declined and closed their businesses; see this list [4] for more information. In 1996, Polaroid, Arthur D. Little, and Lotus were all top employers with over 1,000 employees in Cambridge, but declined or disappeared a few years later. In 2005, alongside Harvard and MIT, health care and biotechnology firms such as Genzyme, Biogen Idec, and Novartis dominate the city economy. Biotech firms are located around Kendall Square and East Cambridge, which decades ago were the center of manufacturing. A number of biotechnology companies are also located in University Park at MIT, a new development in another former manufacturing area. None of the high technology firms that once dominated the economy was among the 25 largest employers in 2005, but by 2008 Akamai and ITA Software had grown to be among the largest employers. Many smaller start-ups and IT companies nonetheless remain as important employers.[citation needed]

Google maintains an office in Cambridge, as does Microsoft Research. Video game developer Harmonix Music Systems is based in Central Square. The city is also the New England headquarters for Miramax Films and Time Warner Cable.

The proximity of Cambridge's universities has also made the city a center for nonprofit groups and think tanks, including the Lincoln Institute of Land Policy, Cultural Survival, and One Laptop per Child.

Transportation

See also: Boston transportation

Road

Several major roads lead to Cambridge, including Route 2, Route 16 and the McGrath Highway (Route 28). The Massachusetts Turnpike does not pass through Cambridge, but provides access by an exit in nearby Allston. Both U.S. Route 1 and I-93 (MA) also provide additional access on the eastern end of Cambridge at Leverett Circle in Boston. Route 2A runs the length of the city, chiefly along Massachusetts Avenue. The Charles River forms the southern border of Cambridge and is crossed by eleven bridges connecting Cambridge to Boston, including the Longfellow Bridge and the Harvard Bridge, eight of which are open to motorized road traffic.

Massachusetts Avenue in Harvard Square

Cambridge has an irregular street network because many of the roads date from the colonial era. Contrary to popular belief, the road system did not evolve from longstanding cow-paths. Roads connected various village settlements with each other and nearby towns, and were shaped by geographic features, most notably streams, hills, and swampy areas. Today, the major "squares" are typically connected by long, mostly straight roads, such as Massachusetts Avenue between Harvard Square and Central Square, or Hampshire Street between Kendall Square and Inman Square.

Mass transit

Cambridge is well served by the MBTA, including the Porter Square stop on the regional Commuter Rail, the Lechmere stop on the Green Line, and five stops on the Red Line (Alewife, Porter Square, Harvard Square, Central Square, and Kendall Square/MIT). Alewife Station, the current terminus of the Red Line, has a large multi-story parking garage (at a rate of $7 per day as of 2009). The Harvard Bus Tunnel, under Harvard Square, reduces traffic congestion on the surface, and connects to the Red Line underground. This tunnel was originally opened for streetcars in 1912, and served trackless trolleys and buses as the routes were converted. The tunnel was partially reconfigured when the Red Line was extended to Alewife in the early 1980s.

Central Red Line Station

Cycling

Cambridge has several bike paths, including one along the Charles River, and the Linear Park connecting the Minuteman Bikeway at Alewife with the Somerville Community Path. Bike parking is common and there are bike lanes on many streets, although concerns have been expressed regarding the suitability of many of the lanes. On several central MIT streets, bike lanes transfer onto the sidewalk. Cambridge bans cycling on certain sections of sidewalk where pedestrian traffic is heavy.

While *Bicycling Magazine* has rated Boston as one of the worst cities in the nation for bicycling (In their words, for "lousy roads, scarce and unconnected bike lanes and bike-friendly gestures from City Hall that go nowhere – such as hiring a bike coordinator in 2001, only to cut the position two years later"), it has listed Cambridge as an honorable mention as one of the best and was called by the magazine "Boston's Great Hope." Cambridge has an active, official bicycle committee.

Walking

Walking is a popular activity in Cambridge. Per year 2000 data, of the communities in the U.S. with more than 100,000 residents, Cambridge has the highest percentage of commuters who walk to work. Cambridge receives a "Walk Score" of 100 out of 100 possible points. Cambridge's major historic squares have been recently changed into a modern walking landscape, which has sparked a traffic calming program based on the needs of pedestrians rather than of motorists.

The Weeks Bridge provides a pedestrian-only connection between Boston and Cambridge over the Charles River

Intercity

Intercity transport is found in Boston, which is adjacent to Cambridge. Intercity buses and Amtrak stop at South Station in Boston, while Logan International Airport is located in East Boston across Boston Harbor from the downtown area. The MBTA also has numerous subway stations in Cambridge and nearby cities and towns that are shared with the regional commuter rail lines it operates.

Media

Newspapers

Cambridge is served by several weekly newspapers. The most prominent is the Cambridge Chronicle, which is also the oldest surviving weekly paper in the United States.

Radio

Cambridge is home to the following commercially licensed and college run radio stations:

Callsign	Frequency	City/town	Licensee	Format
WHRB	95.3 FM	Cambridge	Harvard Radio Broadcasting Co., Inc.	Musical variety
WJIB	740 AM	Cambridge	Bob Bittner Broadcasting	Adult Standards/Pop
WMBR	88.1 FM	Cambridge	Technology Broadcasting Corporation	College radio

Culture, art and architecture

Museums

- Harvard Art Museum, including the Busch-Reisinger Museum, a collection of Germanic art the Fogg Art Museum, a comprehensive collection of Western art, and the Arthur M. Sackler Museum, a collection of Middle East and Asian art
- Harvard Museum of Natural History, including the Glass Flowers collection
- Peabody Museum of Archaeology and Ethnology, Harvard
- Semitic Museum, Harvard
- MIT Museum
- List Visual Arts Center, MIT

Fogg Museum, Harvard

Public art

Cambridge has a large and varied collection of permanent public art, both on city property (managed by the Cambridge Arts Council), and on the campuses of Harvard and MIT. Temporary public artworks are displayed as part of the annual Cambridge River Festival on the banks of the Charles River, during winter celebrations in Harvard and Central Squares, and at university campus sites. An active tradition of street musicians and other performers in Harvard Square entertains an audience of tourists and local residents during the warmer months of the year. The performances are coordinated through a public process that has been developed collaboratively by the performers, city administrators, private organizations and business groups.

Architecture

Despite intensive urbanization during the late 19th century and 20th century, Cambridge has preserved an unusual number of historic buildings, including some dating to the 17th century. The city also contains an abundance of innovative contemporary architecture, largely built by Harvard and MIT.

The Longfellow National Historic Site

Notable historic buildings in the city include:

- The Asa Gray House (1810)
- Austin Hall, Harvard University (1882–84)
- Cambridge City Hall (1888–89)
- Cambridge Public Library (1888)
- Christ Church, Cambridge (1761)
- Cooper-Frost-Austin House (1689–1817)
- Elmwood House (1767), residence of the President of Harvard University
- First Church of Christ, Scientist (1924–30)
- The First Parish in Cambridge (1833)
- Harvard-Epworth United Methodist Church (1891–93)
- Harvard Lampoon Building (1909)
- The Hooper-Lee-Nichols House (1685–1850)
- Longfellow National Historic Site (1759), former home of poet Henry Wadsworth Longfellow
- The Memorial Church of Harvard University (1932)
- Memorial Hall, Harvard University (1870–77)
- Middlesex County Courthouse (1814–48)
- O'Reilly Spite House (1908), built to spite a neighbor who would not sell his adjacent land

Stata Center, MIT

See also: List of Registered Historic Places in Cambridge, Massachusetts

Contemporary architecture:

Simmons Hall, MIT

- Carpenter Center for the Visual Arts, Harvard, the only building by Le Corbusier in North America
- Kresge Auditorium, MIT, by Eero Saarinen
- MIT Chapel, by Eero Saarinen
- Stata Center, MIT, by Frank Gehry
- Simmons Hall, MIT, by Steven Holl

Sister cities

Cambridge has 8 active, official sister cities, and an unofficial relationship with Cambridge, England:

- Cambridge, England, UK (unofficial)
- Coimbra, Portugal
- Cienfuegos, Cuba
- Gaeta, Italy
- Galway, Co. Galway, Ireland
- Yerevan, Armenia
- San José Las Flores, El Salvador
- Tsukuba Science City, Japan
- Kraków, Poland

Ten other official sister city relationships are inactive: Dublin, Ireland; Ischia, Catania, and Florence, Italy; Kraków, Poland; Santo Domingo Oeste, Dominican Republic; Southwark, London, England; Yuseong, Daejeon, Korea; and Haidian, Beijing, China.

And One **Learning Cities**

- Yogjakarta City, Indonesia[citation needed]

Zip codes

- 02138—Harvard Square/West Cambridge
- 02139—Central Square/Inman Square/MIT
- 02140—Porter Square/North Cambridge
- 02141—East Cambridge
- 02142—Kendall Square

General references

- *History of Middlesex County, Massachusetts*, Volume 1 (A-H) [5], Volume 2 (L-W) [6] compiled by Samuel Adams Drake, published 1879-1880.
  - Cambridge article [7] by Rev. Edward Abbott in volume 1, pages 305-358.
- Eliot, Samuel Atkins. *A History of Cambridge, Massachusetts: 1630-1913*. Cambridge: The Cambridge Tribune, 1913.
- Paige, Lucius. *History of Cambridge, Massachusetts: 1630-1877*. Cambridge: The Riverside Press, 1877.
- Survey of Architectural History in Cambridge: Mid Cambridge, 1967, Cambridge Historical Commission, Cambridge, Mass.*[ISBN needed]*
- Survey of Architectural History in Cambridge: Cambridgeport, 1971 ISBN 0-262-53013-9, Cambridge Historical Commission, Cambridge, Mass.
- Survey of Architectural History in Cambridge: Old Cambridge, 1973 ISBN 0-262-53014-7, Cambridge Historical Commission, Cambridge, Mass.
- Survey of Architectural History in Cambridge: Northwest Cambridge, 1977 ISBN 0-262-53032-5, Cambridge Historical Commission, Cambridge, Mass.
- Survey of Architectural History in Cambridge: East Cambridge, 1988 (revised) ISBN 0-262-53078-3, Cambridge Historical Commission, Cambridge, Mass.
- Sinclair, Jill (April 2009). *Fresh Pond: The History of a Cambridge Landscape*. Cambridge, Mass.: MIT Press. ISBN 978-0-262-19591-1.

External links

- Official website [1]
- Cambridge Office for Tourism [8]
- Cambridge (Massachusetts) travel guide from Wikitravel
- Cambridge, Massachusetts [9] at the Open Directory Project

Maps

- Cambridge Maps [10]
- City of Cambridge Geographic Information System (GIS) [11]
- *1871 Atlas of Massachusetts*. [12] by Wall & Gray. Map of Massachusetts. [13] Map of Middlesex County. [14]
- Dutton, E.P. Chart of Boston Harbor and Massachusetts Bay with Map of Adjacent Country. [15] Published 1867. A good map of roads and rail lines around Cambridge.
- Cambridge Citymap – Community, Business, and Visitor Map. [16]
- Old USGS maps of Cambridge area. [17]

Cityscape of Cambridge - Neighborhoods

Kendall Square

Geographical coordinates: 42°21′44″N 71°5′3″W

Kendall Square is a neighborhood in Cambridge, Massachusetts, with the "square" itself at the intersection of Main Street, Broadway, Wadsworth Street, and Third Street (immediately to the east of the secondary entrance of the Kendall/MIT subway station). It may also refer to the broad business district that is east of Portland Street, northwest of the Charles River, north of MIT and south of Binney Street. The One Kendall Square complex is located half a mile to the west of the traditional location of Kendall Square, between Broadway and Binney Street (on the other side of which is the Kendall Square Theatre).

"Galaxy: Earth Sphere" sculpture, a Kendall Sq Landmark by Joe Davis, Fall 1989.

History

Kendall Square has been an important transportation hub since the construction of the West Boston Bridge in 1793, which provided the first direct wagon route from Boston to Cambridge. By 1810, the Broad Canal had been dug, which would connect with a system of smaller canals in this East Cambridge seaport area.

A casual view of Main Street, at Cambridge Center.

Kendall Square area from across the Charles River.

The area became a major industrial center in the nineteenth century, and by the beginning of the twentieth century was home to distilleries, electric power plants, soap and hosiery factories, and the Kendall Boiler and Tank Company (from which the square takes its name). When the Longfellow Bridge replaced the West Boston Bridge in 1907, it included provisions for a future rapid-transit subway link to Harvard Square and Boston (now the Red Line); the original Kendall subway station was opened in 1911. MIT moved to its new Cambridge campus, located south of Kendall Square between Main Street and Massachusetts Avenue, in 1915.

Kendall Square is more recently famous for the number of biotechnology and information technology firms which have chosen to locate there, lured by the proximity of the Massachusetts Institute of Technology (MIT) campus on the south side of Main Street. Many of these firms are in two high-level office complex parks: One Kendall Square and Technology Square, both about half a mile west of the traditional location of Kendall Square. The Cambridge Center development is closest to the Kendall Square intersection.

Restaurants in the area include The Friendly Toast, Cambridge Brewing Company and Legal Sea Foods, both popular for business gatherings. A food plaza on the first floor of the Marriott hotel, and food trucks parked in lots near the corner of Main and Vassar streets (lunch only), sell fast food at low prices, with a variety of cuisines (Asian, Italian, Mexican, etc.) to choose from.

In February of 2009, approximately 80 organizations based in Kendall Square came together to form the Kendall Square Association, with the goal of improving, promoting, and protecting this global center of learning and innovation.

Notable local entities

- Akamai Technologies
- Amgen
- Art Technology Group
- AT&T
- Biogen Idec
- Bitstream Inc.
- Broad Institute
- Cambridge Innovation Center
- Computer Sciences Corp.
- Charles Stark Draper Laboratory ("Draper Lab")
- Equity Residential (Third Square Apartments)
- EMC Corporation
- Endeca Technologies
- Forrester Research
- Genzyme
- Google
- HubSpot
- ITA Software
- John A. Volpe National Transportation Systems Center
- Massachusetts Institute of Technology
- Microsoft
- The MIT Press
- Moshe Safdie and Associates, Inc.
- Nokia
- Novell
- Novartis
- Pegasystems
- Schlumberger
- Sermo
- Verizon
- Vertex Pharmaceuticals
- VMware
- Whitehead Institute for Biomedical Research
- World Wide Web Consortium
- Yahoo

Resident diplomatic missions

See also: List of diplomatic missions in Cambridge, Massachusetts

- ⛉ British Consulate-General – 1 Memorial Drive, 15th Floor

Gallery

Global headquarters of Genzyme.

Global HQ of Akamai Technologies.

See also

- Kendall/MIT Station

External links

- Kendall Square Association [1]

Central Square (Cambridge)

Central Square Historic District	
U.S. National Register of Historic Places	
U.S. Historic District	
Central Square in August 2005	
Location:	Cambridge, Massachusetts
Coordinates:	42°21′54″N 71°6′13″W
Built/Founded:	1793
Architect:	Hartwell & Richardson; Et al.
Architectural style(s):	Late 19th And 20th Century Revivals, Late Victorian, Federal
Governing body:	U.S. POSTAL SERVICE
MPS:	Cambridge MRA
Added to NRHP:	March 2, 1990
NRHP Reference#:	90000128

Central Square is an area in Cambridge, Massachusetts centered around the junction of Massachusetts Avenue, Prospect Street and Western Avenue. Lafayette Square, formed by the junction of Massachusetts Avenue, Columbia Street, Sidney Street and Main Street, is also considered a part of the Central Square area. Harvard Square is to the northwest along Massachusetts Avenue, Inman Square is to the north along Prospect Street and Kendall Square is to the east along Main Street. The section of Central Square along Massachusetts Avenue between Clinton Street and Main Street is designated the "Central Square Historic District," and was added to the National Register of Historic Places on March 2, 1990.

Culture

Central Square is known for its wide variety of ethnic restaurants, churches, bars, and live music and theatre venues. It is gentrifying rapidly, and a number of upscale restaurants have opened in the Square. Many startups, including pharmaceutical, videogame and Internet companies, have moved research and office operations into the Square to take advantage of the proximity to MIT, Boston medical resources and relatively low costs. Some critics have claimed that the recent changes have diminished the Square's edge, as some of the older Square businesses such as Manray have closed. There is also a diverse array of houses of worship in the area, with Christ the King Presbyterian Church, First Baptist Church, Sts. Constantine & Helen Greek Orthodox Church, and other large historic congregations meeting near the Square.

History

Central Square's history has been marked by several waves of immigration. The original population of the Square included people of English and Canadian ancestry. Between 1850 and 1890, the Square attracted many Irish immigrants, and in the late Nineteenth Century also became home to many others from throughout Europe. Later waves of immigration included people from the West Indies, South America and Africa.

Central Square is also the original home of actor Ben Affleck and, since 1927, the Necco factory, which recently relocated to Revere, Massachusetts. The old Necco factory building in Cambridge is now used for labs by Novartis.

Geography and Transportation

Several Cambridge neighborhoods meet at Central Square. To the east, Area 4 lies on the north side of Massachusetts Avenue (aka "Mass Ave.") and Cambridgeport on the south side between Massachusetts Avenue and the Charles River. Both of these neighborhoods were once known as The Port or Old Port region of Cambridge. The area to the west and northwest of Central Square is known as Mid-Cambridge.

Central Square is accessible by the MBTA Red Line subway branch by the station named Central. The intersection of Massachusetts Avenue and Brookline in front of The Middle East in Central Square is named in honor of the late indie rock musician Mark Sandman, who often played there.

Central Square serves as the commercial center for the surrounding neighborhoods of Cambridgeport, Riverside, Mid Cambridge, Area 4 and MIT.

Local government services

Central Square is the seat of government in Cambridge - Cambridge City Hall, and the main branch of the Cambridge Post Office are located in this area. The Cambridge Police Department headquarters was formerly at 5 Western Avenue in the Central Square area however, between November, 2008 - March, 2009 it completed a relocation to a new facility at 125 Sixth Street, near Kendall Square.

Notable Central Square residents

- Ben Affleck, actor
- Ken Brown, filmmaker
- Lisa Crafts, animator
- Matt Damon, actor
- Patrick Ewing, athlete
- Vernon Grant, cartoonist
- John Forbes Nash, mathematician

Notable Central Square businesses

- GamerDNA
- Harmonix Music Systems
- The Middle East (nightclub)
- IDEO
- Novartis
- Quest Diagnostics

Fiction about Central Square

- Central Square (1998), by George Packer. Graywolf Press ISBN 1-55597-277-2

External links

- CentralSquare.com [1]
- Photo comparison of Central Square in 1998 and 2002 [2]

Harvard Square

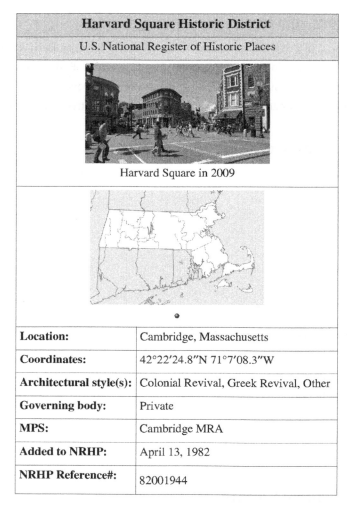

Harvard Square Historic District	
U.S. National Register of Historic Places	
Harvard Square in 2009	
Location:	Cambridge, Massachusetts
Coordinates:	42°22′24.8″N 71°7′08.3″W
Architectural style(s):	Colonial Revival, Greek Revival, Other
Governing body:	Private
MPS:	Cambridge MRA
Added to NRHP:	April 13, 1982
NRHP Reference#:	82001944

Harvard Square is a large triangular area in the center of Cambridge, Massachusetts, at the intersection of Massachusetts Avenue, Brattle Street, and John F. Kennedy Street. Adjacent to the historic heart of Harvard University, Harvard Yard, the Square (as it is called locally) functions as a commercial center for Harvard students, as well as residents of western Cambridge and the inner western and northern suburbs of Boston.

It is also home to Harvard station, a major MBTA Red Line subway and bus transportation hub. In an extended sense, the name "Harvard Square" can also refer to the entire neighborhood surrounding this intersection for several blocks in each direction. The nearby Cambridge Common has a large park area with a playground, baseball field, and a number of monuments, several relating to the Revolutionary

War.

History

Although today a commercial area, the Square boasts famous residents from earlier periods, including the colonial poet Anne Bradstreet. The high pedestrian traffic makes it a gathering place for street musicians; singer-songwriter Tracy Chapman, who attended nearby Tufts University, is known to have played here during her college years.

Until 1984, the Harvard Square stop was the northern terminus of the Red Line, and it still functions as a major transfer station between subway, bus, and trackless trolley. Automobile traffic can be heavy, and parking is difficult. Most of the bus lines serving the area from the north and west run through a tunnel adjacent to the subway tunnel. Originally built for streetcars (which last ran in 1958) and still used by trackless trolleys as well as ordinary buses, the tunnel lessens bus traffic in central Harvard Square, and lets buses cross the Square without encountering automobile traffic.

Transformation

Discussions of how the Square has changed in recent years usually center on the perceived gentrification of the Harvard Square neighborhood and Cambridge in general.

The Square also used to be a neighborhood shopping center, with a grocery store (Sages) and a Woolworth's five and ten. There does remain a small hardware store (Dickson Hardware), but the Square is now more of a regional shopping center, especially for youths.

Harvard Square

In 1981 and 1987 the Harvard Square Theatre was converted into a multiplex cinema; it is now part of the Loews Cineplex Entertainment chain. During the late 1990s, some locally run businesses with long-time shopfronts on the Square—including the unusual Tasty Diner, a tiny sandwich shop open long hours, and the Wursthaus, a beloved old-world German restaurant—closed to make way for national chains.

Following national trends, the local Harvard Trust Company bank has been absorbed into the national Bank of America through a series of mergers. Elsie's sandwiches and Ferranti-Dege cameras are gone. The student co-op, the Harvard Coop, is now managed by Barnes & Noble. *Schoenhof's Foreign Books* is owned by the French Éditions Gallimard.

In 2004, it was announced that the famous Grolier Poetry Bookshop would be sold (although it ended up surviving under different, independent management), and today even the iconic *Out of Town News* is owned by the UK-based Hudson Group. The independent WordsWorth Books closed in 2004, after a tenure of 29 years as a fixture in the Square. Paperback Booksmith and Reading International closed by the end of the 1990s. Still, a few establishments, such as Algiers Coffee House, Leavitt & Pierce tobacconists (est. 1883), Harvard Book Store (est. 1932), the Hong Kong Chinese restaurant (est. 1954), Laflamme Barber Shop (est. 1898), Cardullo's Gourmet Shoppe (est. 1950), Café Pamplona (est. 1959), and Bartley's Burger Cottage (est. 1960) remain as longstanding, locally-run businesses.

Other features

At the center of the Square is the old Harvard Square Subway Kiosk, now a newsstand, *Out of Town News*, stocking newspapers and magazines from around the world. A video of it appears in transitional clips used on CNN. A public motion art installation, Lumen Eclipse, has been introduced at the Tourist Information Booth showing monthly exhibitions of local, national and international artists.

In the southwest part of the Square, on Mount Auburn St, stands the Igor Fokin Memorial. This memorial, created by sculptor Konstantin Simun, pays tribute not only to the late "beloved puppeteer," but to all street performers that are an integral part of the square, especially during summer months.

The office of NPR's *Car Talk* radio show faces the square, with a stencil in the window that reads "Dewey, Cheetham & Howe," the fictional law firm often referenced on the show. The popular show references this by asking its viewers to send in answers to the "Puzzler" to "Puzzler Tower, Car Talk Plaza, Harvard Square, Cambridge (our fair city), MA 02238".

The sunken region next to the newsstand and the subway entrance is called "The Pit." Its arena-like appearance attracts skateboarders and, more generally, young, high-school aged people from surrounding neighborhoods who are associated with countercultural movements such as the punk, hardcore, straight edge, and goth subcultures. The contrast between these congregants and the often older and more conservatively dressed people associated with nearby Harvard University and the businesses in the Square occasionally leads to tension. Harvard sports teams and clubs, including the track teams and all-male social clubs, are known to make use of this contrast through encouraging or sometimes forcing their newest members to engage in humorous or humiliating performances in "The Pit" as part of these members' initiations into the group.

One block east of the pit, an outdoor cafe features always-busy tables for chess players, including Murray Turnbull, with his ever-present "Play the Chessmaster" sign.

A number of other public squares dot the surrounding streets, notably Brattle Square and Winthrop Square, with a wide variety of street performers throughout the year, and the John F. Kennedy Memorial Park, one block further down JFK Street, is on the bank of the Charles River.

The square often attracts activists for the Communist Party USA, Lyndon LaRouche and other non-mainstream political factions. It is also known for its large number of panhandlers; Tom Magliozzi has called it "the bum capital of the world".

"The Garage" is a small, multi-story shopping mall, named thus because it was formerly a parking garage. The original car ramp has been preserved, and is a central feature of this adaptive reuse project. One of the main attractions in The Garage is a Newbury Comics store.

The offices of Dewey, Cheetham, and Howe, home of the radio show *Car Talk*

Notable establishments

- Dewey, Cheatem & Howe office, known for NPR's Car Talk
- American Repertory Theater
- Brattle Theatre, a non-profit movie theater
- Lumen Eclipse public video art display
- In Your Ear and Planet Records, two used record stores
- Newbury Comics, a New England music and pop culture chain
- Million Year Picnic, a comic book store
- Algiers Coffee House, a local hookah cafe
- Pinocchio's Pizza, local mainstay
- Café Pamplona, local Spanish style cafe
- Club Passim, a folk music club
- Grendel's Den, local bar and restaurant

Notable book stores

- Grolier Poetry Bookshop
- Raven Used books Cambridge
- Schoenhof's Foreign Books
- Harvard Book Store
- Globe Corner Bookstore
- Lame duck books
- Harvard Coop

In film

Various parts of the 1997 film *Good Will Hunting* were filmed in and around Harvard Square, most notably at the former Tasty Sandwich Shop and the outdoor seating area of the square's largest Au Bon Pain café.

The 1973 film *The Paper Chase* features Harvard Square landmarks of its era, including the old Out of Town Newsstand, the old MBTA Harvard station kiosk, with its "8 Minutes to Park Street" sign, and the now-defunct Kupersmith's Florists.

The 1977 film *Between the Lines* features similar Harvard Square footage as well as aerial footage of Back Bay.

The 1994 film *With Honors* has a scene filmed in Harvard Square. The Out of Town Newsstand is featured in it. The scene is when Monty approaches Simon as he (Simon) is attempting to sell newspapers he took out of a vending machine.

The 2005 film *Touching History; Harvard Square, the Bank, and The Tasty Diner* chronicles the changing face of the square through the eyes of a small diner serving its last burger and closing its doors to make way for a large surface retail space.

Ben Affleck shot portions of his film *The Town* (2010) in Grendel's Den on Winthrop Street.

See also

- William Brattle House

Gallery

Harvard Square in 1869

Harvard Square with the Out of Town News kiosk, left foreground, May 2004

Harvard Square on a rainy day

Harvard Book Store at dusk

Lowes Movie Theatre,
Church Street

External links

- Harvard Square History and Development [1]
- Cambridge Citymap [16]

Inman Square

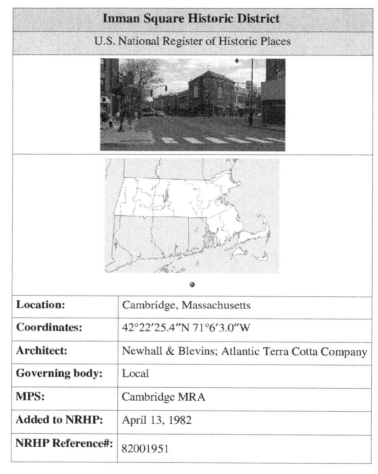

Inman Square Historic District	
U.S. National Register of Historic Places	
Location:	Cambridge, Massachusetts
Coordinates:	42°22′25.4″N 71°6′3.0″W
Architect:	Newhall & Blevins; Atlantic Terra Cotta Company
Governing body:	Local
MPS:	Cambridge MRA
Added to NRHP:	April 13, 1982
NRHP Reference#:	82001951

Inman Square is a neighborhood in Cambridge, Massachusetts. It lies north of Central Square, at the junction of Cambridge, Hampshire, and Inman Streets near the Cambridge–Somerville border.

Location

Like many squares in the Boston area, Inman Square refers both to an intersection and to a retail district and neighborhood. Current residents of the area seem to converge on a broad definition of Inman Square as the region centered on the intersection of Cambridge and Hampshire Streets that radiates out around 500 feet (150 m) along Cambridge Street to Prospect and encompasses the business district and outlying houses.

Geologically, the area is part of the larger Boston Basin and attaches to the relative lowland known as the Cambridge plain. Originally, the land was both flat and surrounded by an irregular, swampy region that formed a natural boundary. Situated a short walk east of Harvard Square, north of Central Square, south of Union Square, and west of Lechmere (also known as East Cambridge), Inman Square is fairly centralized within the Mid-Cambridge/Somerville area. Hampshire Street connects it with Porter Square to the northwest and Kendall Square to the southeast.

History

Inman Square likely owes its name to Ralph Inman (1713–1788), described as a gentleman of fortune and a Boston merchant. The details of his life can be pieced together from articles in the New England and Genealogical Register, vols. 12, 14, 25, 26, 30, 55, 84, 112, and 136, as well as numerous other sources. He had extensive business interests along the Boston wharf and with Thomas Sodden owned 400 acres (1.6 km^2) making up "what is now the Port."

Inman also owned a "large, three-story rambling mansion" in a "little genteel Town about 4 Miles off (from Boston) calld Cambridge, where a number of Gentlemen's Families live upon their Estates." This included the Brattles, after whom Brattle Square was named.

During the American Revolutionary War, in 1775, American general Israel Putnam took over Inman's house as his headquarters. Inman was intent on remaining neutral in the war, but his intentions went for naught when his son joined the British Army, causing authorities to begin confiscating his property. He fled, leaving Mrs. Inman to deal with General Putnam. He apparently recovered from this, because he was at home again in Cambridge after the war.

Inman's wife, his second, was a business woman in her own right. She owned the sugar warehouse in Boston that the British troops took over as a barracks when they came to settle the unrest in Boston. It was from there that they marched to the Battles of Lexington and Concord.

An extensive description of the house is given in NE & GR, July 1871, vol. 25, page 232. "On the Inman street side" and "looking toward Boston road" are mentioned. It was "the first object of any interest in approaching the colleges from Boston ..." At the time of the description, 6 acres (24000 m^2) were still attached to it. Inman died there in 1788. His wife predeceased him.

Inman Square's origins lie in the growth of East Cambridge, starting at around 1790, when a group of financiers led by Andrew Craigie began buying up land around Lechmere Point, home to present-day CambridgeSide Galleria shopping mall, in an effort to build a toll bridge over the Charles River. After Craigie's bridge was built, he constructed roads from the Lechmere area that had been laid out with a gridwork of streets. One of these roads was the Middlesex Turnpike, the present-day Hampshire Street, which connected Cambridge with Lowell and Boston, bringing regional traffic through the area. Craigie also laid out Cambridge Street, which would intersect with Hampshire, producing Inman Square in 1809.

By the 1860s, horse carts were common in the area and contributed to dwellings popping up along their routes. By 1900, full streetcar service was in the area, led by the Charles River Street Railway, which built its first railway through Inman Square in 1881. By 1874 the region was an urban center called both "Atwood's Corner" and "Inman Square." This ambiguity was fixed a year later in a petition that would make official the Inman Square moniker.

After transportation brought people and commerce to the region, a new era of stability overtook Inman Square. From 1910 up until the early 1950s, streetcar, automobile, and foot traffic shuffled people to and from the square where architectural instead of transportation construction was taking place. During this period commercial dwellings popped up to service the local community: drugstores, taverns, markets, bakeries, delis, and an insurance company were among the many stores that called Inman Square home.

After the streetcars left Cambridge Street around 1950 the square became "just a little bit out of the way" yet remained "around the corner from Harvard, Central, Kendall and Lechmere." Even though there is not direct rapid transit, three MBTA bus lines (69, 83, 91) stop in the square, making it accessible by mass transit. Post-streetcar visitors still regularly frequent the area's restaurant and entertainment attractions.

2000s

In the 2000s, Inman Square is a culturally diverse neighborhood, home to professionals, working people, and students and professors from neighboring MIT and Harvard. Inman Square also has strong Brazilian and Portuguese influences,[citation needed] as can be seen in the storefronts lining Cambridge Street, especially to the East of Prospect Street.

S&S Deli

The regional restaurant chain Legal Sea Foods began in Inman Square in 1950 as a fish market that also did a takeout business. Legal Sea Foods grew to a chain of 31 restaurants, including some in Kendall Square and Copley Square in Boston), as well as in suburbs and cities throughout the region. After the original Legal Sea Foods burned in a fire, it was rebuilt and became Rosie's Bakery.

Firehouse 1384

From the 1960s through the late 1970s, next to Legal Seafoods one could find the home of the improvisational troupe The Proposition. Alumni of the troupe include actor Josh Mostel and original *Saturday Night Live* cast member Jane Curtin. Later in the 1980s, at the Ding Ho restaurant on Springfield Street (later home of Ole Mexican Grill), such comedians as Steven Wright, Jimmy Tingle, Bobcat Goldthwait, and club founder Barry Crimmins got their start. Most, including future *Tonight Show* host Jay Leno, began by performing between sets of musical acts at the "Ding", as it was known to locals.[citation needed] Leno's first stage appearance took place there between sets of JT's Mardi Gras Band and the Lawnchair Ladies.[citation needed]

Boston's oldest continuously operating improvisational theater troupe, ImprovBoston, has recently moved from its longtime home in Inman square to nearby Central square on Prospect street. ImprovBoston alumni include *Wait Wait... Don't Tell Me!* panelist Adam Felber.

Inman Square was also home to the Center for New Words (originally the New Words Bookstore), one of the oldest and longest-running women's bookstores in the country. Located at 186 Hampshire Street, it closed its retail business in the early 2000s. Meanwhile, from 2003 to early 2006, the Zeitgeist Gallery resided at 1353 Cambridge Street, after a fire drove it from its former home at the corner of Norfolk Street and Broadway. Run by a group of artists, musicians and activists, it was a focal point for art, music and community

Bukowski Tavern on Cambridge St.

activism, and fostered avant garde, experimental and underground work. It was evicted by its landlord in a hostile takeover in early 2006.[citation needed] A related space called Zeitgeist Outpost or Outpost 186, opened by former Zeitgeist volunteers, is now on the other side of Inman Square. It is, in fact, in the former New Words back room, where the women's bookstore once held poetry readings, author presentations and acoustic concerts. The Zeitgeist's former landlord went on to open a more upscale jazz nightclub in his building, called the Lilypad.

External links

- InmanSquare.com [1]

Lechmere Square

Geographical coordinates: 42°22'15"N 71°4'36"W

Lechmere Square (pronounced "leech-meer") is located at the intersection of Cambridge St. and First St. in East Cambridge, Massachusetts. It was originally named for the Colonial-era landowner Richard Lechmere, a Loyalist who returned to England at the beginning of the American Revolution. His lands were later seized by the new American government. The shoreline is shown as **"Lechmere's Point"** on Revolutionary War maps, and was the landing point for British troops en route to the Battles of Lexington and Concord.[1]

The area was developed by land speculator Andrew Craigie in the early 19th century. Later, a store (Lechmere) was founded in the area and named for it. The store expanded into a regional chain, which was purchased by Montgomery Ward in 1994 and closed in 1997 as Montgomery Ward filed for Chapter 11 bankruptcy.

The area is now best known for the CambridgeSide Galleria, one of the few full-fledged interior shopping malls within the city limits of Boston and Cambridge, which is on the site of the original Lechmere store (and, when built, incorporated a newly-built Lechmere Sales store as one of its anchor tenants). In years past, Lechmere Square was a manufacturing center producing candy, furniture and caskets.

Lechmere Square and the surrounding East Cambridge are currently undergoing a revival of sorts. The area's factories have been or are being converted into office buildings and condominiums. Several large-scale development projects were begun in 2004 and 2005. The results of these projects are yet to be seen. It does appear, however, that East Cambridge and Lechmere Square are undergoing a gentrification process similar to what has been seen in other areas of Cambridge.

Lechmere Square is served by the MBTA's Lechmere station. Many MBTA bus lines also stop here. Lechmere is the northern terminus of the Green Line and is an above-ground stop. Service to Lechmere and nearby Science Park was interrupted from June, 2004 until November 12, 2005 for replacement of the Causeway Street Elevated with a tunnel under North Station [2]. The historic concrete Lechmere Viaduct across the Charles River remains. Planning is ongoing to move Lechmere station across Monsignor OBrien Highway, where it will serve the new North Point development and facilitate a Green Line extension to the north.

The Charles River, Lechmere Canal, and Memorial Drive are nearby. Lechmere is also located close to the Museum of Science.

References

- Cambridge Historical Commission, "History of Cambridge, Massachusetts, USA" [3]. Retrieved May 29, 2005.
- Discount Store News (1994), "Montgomery Ward buys Lechmere; continues growth through acquisition" [4]. Retrieved May 29, 2005.
- Boston Business Journal (1997), "Lechmere: Joining the ghosts of retailers past" [5]. Retrieved May 29, 2005.

Porter Square

Geographical coordinates: 42°23′19″N 71°07′10″W

Porter Square is a neighborhood of Cambridge, Massachusetts in the USA, located around the intersection of Massachusetts Avenue and Somerville Avenue, between Harvard and Davis Squares. The Porter Square station serves both the MBTA Red Line, and the Commuter Rail. The station is approximately 200 yards from the border with Somerville, so "Porter Square" inhabitants include residents of both cities.

Attractions

A prominent feature of the Porter Square skyline is the tower on the Art Deco-style University Hall building, which was a Sears, Roebuck store from 1928 to 1985. In 1991, Lesley University began leasing classroom space there, and in 1994 it bought the building, known then as the Porter Exchange building, in which it now houses its bookstore and art and dance studios, in addition to classrooms.

Lesley University continues to expand in the Porter Square neighborhood, with current plans [1] to relocate the Art Institute of Boston to the site occupied by the North Prospect Church on Massachusetts Avenue, across Roseland Street from University Hall.

In addition to its Lesley facilities, University Hall contains many (mostly Japanese) small shops and restaurants, including Bluefin (Japanese cuisine), and a Bally Total Fitness gym. The concentration of Japanese establishments has resulted in some referring to it unofficially as "Japantown-Cambridge" or "Little Japan". In May 2009, Lesley University ousted the Japanese grocery store Kotobukiya from Porter Exchange in favor of plans to expand its textbook store, prompting rumors that Lesley is seeking to replace "Little Japan" with its own student center.

The Porter Square Shopping Center contains a Shaw's (formerly Star Market), Tags Hardware, CVS/pharmacy, an independent bookstore called Porter Square Books, a Cambridge Naturals store, Mudflat pottery gallery, Emack & Bolio's, Gentle Dental, and a parking lot known for its lack of parking and its strict two-hours-or-you're-towed policy.

Porter Square Shopping Center, 2009

Restaurants in the area include Zing Pizza, Wok & Roll (Chinese), Tacos Lupita (Salvadoran), Anna's Taqueria, Sugar & Spice (Thai), Christopher's (American), Passage to India, and Elephant Walk (Cambodian). Porter Square is also home to Toad, a bar that features a live band every night.

From 2004 to mid-2006 the intersection of Massachusetts and Somerville Avenue, including the area in front of the strip mall, underwent extensive construction to improve access for pedestrians, bicyclists, and mass transit users, and improve drainage and stormwater conditions. The artist Toshihiro Katayama of Harvard University, in conjunction with the landscape architect Cynthia Smith, designed a new visual look for the square including contrasting light and dark concrete paving, stone walls and boulders.

History

Porter Square was named for the now-vanished Porter's Hotel, operated by Zachariah B. Porter, who also left his name to the hotel's specialty, the cut of steak known as porterhouse. The square, formerly flanked by cattle yards that used the Porter rail head to transport their beef throughout the US, was an important center for commerce and light industry as early as the late 18th century. The hotel was demolished in 1909. A relic of the cattle trade, a tunnel for moving cattle to and from the railroad without interfering with street traffic, survives under the nearby Walden Street Bridge, and has been preserved and restored. The "most dramatic loss" of 19th century landscape in the square was the leveling of the old Rand Estate in 1952 to make way for the Porter Square Shopping Center.

In 1984 the Red Line was extended from Harvard through Porter and Davis Square to its present terminus at Alewife, a project that also left Porter with its most visible landmark, Susumu Shingu's 46-foot stainless steel kinetic sculpture entitled "Gift of the Wind."

Chronic homelessness

The presence of chronically homeless and impoverished individuals persists despite Porter Square's recent improvements and distinct aesthetic charm. Panhandlers in the Square are regularly stationed outside the entryways of certain shops. Others have taken up residence inside the route 83 bus shelter at Porter Square Station, partially inhibiting its intended use.

Frequent inhabitant of the MBTA bus stop
at Porter Square, 2010

External links

- Description of Porter Square design project [2] from Cambridge community development site
- Article about University Hall building [3] in Lesley University magazine
- PSNA [4] Porter Square Neighbors Association

Cambridgeport

Cambridgeport is one of the neighborhoods of Cambridge, Massachusetts. It is bounded by Massachusetts Avenue, the Charles River, the Grand Junction Railroad, and River Street. The neighborhood contains predominantly residential homes, many of the triple decker style common in New England. Central Square, at the northernmost part of Cambridgeport, is an active commercial district and transportation hub, and University Park is a collection of renovated or recently constructed office and apartment buildings. The neighborhood also includes Fort Washington Park, several MIT buildings, and Magazine Beach.

The neighborhood is Area 5 of Cambridge.

History

In the late 1800s the Fig Newton cookie (named after nearby Newton, Massachusetts) was first manufactured in Cambridgeport at the F. A. Kennedy Steam Bakery.

Large portions of the neighborhood would have been demolished as part of the Inner Belt highway project. The interstate would have followed the path of Brookline Street to the Boston University Bridge.

Demographics

In 2005 the neighborhood had a population of 10,052 residents living in 4,203 households. The average household income was $45,294.

Cambridge Common

Cambridge Common is a public park in Cambridge, Massachusetts, United States. It is located near Harvard Square and borders on several parts of Harvard University.

View of the Cambridge Common, ca. 1808-9, with Harvard College on the left and Christ Church on the right.

History

During the American Revolutionary War, General George Washington first gathered his troops here. The tree under which legend has it they gathered, called the Washington Elm, no longer stands but its location is marked with a commemorative plaque. Nearby is a trio of bronze cannons, a plaque for Henry Knox and another for Tadeusz Kościuszko.

Cambridge Common is also the site of an Irish Famine Memorial, dedicated on July 23, 1997 by then President of Ireland, Mary Robinson, and unveiled to an audience of 3,000 people. The Memorial sculpture was created by Maurice Harron, a sculptor from Derry, Northern Ireland. There is a very similar memorial in downtown Boston.

See also

• Cambridge Common Historic District

References

• Cambridge Common Irish Famine Memorial [1] (archived 2007)

Geographical coordinates: 42°22′35″N 71°07′14″W

Wellington-Harrington

Wellington-Harrington is a neighborhood in Cambridge, Massachusetts, bounded by Hampshire Street on the southwest, the railroad tracks on the east, and the Somerville town line on the north. In 2005, it had a population of 7,345 residents living in 2,734 households. The average household income was $39,899.

References

- Cambridge Police Department [1]

Geographical coordinates: 42°22′21″N 71°5′31″W

Mid-Cambridge

Mid-Cambridge is a neighborhood of Cambridge, Massachusetts. It is bounded by Massachusetts Avenue on the south and west, Prospect Street on the east, and Hampshire Street, the Somerville border, Kirkland Street, Quincy Street, and Cambridge Street on the north.

In 2005, the neighborhood had a population of 13,285 residents in 5,989 households. The average household income was $50,410.

References

- Cambridge Police Department [1]

Historic Christ the King Presbyterian Church on Prospect Street in Mid-Cambridge was constructed in 1851 by Alexander Esty

Area 4, Cambridge

Area 4 is one of the neighborhoods of Cambridge, Massachusetts, roughly between Central Square, Inman Square, and MIT. It is bounded on the south by Massachusetts Avenue and Main Street, on the west by Prospect Street, on the north by Hampshire Street, and on the east by the Grand Junction Railroad tracks. Area 4 is a densely populated residential neighborhood with about 7,000 residents.

History and name

Prior to the filling in of Boston's Back Bay and Charles River marshes, brackish saltwater reached into what is now Area 4. After landfill allowed Cambridge to expand over the area now known as Cambridgeport, this entire portion of Cambridge was known as the "Old Port". Cambridge's Old Port was split into two planning zones, Area 4 and Area 5, by the Cambridge Community Development department, with Massachusetts Avenue as the dividing line. The "Port" name went to Area 5, aka Cambridgeport, where the waterfront is currently located, and inland Area 4 lost its name and became known by its neighborhood planning designation (which is also its police zone).

Elias Howe, Jr. invented the sewing machine at 55 Cherry Street in Area 4 in 1846. Howe's was the first patented functional sewing machine. Isaac Singer, who made sewing machines commercially successful, was forced to pay patent royalties to Howe.

Area 4 was the site of the first reciprocal telephone conversation, which took place between Alexander Graham Bell and Thomas A. Watson on October 9, 1876. Watson was at an office in Area 4, and Bell was at an office on Cambridge Street in Boston.

Candy industry

Area 4 was the early hub of the candy industry in the United States, beginning with the first candy factory in Cambridge, started by Robert Douglass in 1826 on Windsor Street. Notable Area 4 candy factories included Cambridge Brands, makers of Junior Mints, still in operation on Main Street; the Squirrel Brands company, makers of Squirrel nut caramel (the inspiration for the band name Squirrel Nut Zippers); and Necco (New England Confectionery Company), whose factory located across Massachusetts Avenue from today's Area 4 was the largest candy factory in the world.

Notable people and places

The Garment District is a low cost new and used clothing store located in a historic building. It is widely known throughout the Boston area, especially its "Dollar a Pound" section. In 2004-2005 the store was threatened with redevelopment into condominiums, but was saved with help by the Area 4 neighborhood coalition and a historical designation for the building by the City of Cambridge.

Squirrel Brand Park is located on the grounds of the old Squirrel Brand candy factory.

Clement G. Morgan, 1859–1929, was the first black Cambridge City Councilor, and founded the Niagara Movement, a predecessor of the National Association for the Advancement of Colored People (NAACP). Morgan grew up on Columbia Street and on Prospect Street. Morgan Park in Area 4 is named after him.

Denise Simmons, Mayor of Cambridge, lives in Area 4 and gets most of her support in elections from this neighborhood. She is seen as Area 4's representative to city government.

David Scondras, the first openly gay member of the Boston City Council and founder of Fenway Community Health Center in Boston's Fenway neighborhood, moved to Area 4 in early 2005 and became the neighborhood coalition's community organizer. He was forced to resign from this position after being arrested in Lowell Mass for soliciting sex from what he thought was an underaged boy he met over the internet. He later pleaded guilty to the charge and was required to register as a sex offender.

Demographics

Per city data, in 2005 Area 4 had a population of 7,263 residents living in 2,523 households. The average household income was $34,306.

External links

- Cambridge Community Development Area 4 page [1]
- Cambridge Area 4 Neighborhood Coalition [2]

Geographical coordinates: 42°22′1″N 71°5′52.″W**unknown operator: u'.'unknown operator: u'.'**

East Cambridge, Massachusetts

East Cambridge is a neighborhood of Cambridge, Massachusetts. Referred to as Area 1, East Cambridge is bounded by the Charles River on the East, the Somerville border on the North, Broadway and Main Street on the South, and the railroad tracks on the West. "East Cambridge Begins at The Tracks" was a controversial slogan in the early 20th Century which challenged neighborhood honor between the residents of East Cambridge (Area 1) and Wellington-Harrington (Area 3).

During the late 1990s and early 2000s, East Cambridge and its neighbor Lechmere Square have been undergoing a gentrification process, as old factories are converted into condominiums and office space.

Dorothea Lynde Dix became an advocate for the humane treatment of the mentally insane in the Antebellum era when she volunteered as a Sunday School teacher at East Cambridge, Massachusetts.

East Cambridge, Massachusetts is roughly a five block area of condensed homes. There are predominately Irish and Portuguese natives with also a mix of Polish and Italian. It is predominately a middle class neighborhood. The neighborhood is currently the site of most of large scale developments in Cambridge, including North Point, which will consist of over a dozen residential towers.

Demographics

Per city data, in 2005 East Cambridge had a population of 7,294 residents living in 2,726 households. The average household income was $57,979.

References

Geographical coordinates: 42°22′00″N 71°04′48″W

Riverside, Cambridge

Riverside is a neighborhood of Cambridge, Massachusetts bounded by Massachusetts Avenue on the north, River Street on the east, the Charles River on the south, and JFK Street on the west. In 2005 it had a population of 11,201 residents in 3,341 households, and the average household income was $40,753.

References

- Cambridge Police Department [1]

Geographical coordinates: 42°22′4″N 71°6′53″W

Agassiz, Cambridge, Massachusetts

Geographical coordinates: 42°23′1″N 71°6′58″W

Agassiz, also called **Harvard North**, is a neighborhood of Cambridge, Massachusetts, bounded by Massachusetts Avenue on the west, Cambridge Street, Quincy Street, and Kirkland Street on the south, Porter Square on the north, and the Somerville border on the northeast.

In 2005 it had a population of 5,241 residents living in 1,891 households, and the average household income was $55,380.

References

- Cambridge Police Department [1]

North Cambridge, Massachusetts

North Cambridge is a neighborhood of Cambridge, Massachusetts bounded by Porter Square and the Fitchburg Line railroad tracks on the south, the city of Somerville on the northeast, Alewife Brook and the town of Arlington on the northwest, and the town of Belmont on the west. In 2005 it had a population of 10,642 residents living in 4,699 households, and the average income was $44,784.

Autumn in the Alewife Linear Park, near the corner of Cedar Street and Massachusetts_Avenue_(Boston)Massachusetts Avenue, North Cambridge

The main commercial areas of North Cambridge are situated along Alewife Brook Parkway and Massachusetts Avenue. However, a third area, Davis Square, in Somerville, exerts considerable influence on the North Cambridge neighborhood.

Four roads span the railroad tracks, connecting the vast majority of North Cambridge with other neighborhoods of Cambridge. From east to west, these are: *Mass. Ave.* (route MA-2A), Walden Street, Sherman Street (grade crossing), and *Alewife Brook Parkway* (carrying routes MA-2, MA-16, and US-3).

See also

- Alewife Linear Park
- Lexington and West Cambridge Railroad
- St. John's Roman Catholic Church
- Walden Street Cattle Pass

References

- Cambridge Police Department map & statistics [1]

Geographical coordinates: 42°23′45″N 71°07′48″W

West Cambridge (neighborhood)

West Cambridge is a neighborhood in Cambridge, Massachusetts. It is bounded by the Charles River on the south, JFK Street on the east, Concord Avenue on the north, and Fresh Pond, Aberdeen Avenue, and the Watertown line on the west.

In 2005 it had a population of 8,266 residents living in 3,887 households, and the average household income was $80,746.

References

- Cambridge Police Department [1]

Geographical coordinates: 42°22′40″N 71°7′49″W

Peabody, Cambridge, Massachusetts

Peabody is a neighborhood in Cambridge, Massachusetts. It is bounded by Concord Avenue and Garden Street on the south, Massachusetts Avenue on the east, and the railroad tracks on the north and west. In 2005 it had a population of 11,794 residents living in 5,208 households, and the average household income was $58,708.

Gardens at the Cooper-Frost-Austin House

References

- Cambridge Police Department [1]

Geographical coordinates: 42°23′2″N 71°7′45″W

Cambridge Highlands

Cambridge Highlands is a neighborhood of Cambridge, Massachusetts bounded by the railroad tracks on the north and east, the Belmont town line on the west, and Fresh Pond on the south. In 2005 it had a population of 673 residents living in 281 households, and the average household income was $56,500.

References

- Cambridge Police Department [1]

Geographical coordinates: 42°23′25″N 71°9′3″W

Strawberry Hill, Cambridge

Strawberry Hill is a neighborhood in Cambridge, Massachusetts. It is bounded by the town of Belmont on the west, Watertown on the south, Aberdeen Avenue on the east, and Fresh Pond on the north. In 2005 it had a population of 2,335 residents living in 1,061 households, and the average household income was $44,107.

References

- Cambridge Police Department [1]

Geographical coordinates: 42°22′40″N 71°9′7″W

Cityscape of Cambridge - Architecture

Asa Gray House

Asa Gray House	
U.S. National Register of Historic Places	
U.S. National Historic Landmark	
Asa Gray House.	
Location:	88 Garden St., Cambridge, Massachusetts
Coordinates:	42°22′58.7″N 71°7′40.8″W
Built/Founded:	1810
Architect:	Town,Ithiel
Governing body:	Private
Added to NRHP:	October 15, 1966
Designated NHL:	January 12, 1965
NRHP Reference#:	66000655

The **Asa Gray House** is a historic house located at 88 Garden Street, Cambridge, Massachusetts. It is a National Historic Landmark.

The house was designed in 1810 by architect Ithiel Town in the Federal style for the first head of the Harvard Botanic Garden, and has been the residence of ornithologist Thomas Nuttall and botanist Asa Gray.

It was declared a National Historic Landmark in 1965.

Elmwood (Cambridge, Massachusetts)

Elmwood	
U.S. National Register of Historic Places	
U.S. National Historic Landmark District	
Location:	33 Elmwood Avenue, Cambridge, Massachusetts
Coordinates:	42°22′30.74″N 71°8′19.48″W
Built/Founded:	1767
Architect:	Thomas Oliver
Architectural style(s):	Georgian
Governing body:	Local
Added to NRHP:	October 15, 1966
Designated NHLD:	December 29, 1962
NRHP Reference#:	66000364

Elmwood, also known as the **Oliver-Gerry-Lowell House**, is a registered historic house in Cambridge, Massachusetts, known for its several prominent former residents, including: Andrew Oliver (1706–74), royal Lieutenant Governor of Massachusetts; Elbridge Gerry (1744–1814), signer of the US Declaration of Independence and whose political tactics earned the term gerrymandering, and Vice President of the United States; and James Russell Lowell (1819–1891), noted American writer, poet, and foreign diplomat. It is now the residence of the President of Harvard University.

History

Early history

The house was built in 1767 by Thomas Oliver, Lieutenant-Governor of Massachusetts for a short period until he was forced to resign in September 1774. He fled the colony, initially to Nova Scotia, and then to Bristol, England, where he died in 1815. The house was confiscated at some point during the American Revolution. In 1787 Elbridge Gerry purchased the estate, and in March 1813 took the oath of office as Vice President in the house, where he lived until his death in 1814.

Lowell family

Not long after the death of Elbridge Gerry, Elmwood was purchased by the Lowell family. It was in this home that James Russell Lowell was born on February 22, 1819, the son of Charles Russell Lowell, Sr. and Harriett Brackett Spence Lowell. James Russell Lowell was the youngest of six children; his older siblings were Charles, Rebecca, Mary, William, and Robert.

In the 1850s, Lowell dealt with many personal tragedies, including the sudden death of his mother and his third daughter, Rose. His personal troubles as well as the Compromise of 1850 convinced him to spend a winter in Italy after coaxing from William Wetmore Story. The trip was financed by the sale of land around Elmwood, and Lowell intended to sell off even further. Ultimately, 25 of the original 30 acres were sold to supplement Lowell's income. His personal troubles continued: his son Walter died while overseas, his wife Maria White Lowell died in October 1853, his father became deaf, and his sister Rebecca was deteriorating mentally, such that she often went without speaking for weeks. He had difficulty coping and became a recluse at Elmwood for a time until an invitation to speak at the Lowell Institute resulted in a job offer at Harvard College. He accepted the job, with the request he be allowed to study abroad for a year first.

Lowell returned to the United States and began his duties at Harvard in the summer of 1856. Still grieving the loss of his wife, however, he avoided Elmwood. Instead, he lodged in an area known as Professors' Row on Kirkland Street in Cambridge along with his daughter Mabel and her governess Frances Dunlap. Lowell and Dunlap married in 1857. After the death of Lowell's father in January 1861 due to a heart attack, he moved back to Elmwood with his family. Despite avoiding the home for so long, he was pleased to be back. He wrote to his friend Charles Frederick Briggs: "I am back again to the place I love best. I am sitting in my old garret, at my old desk, smoking my old pipe... I begin to feel more like my old self than I have these ten years". However, Elmwood's expenses drained him, with taxes at $1,000 a year. As early as 1867, he considered renting out Elmwood and moving into a smaller home elsewhere but never did. Instead, to ease his financial plight, he began to sell off land in 1870 until only 2 and a half acres remained his surrounding Elmwood.

Lowell remained at Elmwood for the remainder of his life, except during the period between 1877 and 1885, when he served as Minister to Spain and Great Britain. At Elmwood, he wrote some of his best-known works, including *The Vision of Sir Launfal*, *The Biglow Papers*, and *A Fable for Critics*, all published in 1848. It was Lowell who named the house "Elmwood". He mentions the home in some of his poetry:

> My Elmood chimneys seem crooning to me,
>
> As of old in their moody, minor key,
>
> And out of the past the hoarse wind blows.

Lowell's friend and fellow poet Henry Wadsworth Longfellow also wrote a poem about the house called "The Herons of Elmwood".

In the summer of 1872, when Lowell traveled to Europe, he rented the house to Thomas Bailey Aldrich. Years later, in 1877, when Lowell was appointed Ambassador to Spain, he rented the home to the violinist Ole Bull. Shortly after Bull's death in 1880, the Norwegian poet, playwright, and novelist Bjørnstjerne Bjørnson was the guest of Bull's widow at Elmwood for three months. Upon Lowell's return to the United States in 1885, he stayed at Elmwood until his death. He died in the home on August 12, 1891.

Recent history

Elmwood has been owned by Harvard University since 1962 and served as residence for the university's presidents since 1971 when acting Harvard President Derek Bok (1971–1991 & 2006–2007) moved his young family to these bucolic grounds to escape the din of student activity on Quincy Street. Elmwood has continued to serve as the residence of University Presidents since.

Architecture

Although parts of Elmwood's interior have been altered, its exterior has not changed greatly over the years. It is a large, square, clapboarded structure in Georgian style with brick-lined walls and two interior chimneys. All three floors in the main section are bisected into two rooms on either side by a central hall. Its first- and second-story windows are topped by cornices, and a balustrade encloses the low-pitched hip roof. The most striking exterior feature is the entranceway, which is flanked by Tuscan pilasters supporting a classic entablature decorated with a frieze. A large window sits above the entablature and is flanked by Ionic pilasters and

Elmwood was designed in the traditional Georgian style in 1767.

topped by a triangular pediment. A one-story porch with balustraded roof deck on the north side of the house, as well as a terrace on the south side, are later additions.

External links

- "Fords Occupy Restored Elmwood [1]" by Andrew T. Weil, *The Harvard Crimson*, September 23, 1963.
- "Elmwood: Molasses, Gerrymandering and Derek [2]" by J. Anthony Day, *The Harvard Crimson*, March 24, 1971

Hooper-Lee-Nichols House

Hooper-Lee Nichols House	
U.S. National Register of Historic Places	
The Hooper-Lee-Nichols House, front facade.	
Location:	Cambridge, Massachusetts
Coordinates:	42°22′37″N 71°8′11″W
Built/Founded:	1680
Architect:	Chandler,Joseph E.
Architectural style(s):	No Style Listed
Governing body:	Private
Added to NRHP:	June 15, 1979
NRHP Reference#:	79000355

The **Hooper-Lee-Nichols House** is a historic Colonial American house, initially constructed 1685, but enlarged and remodeled many times. It is located at 159 Brattle Street, Cambridge, Massachusetts, USA, and is the second-oldest house in Cambridge (after the Cooper-Frost-Austin House, c. 1681-1682). The house is now headquarters for the Cambridge Historical Society; tours are given several times a week.

History

The house was originally built in 1685 by Dr. Richard Hooper as a typical "first-period" farmhouse, although its ceilings were plastered, which was unusual for a modest house. When Hooper died in 1691, his wife took in boarders and the property then began fall into disrepair. She in turn died in 1701, and the house continued its decline until 1717, when it was inherited by Hooper's son, Dr. Henry Hooper. He added a lean-to and rebuilt the chimney with cooking ovens. In 1733, he sold the house to Cornelius Waldo, who added a third story and wooden quoins at the house's corners. Waldo also installed larger windows. The result was a house that looked thoroughly Georgian.

Judge Joseph Lee bought the house in 1758, adding the enclosed entry porch and applying stucco to the west wall. Lee was a British Loyalist and hence vacated his house during the first days of the American Revolution; he returned however in 1777.

In 1850, George and Susan Nichols rented and began to renovate the house. They enlarged the rear and installed the roof balustrade, containing balusters once part of the chancel of Saint Paul's Cathedral in Boston. In 1916 their grandson raised the rear of the house to a full three stories. Finally in 1923 William and Frances Emerson purchased the house. He was for many years Dean of Architecture at MIT; and she deeded the house to the Cambridge Historical Society which came into its possession in 1957. In the early 1980s, the Society made extensive exterior restorations.

The house is open for tours on Tuesdays and Thursdays at 2 and 3 PM.

External Link and references

- Cambridge Historical Society: Hooper-Lee-Nichols House [1]

Cooper-Frost-Austin House

Cooper-Frost-Austin House	
U.S. National Register of Historic Places	
Part of front facade with enclosed porch	
Location:	21 Linnaean St Cambridge, Massachusetts
Added to NRHP:	September 22, 1972
NRHP Reference#:	72000124

The **Cooper-Frost-Austin House** is a historic Colonial American house, currently estimated to have been constructed circa 1681-1682. It is located at 21 Linnaean Street, Cambridge, Massachusetts. It is the oldest extant home in Cambridge and operated as a non-profit museum by Historic New England. The house is rarely open for public tours, but private tours can be arranged during the summer months.

The house was built by Samuel Cooper on land that his father, Deacon John Cooper, had owned since 1657, and was first documented in 1689 in *The Register Book of the Lands and Houses in the "New Towne"* (as Cambridge was then named). Its original structure was a single room and chimney bay in width, two and one half stories in height with an integral lean-to, containing a "low room," "little room," "kitchin," "Chamber," "kitchin Chamber," "Garret," and "Cellar," all of which still exist, as do the original chimney and a facade gable. The house was extended in 1690 by Cooper's son, and then again between 1807-1816 by Martha Frost Austin and Thomas Austin who added an enclosed porch and Federal style stairway and trim. The house was acquired by Historic New England in 1912.

In 2002 the Oxford Dendrochronology Laboratory [1] analyzed wooden beams from the original structure and ascertained that donor trees were felled at the following times: Winter 1675/6, Winter 1680/81, and Spring 1681. The oldest timber may have been stockpiled before construction.

External links

- Historic New England - Cooper-Frost-Austin Home [2]

Geographical coordinates: 42°23′04″N 71°07′19″W

Cambridge Public Library

Cambridge Public Library	
U.S. National Register of Historic Places	
Location:	Cambridge, Massachusetts
Coordinates:	42°22′27″N 71°6′38″W
Built/Founded:	1888
Architect:	Van Brunt & Howe (1888), William Rawn Associates (2009)
Architectural style(s):	Other, Romanesque
Governing body:	Local
MPS:	Cambridge MRA
Added to NRHP:	April 13, 1982
NRHP Reference#:	82001931

The **Cambridge Public Library** in Cambridge, Massachusetts is part of the Minuteman Library Network. The library includes a headquarters and several branch buildings throughout the city.

In fiscal year 2008, the city of Cambridge spent 1.39% ($4,689,660) of its budget on the library -- some $44 per person.

Main building

The main branch of the Cambridge Public Library is an historic library building at 449 Broadway. It was built in 1888. Its land and full construction funding were provided by Frederick H. Rindge, a Cambridge native and philanthropist. It was added to the National Historic Register in 1982.

A $90 million expansion and renovation of the library, led by the Boston architectural firms William Rawn Associates and Ann Beha Architects, opened on November 8, 2009. The new addition more than triples the square footage of the building, and is the first building in the USA to make use of European Double-Skin Curtainwall technology. Architectural drawings and construction photos are available here [1]. During most of the construction, the library collection had been relocated to the Longfellow School.

Branches

Six smaller neighborhood branch libraries are scattered throughout the City of Cambridge. These are:

- Boudreau Branch, 245 Concord Avenue, West Cambridge
- Central Square Branch, 45 Pearl Street, Cambridgeport
- Collins Branch, 64 Aberdeen Avenue, West Cambridge
- O'Connell Branch, 48 Sixth Street, East Cambridge
- O'Neill Branch, 70 Rindge Avenue, North Cambridge
- Valente Branch, 826 Cambridge Street, East Cambridge

External links

- Cambridge Public Library Website [2]
- Main Library Expansion Project [3]

Middlesex County Courthouse (Massachusetts)

Middlesex County Courthouse

The **Middlesex County Courthouse** is a historic courthouse building in East Cambridge, Massachusetts, now on the National Register of Historic Places. It was initially designed in 1814-1816 by noted architect Charles Bulfinch (1763–1844), and subsequently enlarged in 1848 by Ammi B. Young.

The original courthouse was given by Andrew Craigie as part of his scheme to develop East Cambridge. Bulfinch created its plans, and it was erected 1814-1816 on Third Street between Otis and Thorndike Streets. His original stuccoed building is now known by only one surviving sketch, and forms the central core of today's building.

In 1848 architect Young enlarged and refaced the building in brick, adding late Federal and Greek Revival details such as a monumental cupola, Palladian windows, and recessed wall arches. A later 1924 addition obscured his 1848 entry facade. In 1973 the buildings were slated for demolition to make a parking lot, but saved by a preservation effort led by architect Graham Gund. Restoration efforts removed the 1924 addition, recreated Young's entry portico, restored its large clock tower, and cleaned and repaired the cupola's gold dome, brickwork, cast-iron trim, wrought-iron fencing, and slate and copper roofs.

Other buildings in the restored Bulfinch Square include the imposing Registry of Deeds and Probate Court (1896) with its four giant brick-columned porticoes, the Clerk of Courts Building (1889), and the Third District Court Built (1931, architect Charles Greco).

The Middlesex County Courthouse building is situated adjacent to the iconic 16 story former Edward J. Sullivan "Hi-rise" Superior court building.

References

- Historical & Archaeologial Resources of the Boston Area, Massachusetts Historical Commission [1]
- Eastern Cambridge Planning Study [2]
- "Preserving America's Past", The New York Times, January 18, 1987.
- WalkBoston description [3]
- Local historical signs and markers, Bulfinch Square, Cambridge, Massachusetts

Cambridge, Massachusetts City Hall

The **Cambridge, Massachusetts City Hall** is the city hall for Cambridge, Massachusetts, located at 795 Massachusetts Avenue, and built in the Richardsonian Romanesque style. The building additionally serves as a centerpiece of the surrounding City Hall Historic District and adjacent Central Square Historic District.

Cambridge, Massachusetts City Hall.

History

The hall was built between 1888–1889, and was largely funded through a donation from Frederick Hastings Rindge. The architects were Longfellow, Alden & Harlow (Alexander Wadsworth Longfellow, Jr., 1854–1934; Frank E. Alden, 1859–1908; and Alfred B. Harlow, 1857–1927). The building is three stories tall, with a bell tower that rises to 158 feet. Load-bearing stone walls are of Milford granite trimmed with Longmeadow brownstone.

Cambridge City Hall houses offices for the city council, the city manager and several municipal departments. In addition to the main building, the city of Cambridge also houses several other departments a couple of city blocks away in the City Hall Annex, located at Broadway and Inman Street.

On May 17, 2004, shortly after midnight, the first legal applications in the United States for marriage licenses for same-sex couples were issued at Cambridge City Hall. At 9:15 a.m. that day, the Cambridge City Clerk began solemnizing same-sex marriages. *See* same-sex marriage in Massachusetts.

External links

- Official page for city of Cambridge [1]
- Datasheet at Towerclocks.org [1]

Geographical coordinates: 42°22′02″N 71°06′20″W

Austin Hall (Harvard University)

Austin Hall	
U.S. National Register of Historic Places	
 Austin Hall	

Location:	Cambridge, Massachusetts
Coordinates:	42°22′36.58″N 71°7′9.72″W
Built/Founded:	1881
Architect:	Henry Hobson Richardson
Architectural style(s):	Other, Romanesque
Governing body:	Private
Added to NRHP:	April 19, 1972
NRHP Reference#:	72000128

Austin Hall is a classroom building of the Harvard Law School designed by noted American architect H. H. Richardson. The first building purpose built for an American law school, it was also the first dedicated home of Harvard Law. It is located on the Harvard University campus in Cambridge, Massachusetts.

The hall was built 1882–1884 in Romanesque Revival style. Single-story wings flank a heavy, two-story central mass, with the reading room extending rearwards to form an overall T shape. A central entryway framed with Romanesque triple arch is set deep within the building's flat front facade, with an asymmetric stairway tower protruding forwards to its right. The building is faced with Longmeadow sandstone in striking polychrome patterns, the light stones forming checkerboards within dark, reddish walls. The arches are of pale Ohio sandstone, as is the thick cornice band incised with a lengthy and sententious motto.

Austin Hall's first floor contains three large classrooms; these were designed to complement the new law school curriculum that was being implemented at the time by Dean Christopher Columbus Langdell, including large core classes employing the Socratic method. As this curriculum has been imitated by other American law schools, so has the classroom layout first employed at Austin Hall.

The building's second floor contains the Ames Courtroom, where students argue moot cases

Austin Hall, shortly after its construction, albumen print, ca. 1883-1895

Entryway detail

before panels of judges. A United States Supreme Court justice usually presides over the moot court's final round. The reading room's interior has been judged particularly fine for its ornamented fireplace and tie beams carved with the heads of dragons and boars.

References

- Jeffrey Karl Ochsner, *H. H. Richardson: Complete Architectural Works*, MIT Press, 1985, page 76. ISBN 0262650150.
- Harvard Law School walking tour [1]
- Harvard Law School map [2]

Memorial Hall (Harvard University)

Memorial Hall, Harvard University	
U.S. National Register of Historic Places	
U.S. National Historic Landmark	
 Memorial Hall	
Location:	Cambridge, Massachusetts
Coordinates:	42°22′33″N 71°6′57″W
Built/Founded:	1870
Architect:	William Robert Ware; Henry Van Brunt
Architectural style(s):	Gothic
Governing body:	Harvard University
Added to NRHP:	December 30, 1970
Designated NHL:	December 30, 1970
NRHP Reference#:	70000685

Memorial Hall is an imposing brick building in High Victorian Gothic style, located on the Harvard University campus in Cambridge, Massachusetts. It is now a National Historic Landmark.

Memorial Hall was erected in honor of Harvard graduates who fought for the Union in the American Civil War. From 1865 to 1868, a fund-raising committee gathered $370,000, then equal to one-twelfth of Harvard's total endowment, which was augmented by an additional $40,000 bequest from Charles Sanders, class of 1802 and college steward 1827-1831, for "a hall or theatre to be used on Commencement days, Class days, Exhibition days, days of the meetings of the society of Alumni, or any other public occasion connected with the College, whether literary or festive."

An architectural competition began in December 1865, with the winning designs submitted by William Robert Ware, class of 1852, and Henry Van Brunt, class of 1854. (These initial designs were altered as plans proceeded.) In 1870 the building was named Memorial Hall and its cornerstone laid; Oliver Wendell Holmes, Sr., composed a hymn for the occasion. The hall was dedicated for use in 1874, with Sanders Theatre substantially complete in 1875, and the tower completed in 1877. The tower was subsequently destroyed in a 1956 fire but rebuilt in 1999.

In *The Bostonians*, Henry James described it thus: "The Memorial Hall of Harvard consists of three main divisions: one of them a theater, for academic ceremonies; another a vast refectory, covered with a timbered roof, hung about with portraits and lighted by stained windows, like the halls of the colleges of Oxford; and the third, the most interesting, a chamber high, dim and severe, consecrated to the sons of the university who fell in the long Civil War." Principal interior features of Memorial Hall are as follows:

- Sanders Theatre is a lecture and concert hall of 1,166 seats, wood-paneled with statues of James Otis (by Thomas Crawford) and Josiah Quincy (by William Wetmore Story), and inspired by Christopher Wren's Sheldonian Theatre at Oxford, England. It contains John La Farge's stained glass window *Athena Tying a Mourning Fillet.*

- The hall's great room (9,000 square feet), now known as Annenberg Hall, is shaped by massive wooden trusses, walnut paneling, and a blue, stenciled ceiling. It was converted to a student commons soon after construction, and served as the college's main dining hall until 1926. From 1926 until 1994, it was only lightly used but after extensive renovation reopened in 1996 as the dining hall for all freshmen.

- The Memorial Transept [2600 square feet (240 m^2)] consists of a 60-foot-high (18 m) gothic vault above a marble floor, black walnut paneling and stenciled walls, two stained glass windows, and 28 white marble tablets commemorating 136 Civil War casualties.

- Twenty-two stained glass windows throughout the building, installed between 1879 and 1902, include works by John La Farge (4 windows), Louis Comfort Tiffany Studios (3 windows), Donald MacDonald (2 windows), and Sarah Wyman Whitman (2 windows).

Gallery

Wide view of entire building

Exterior details

The hallway leading to Sanders Theatre

References

- Memorial Hall (Harvard University) [1]
- High Victorian Gothic photographs [2]

Kresge Auditorium

Kresge Auditorium is an auditorium building for the Massachusetts Institute of Technology, located at 48 Massachusetts Avenue, Cambridge, Massachusetts. It was designed by the noted architect Eero Saarinen, with ground-breaking in 1953 and dedication in 1955. It was designed together with the MIT Chapel, the two buildings separated by a "green," referred to by students as the "Kresge Oval." The ensemble is recognized as one of the best examples of mid-Century modern architecture in the US. Though unassuming by

Kresge Auditorium from rear, looking toward I. M. Pei's Green Building.

today's standards, the buildings were part of an attempt to define MIT's social cohesion. The Auditorium was where MIT students and faculty could gather for formal events, the chapel was intended for marriages and memorial; the green that stretches between the two buildings, in the tradition of early-American urban planning, was to serve as the setting for civic events. Though the campus has grown around the buildings, the essential features of this idea are still easily legible. The building was named for its principal funder, Sebastian S. Kresge, founder of Kresge Stores (corporate predecessor of K-Mart) and the Kresge Foundation.

Roof detail.

The auditorium is defined by an elegant thin-shell structure, one-eighth of a sphere rising to a height of 50 feet, and sliced away by sheer glass walls so that it comes to earth on only three points. Thin shelled concrete technology was innovative for the times. The dome weighs only 1200 tons and is clad with copper. Sitting on a circular brick platform, the dome contains a concert hall (with seating for 1226 people), with a lower level that houses a small theater (seating 204), two rehearsal rooms, dressing rooms, offices, bathrooms, and lounges. The concert hall also contains a Holtkamp organ. The opening ceremony in 1955, that featured the

Interior view, with the MIT Summer Philharmonic Orchestra.

organ, included a piece of music that was commissioned for the event, Aaron Copland's "Canticle of Freedom."

Every seat in concert hall has an unobstructed view since there are no interior supports for the overarching dome. Working with renowned acoustical architects Bolt, Beranek and Newman, Saarinen employed free-hanging acoustic "clouds" that absorb and direct sound, instead of a traditional plaster ceiling. These clouds also contained lights, loudspeakers, and ventilation.

While standing on either side of the entry lobby, one can distinctly hear people on the other side speaking in as low a voice as a whisper.

The first professional recording at the Kresge Auditorium was a performance by soloist James Stagliano on the French Horn, playing Mozart's 4 Concerti for Horn, accompanied by the Zimbler Sinfonietta. The recording was made using a single Telefunken microphone, positioned 10 feet from the concert platform. The performance was recorded on an Ampex tape recorder, and released on LP under the 'Boston Records' Label.

See also

- Eero Saarinen structures
- MIT Chapel
- List of concert halls
- Thin-shell structure
- List of thin shell structures
- Architecture of the Massachusetts Institute of Technology
- Kresge Auditorium at Interlochen Center for the Arts in Interlochen, Michigan
- Centre des nouvelles industries et technologies

External links

- Kresge Auditorium [1].
- Facade of Kresge Auditorium, MIT [2].

Geographical coordinates: 42°21′29″N 71°05′42″W

Stata Center

The **Ray and Maria Stata Center** or *Building 32* is a 720000-square-foot (67000 m^2) academic complex designed by Pritzker Prize-winning architect Frank Gehry for the Massachusetts Institute of Technology (MIT). The building opened for initial occupancy on March 16, 2004. It sits on the site of MIT's former Building 20, which housed the historic Radiation Laboratory, in Cambridge, Massachusetts.

Stata Center

Major funding for this project was provided by Ray Stata (MIT class of 1957) and Maria Stata. Other major funders include Bill Gates, Alexander W. Dreyfoos, Jr. (MIT class of 1954), and Morris Chang of TSMC. Above the fourth floor, the building splits into two distinct structures: the Gates tower and the Dreyfoos tower.

Contained within the building are the Computer Science and Artificial Intelligence Laboratory, the Laboratory for Information and Decision Systems, as well as the Department of Linguistics and Philosophy. Academic celebrities such as Noam Chomsky, Rodney Brooks and Ron Rivest have offices there. World Wide Web Consortium founder Tim Berners-Lee and free software movement founder Richard Stallman also have offices within.

Several MIT classes, including many taught by the computer science and electrical engineering department (Course VI) are held inside. The Forbes Family Café is also located in the Stata Center, serving coffee and lunch to the public.

In contrast to the trend at MIT of referring to buildings by their numbers rather than their official names, the complex is usually referred to as "Stata", or "the Stata Center". The two towers are often called "G Tower" and "D tower".

Building 20

Main article: Building 20

The Stata Center necessitated the removal of the much-beloved Building 20 in 1998. Building 20 was erected hastily during World War II as a temporary building that housed the historic Radiation Laboratory. Over the course of fifty-five years, its "temporary" nature allowed research groups to have more space, and to make more creative use of that space, than was possible in more respectable buildings (including providing permanent rooms for official Institute clubs and groups, most notably the Tech Model Railroad Club). Professor Jerome Y. Lettvin once quipped, "You might regard it as the womb of the Institute. It is kind of messy, but by God it is procreative!"

Building 20 time capsule to be opened in 2053

Critical response

The Boston Globe architecture columnist Robert Campbell wrote a glowing appraisal of the building on April 25, 2004. According to Campbell, "the Stata is always going to look unfinished. It also looks as if it's about to collapse. Columns tilt at scary angles. Walls teeter, swerve, and collide in random curves and angles. Materials change wherever you look: brick, mirror-surface steel, brushed aluminum, brightly colored paint, corrugated metal. Everything looks improvised, as if thrown up at the last moment. That's the point. The Stata's appearance is a metaphor for the freedom, daring, and creativity of the research that's supposed to occur inside it." Campbell stated that the cost overruns and delays in completion of the Stata Center are of no more importance than similar problems associated with the building of St. Paul's Cathedral. The 2005 Kaplan/Newsweek guide "How to Get into College," which lists twenty-five universities its

View from the 7th floor

editors consider notable in some respect, recognizes MIT as having the "hottest architecture," placing most of its emphasis on the Stata Center.

Though there are many who praise this building, and in fact from the perspective of Gehry's other work it is considered by some as one of his best, there are certainly many who are less enamoured of the structure. The use of glass for walls on the inside means that those who work in the building have to give up a sense of privacy.[*citation needed*] There is also one lecture room where, because of the slight lean of the wall panels, some people have been known to experience vertigo.[*citation needed*] Sound insulation is almost absent.[*citation needed*] The building has also been criticized as insensitive to the needs of its inhabitants, poorly designed for day-to-day use, and at an official cost \$283.5 million, overpriced.[*citation needed*] Probably one of the more successful aspects of the building is the inner circulation system with niches for impromptu meetings and blackboards along the wall.[*citation needed*]

Interior, main floor, Gates tower

Mathematician and architectural theorist Nikos Salingaros has harshly criticized the Stata Center:

An architecture that reverses structural algorithms so as to create disorder—the same algorithms that in an infinitely more detailed application generate living form—ceases to be architecture. Deconstructivist buildings are the most visible symbols of actual deconstruction. The randomness they embody is the antithesis of nature's organized complexity. This is despite effusive praise in the press for "exciting" new academic buildings, such as the Peter B. Lewis Management Building at Case Western Reserve University in Cleveland, the Vontz Center for Molecular Studies at the University of Cincinnati Medical Center, and the Stata Center for Computer, Information, and Intelligence Sciences at MIT, all by Frank Gehry. Housing a scientific department at a university inside the symbol of its nemesis must be the ultimate irony.

Former Boston University president John Silber said the building "really is a disaster." Architecture critic Robert Campbell praised Gehry for "break[ing] up the monotony of a street of concrete buildings" and being "a building like no other building." The style of the building has been likened to the German Expressionism of the 1920s.

Lawsuit

Water from a fire sprinkler system failure in 2007

On October 31, 2007, MIT sued architect Frank Gehry and the construction company, Skanska USA Building Inc., for "providing deficient design services and drawings" which caused leaks to spring, masonry to crack, mold to grow, drainage to back up, and falling ice and debris to block emergency exits. A Skanska spokesperson said that prior to construction Gehry ignored warnings from Skanska and a consulting company regarding flaws in his design of the amphitheater, and rejected a formal request from Skanska to modify the design.

In an interview, Mr. Gehry, whose firm was paid $15 million for the project, said construction problems were inevitable in the design of complex buildings. "These things are complicated," he said, "and they involved a lot of people, and you never quite know where they went wrong. A building goes together with seven billion pieces of connective tissue. The chances of it getting done ever without something colliding or some misstep are small." "I think the issues are fairly minor," he added. "M.I.T. is after our insurance." Mr. Gehry said value engineering—the process by which elements of a project are eliminated to cut costs—was largely responsible for the problems. "There are things that were left out of the design," he said. "The client chose not to put certain devices on the roofs, to save money."

The 2007 MIT lawsuit against Frank O. Gehry & Associates, Beacon Skanska Construction, and NER Construction Management was reportedly settled in 2010 with most of the issues having been resolved.

Occupants

- Computer Science and Artificial Intelligence Laboratory (CSAIL[1])
  - World Wide Web Consortium
- Laboratory for Information and Decision Systems (LIDS)
- Department of Linguistics and Philosophy
- Childcare Center
- Fitness Center
- Forbes Cafe
- MIT Library cube

References

- Joyce, Nancy E. (2004). *Building Stata: The Design and Construction of Frank O. Gehry's Stata Center at MIT.* afterword by William J. Mitchell, photography by Richard Sobol. Cambridge, Mass.: The MIT Press. ISBN 978-0262600613.
- Mitchell, William J. (2007). *Imagining MIT: Designing a Campus for the Twenty-First Century.* Cambridge, Mass.: The MIT Press. ISBN 978-0-262-13479-8.

External links

- "Stata Center" [1]. MIT Department of Facilities, Massachusetts Institute of Technology. Retrieved 2007-09-23.
- "A multimedia walking tour of the Stata Center" [2]. Untravel Media, Massachusetts Institute of Technology startup. Retrieved 2008-06-19.
- "Ray and Maria Stata Center" [3]. MIT Computer Science and Artificial Intelligence Laboratory, Massachusetts Institute of Technology. Archived from the original [4] on 2007-09-18. Retrieved 2007-09-23.
- Reiss, Spencer (May 2004). "Frank Gehry's Geek Palace" [5]. *Wired, CondéNet Inc.* **8** (12.05): 518. doi:10.1007/s11916-004-0076-y [6]. Retrieved 2007-09-23.
- Beam, Alex (2004-05-04). "After buildup, MIT center is a letdown" [7]. *The Boston Globe* (The New York Times Company). Retrieved 2007-09-23.
- Ted Smalley Bowen (2004-05-19). "MIT's Stata Center Opens, Raises Questions about Cost Control" [8]. *Architectural Record* (The McGraw-Hill Companies, Inc. (construction.com)). Archived from the original [9] on 2007-09-29. Retrieved 2007-09-23.
- Wollman, Garrett A. (2005-12-20, presented 2005-12-07). "Building MIT's Stata Center: An IT Perspective" [10] (KPresenter). *Lisa'05 Conference Proceedings*. USENIX (usenix.org). Retrieved 2007-09-23.

- Virtual tour: MIT Computer Science and Artificial Intelligence Laboratory (undated). "CSAIL Lab Virtual Tours - Information Desk" [11]. Retrieved 2006-12-26.

Maps

- "Campus Map: Building 32 (Ray and Maria Stata Center)" [12]. MIT Department of Facilities and Information Services & Technology, Massachusetts Institute of Technology. Retrieved 2007-09-23.

Geographical coordinates: 42°21′42″N 71°05′25″W

The Massachusetts Institute of Technology

Massachusetts Institute of Technology

Massachusetts Institute of Technology	
Motto	*Mens et Manus*
Motto in English	Mind and Hand
Established	1861 (opened 1865)
Type	Private
Endowment	US $8.3 billion
Chancellor	Phillip Clay
President	Susan Hockfield
Provost	L. Rafael Reif
Academic staff	1,009
Students	10,384
Undergraduates	4,232
Postgraduates	6,152
Location	Cambridge, Massachusetts, United States
Campus	Urban, 168 acres (68.0 ha)
Nobel Laureates	76
Colors	Cardinal Red and Steel Gray[a]
Mascot	Tim the Beaver
Athletics	Division III (except for Rowing) 33 varsity teams
Affiliations	NEASC, AAU, COFHE, NASULGC

Website	web.mit.edu [1]

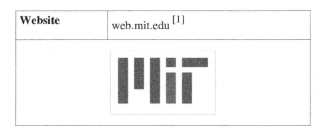

The **Massachusetts Institute of Technology (MIT)** is a private research university located in Cambridge, Massachusetts. MIT has five schools and one college, containing a total of 32 academic departments, with a strong emphasis on scientific and technological research. MIT is one of two private land-grant universities[b] and is also a sea-grant and space-grant university.

Founded by William Barton Rogers in 1861 in response to the increasing industrialization of the United States, the university adopted the European polytechnic university model and emphasized laboratory instruction from an early date. Its current 168-acre (68.0 ha) campus opened in 1916 and extends over 1 mile (1.6 km) along the northern bank of the Charles River basin. MIT was elected to the Association of American Universities in 1934 and researchers were involved in efforts to develop computers, radar, and inertial guidance in connection with defense research during World War II and the Cold War. In the past 60 years, MIT's educational disciplines have expanded beyond the physical sciences and engineering into fields like biology, economics, linguistics, political science, and management.

MIT enrolled 4,232 undergraduates and 6,152 graduate students for 2009–2010. It employs about 1,009 faculty members. 76 Nobel Laureates, 50 National Medal of Science recipients, and 35 MacArthur Fellows are currently or have previously been affiliated with the university. MIT has a strong entrepreneurial culture and the aggregated revenues of companies founded by MIT alumni would be the seventeenth largest economy in the world. MIT managed $718.2 million in research expenditures and a $8.0 billion endowment in 2009.

The Engineers sponsor 33 sports, most of which compete in the NCAA Division III's New England Women's and Men's Athletic Conference; the Division I rowing programs compete as part of the EARC and EAWRC.

History

Main article: History of the Massachusetts Institute of Technology

Foundation and early years (1861–1915)

Institute of Technology, Boston, 19th c. (photo by E.L. Allen)

Institute of Technology, Back Bay, Boston, 19th c. (photo by E.L. Allen)

As early as 1859, the Massachusetts General Court was given a proposal for use of newly opened lands in Back Bay in Boston for a museum and Conservatory of Art and Science. In 1861, The Commonwealth of Massachusetts approved a charter for the incorporation of the "Massachusetts Institute of Technology and Boston Society of Natural History" submitted by William Barton Rogers. Rogers sought to establish a new form of higher education to address the challenges posed by rapid advances in science and technology during the mid-19th century with which classic institutions were ill-prepared to deal. Barton believed, "The true and only practicable object of a polytechnic school is, as I conceive, the teaching, not of the minute details and manipulations of the arts, which can be done only in the workshop, but the inculcation of those scientific principles which form the basis and explanation of them, their leading processes and operations in connection with physical laws."

The Rogers Plan, as it has come to be known, reflected the German research university model, emphasizing an independent faculty engaged in research as well as instruction oriented around seminars and laboratories. Rogers proposed that this new form of education be rooted in three principles: the educational value of useful knowledge, the necessity of "learning by doing", and integrating a professional and liberal arts education at the undergraduate level.

❝ ...a school of industrial science [aiding] the advancement, development and practical application of science in connection with arts, agriculture, manufactures, and commerce. ❞

—, Act to Incorporate the Massachusetts Institute of Technology, *Acts of 1861, Chapter 183*

Because open conflict in the Civil War broke out only weeks after receiving the charter, MIT's first classes were held in rented space at the Mercantile Building in downtown Boston in 1865. Though it was to be located in the middle of Boston, the mission of the new institute matched the intent of the 1862 Morrill Land-Grant Colleges Act to fund institutions "to promote the liberal and practical education of the industrial classes." Although the Commonwealth of Massachusetts founded what was to become the University of Massachusetts under this act,[d] MIT was also named a land grant school. The proceeds went toward new buildings in Boston's Back Bay in 1866; MIT was called "Boston Tech." During the next half-century, the focus of the science and engineering curriculum drifted towards vocational concerns instead of theoretical programs. Over the next 40 years, the MIT faculty and alumni repeatedly rejected overtures from Harvard University president Charles W. Eliot to merge MIT with Harvard's Lawrence Scientific School.

Development and post-war growth (1916–1965)

Industrialist George Eastman, donated the funds to build a new campus along a mile-long tract on the Cambridge side of the Charles River, almost entirely on landfill. In 1916, MIT moved into the handsome new neoclassical campus designed by William W. Bosworth.

In the 1930s President Karl Taylor Compton and Vice-President (effectively Provost) Vannevar Bush drastically reformed the curriculum by re-emphasizing the importance of "pure" sciences like physics and chemistry and reducing the work required in shops and drafting. Despite the challenges of the Great Depression, the reforms "renewed confidence in the ability of the Institute to develop leadership in science as well as in engineering." The expansion and reforms cemented MIT's academic reputation and it was elected to the Association of American Universities in 1934.

MIT was substantially changed by its involvement in military research during World War II. Bush was appointed head of the enormous Office of Scientific Research and Development and directed funding to only a select group of universities, including MIT. MIT's Radiation Laboratory was established in 1940 to assist the British in developing a microwave radar and the first mass-produced units were installed on front-line units within months. Other defense projects included gyroscope-based and other complex control systems for gun and bombsights and inertial navigation under Charles Stark Draper's Instrumentation Laboratory, the development of a digital computer for flight simulations under Project Whirlwind, and high-speed and high-altitude photography under Harold Edgerton. By the end of the war, MIT employed a staff of over 4,000 (including more than a fifth of the nation's physicists) and was the nation's single largest wartime R&D contractor.

In the post-war years, government-sponsored research such as SAGE and guidance systems for ballistic missiles and Project Apollo combined with surging student enrollments under the G.I. Bill contributed to a rapid growth in the size of the Institute's research staff and physical plant as well as placing an increased emphasis on graduate education. The profound changes that occurred at MIT between 1930 and 1957 included the doubling of its faculty and a quintupling of its graduate student population. These changes were significantly guided and shaped by the institution-building strategies of Karl Taylor Compton, president of MIT between 1930 and 1948, James Rhyne Killian, president from 1948 to 1957, and Julius Adams Stratton, chancellor from 1952 to 1957.

While the school mainly served the needs of industrial patrons in the 1920s, by the 1950s it had gained considerable autonomy from industrial corporations while attracting new patrons and building a close relationship with philanthropic foundations and the federal government. As the Cold War and Space Race intensified and concerns about the technology gap between the U.S. and the Soviet Union grew more pervasive throughout the 1950s and 1960s, MIT's involvement in the military-industrial complex was a source of pride on campus.

Recent history (1966–present)

Following a comprehensive review of the undergraduate curriculum in 1949 and the successive appointments of more humanistically oriented Presidents Howard W. Johnson and Jerome Wiesner between 1966 and 1980, MIT greatly expanded its programs in the humanities, arts, and social sciences. Previously marginalized faculties in the areas of economics, management, political science, and linguistics emerged into cohesive and assertive departments by attracting respected professors, launching competitive graduate programs, and forming into the School of Humanities, Arts, and Social Sciences and Sloan School of Management in 1950 to compete with the powerful Schools of Science and Engineering.

The MIT Media Lab houses researchers developing novel uses of computer technology. Shown here is the 1982 building, designed by I.M. Pei, with an extension (background) designed by Fumiko Maki and opened in March 2010.

In late 1960s and early 1970s, student and faculty activists protested against the Vietnam War and MIT's defense research. The Union of Concerned Scientists was founded on March 4, 1969 during a meeting of faculty members and students seeking to shift the emphasis on military research towards environmental and social problems. Although MIT ultimately divested itself from the Instrumentation Laboratory and moved all classified research off-campus to the Lincoln Laboratory facility in 1973 in response to the protests, the student body, faculty, and administration remained comparatively unpolarized during the tumultuous era.

In addition to developing the predecessors to modern computing and networking technologies, students, staff, and faculty members at the Project MAC, Artificial Intelligence Laboratory, and Tech Model Railroad Club wrote some of the earliest interactive computer games like *Spacewar!* and created much of modern hacker slang. Several major computer-related organizations have originated at MIT since the 1980s; Richard Stallman's GNU Project and the subsequent Free Software Foundation were founded in the mid-1980s at the AI Lab, the MIT Media Lab was founded in 1985 by Nicholas Negroponte and Jerome Wiesner to promote research into novel uses of computer technology, the World Wide Web Consortium standards organization was founded at the Laboratory for Computer Science in 1994 by Tim Berners-Lee, the OpenCourseWare project has made course materials for over 1,800 MIT classes available online free of charge since 2002, and the One Laptop per Child initiative to expand computer education and connectivity to children worldwide was launched in 2005. Upon taking office in 2004, President Hockfield launched an Energy Research Council to investigate how MIT can respond to the interdisciplinary challenges of increasing global energy consumption.

MIT was named a sea-grant college in 1976 to support its programs in oceanography and marine sciences and was named a space-grant college in 1989 to support its aeronautics and astronautics programs. Despite diminishing government financial support over the past quarter century, MIT launched several development campaigns to significantly expand the campus: new dormitories and athletics buildings on west campus, the Tang Center for Management Education, several buildings in the northeast corner of campus supporting research into biology, brain and cognitive sciences, genomics, biotechnology, and cancer research, and a number of new "backlot" buildings on Vassar Street including the Stata Center. Construction on campus continues to expand the Media Lab, Sloan's eastern campus, and graduate residences in the northwest.

Campus

Main article: Campus of the Massachusetts Institute of Technology

MIT's 168-acre (68.0 ha) campus spans approximately a mile of the north side of the Charles River basin in the city of Cambridge. The campus is divided roughly in half by Massachusetts Avenue, with most dormitories and student life facilities to the west and most academic buildings to the east. The bridge closest to MIT is the Harvard Bridge, which is known for being marked off in a non-standard unit of length – the smoot. The Kendall MBTA Red Line station is located on the far northeastern edge of the campus in Kendall Square. The Cambridge neighborhoods surrounding MIT are a mixture of high tech companies occupying both modern office and rehabilitated industrial buildings as well as socio-economically diverse residential neighborhoods.

The central and eastern sections of MIT's campus as seen from above Massachusetts Avenue and the Charles River. In the center is the Great Dome overlooking Killian Court with Kendall Square in the background.

MIT buildings all have a number (or a number and a letter) designation and most have a name as well. Typically, academic and office buildings are referred to only by number while residence halls are referred to by name. The organization of building numbers roughly corresponds to the order in which the buildings were built and their location relative (north, west, and east) to the original, center cluster of Maclaurin buildings. Many are connected above ground as well as through an extensive network of underground tunnels, providing protection from the Cambridge weather as well as a venue for roof and tunnel hacking.

MIT's on-campus nuclear reactor is one of the largest university-based nuclear reactors in the United States. The prominence of the reactor's containment building in a densely populated area has been controversial, but MIT maintains that it is well-secured. Other notable campus facilities include a pressurized wind tunnel and a towing tank for testing ship and ocean structure designs. MIT's campus-wide wireless network was completed in the fall of 2005 and consists of nearly 3,000 access points covering 9400000 square feet (870000 m^2) of campus.

In 2001, the Environmental Protection Agency sued MIT for violating Clean Water Act and Clean Air Act with regard to its hazardous waste storage and disposal procedures. MIT settled the suit by paying a $155,000 fine and launching three environmental projects. In connection with capital campaigns to expand the campus, the institute has also extensively renovated existing buildings to improve their energy efficiency. MIT has also taken steps to reduce its environmental impact by running alternative fuel campus shuttles, subsidizing public transportation passes, and a low-emission cogeneration plant that serves most of the campus electricity and heating requirements.

Between 2006 and 2008, MIT reported 16 forcible sex offenses, 4 robberies, 13 aggravated assaults, 536 burglaries, 2 cases of arson, and 16 cases of motor vehicle theft.

Architecture

MIT's School of Architecture was the first in the United States, and it has a history of commissioning progressive buildings. The first buildings constructed on the Cambridge campus, completed in 1916, are known officially as the *Maclaurin buildings* after Institute president Richard Maclaurin who oversaw their construction. Designed by William Welles Bosworth, these imposing buildings were built of concrete, a first for a non-industrial — much less university — building in the U.S. The utopian City Beautiful movement greatly influenced Bosworth's design which features the Pantheon-esque Great Dome, housing the Barker Engineering Library, which overlooks Killian Court,

The Stata Center houses CSAIL, LIDS, and the Department of Linguistics and Philosophy

where annual Commencement exercises are held. The friezes of the limestone-clad buildings around Killian Court are engraved with the names of important scientists and philosophers.[k] The imposing Building 7 atrium along Massachusetts Avenue is regarded as the entrance to the Infinite Corridor and the rest of the campus.

Alvar Aalto's Baker House (1947), Eero Saarinen's Chapel and Auditorium (1955), and I.M. Pei's Green, Dreyfus, Landau, and Wiesner buildings represent high forms of post-war modern architecture. More recent buildings like Frank Gehry's Stata Center (2004), Steven Holl's Simmons Hall (2002),

Charles Correa's Building 46 (2005), Fumihiko Maki's Media Lab Extension (2009) are distinctive amongst the Boston area's classical architecture and serve as examples of contemporary campus "starchitecture." These buildings have not always been popularly accepted; in 2010, *The Princeton Review* included MIT in a list of twenty schools whose campuses are "tiny, unsightly, or both."

Housing

Main article: Housing at MIT

Undergraduates are guaranteed four-year housing in one of MIT's twelve dormitories, although 8% of students live off campus or commute. On-campus housing provides live-in graduate student tutors and faculty housemasters who have the dual role of both helping students and monitoring them for medical or mental health problems. Students are permitted to select their dorm and floor upon arrival on campus, and as a result diverse communities arise in living groups; the dorms on and east of Massachusetts Avenue have typically been more involved in countercultural activities. MIT also has five dormitories

Simmons Hall was completed in 2002

for single graduate students and two apartment buildings on campus for families.

MIT has a very active Greek and co-op system which includes 36 fraternities, sororities, and independent living groups (FSILGs). 50% of male undergraduates join a fraternity and 34% of women join sororities. Most FSILGs are located across the river in the Back Bay owing to MIT's historic location there, but eight fraternities are located on MIT's West Campus and in Cambridge. After the 1997 death of Scott Krueger, a new member at the Phi Gamma Delta fraternity, MIT required all freshmen to live in the dormitory system starting in 2002. Because the fraternities and independent living groups had previously housed as many as 300 freshmen off-campus, the new policy did not take effect until 2002 after Simmons Hall opened.

Organization and administration

MIT is chartered as a non-profit organization and is owned and governed by a privately appointed board of trustees known as the MIT Corporation. The current board consists of 43 members elected to five year terms, 25 life members who vote until their 75th birthday, three elected officers (President, Treasurer, and Secretary), and four *ex officio* members including the president of the alumni association, the Governor of Massachusetts, the Massachusetts Secretary of Education, and the Chief Justice of the Massachusetts Supreme Judicial Court. The board is chaired by John S. Reed, the former chairman of the New York Stock Exchange and Citigroup. The corporation approves the budget, new programs, degrees, and faculty appointments as well as electing the President to serve as the chief executive officer of the university and presiding over the Institute's faculty. The sixteenth and current president, Susan Hockfield, a molecular neurobiologist, succeeded Charles M. Vest's fourteen year tenure in December 2004 and is the first woman to hold the post. MIT's endowment and other financial assets are managed through a subsidiary MIT Investment Management Company (MITIMCo). Valued at $8.0 billion in 2009, MIT's endowment is the sixth-largest among American colleges and universities.

MIT is "a university polarized around science, engineering, and the arts." It has five schools (Science, Engineering, Architecture and Planning, Management, and Humanities, Arts, and Social Sciences) and one college (Whitaker College of Health Sciences and Technology), but no schools of law or medicine.[e] The chair of each of MIT's 32 academic departments reports to the dean of that department's school, who in turn reports to the Provost under the President. However, faculty committees assert substantial control over many areas of MIT's curriculum, research, student life, and administrative affairs.

Collaborations

The university historically pioneered research and training collaborations between the academy, industry and government. Fruitful collaborations with industrialists like Alfred P. Sloan and Thomas Alva Edison led President Compton to establish an Office of Corporate Relations and an Industrial Liaison Program in the 1930s and 1940s that now allows over 600 companies to license research and consult with MIT faculty and researchers. Throughout the late 1980s and early 1990s, American politicians and business leaders accused MIT and other universities of contributing to a declining economy by transferring taxpayer-funded research and technology to international — especially Japanese — firms that were competing with struggling American businesses.

MIT's extensive collaboration with the federal government on research projects has also led to several MIT leaders serving as Presidential scientific advisers since 1940.[j] MIT established a Washington Office in 1991 to continue to lobby for research funding and national science policy. In response to MIT, eight Ivy League colleges, and 11 other institutions holding "Overlap Meetings" to prevent bidding wars over promising students from consuming funds for need-based scholarships, the Justice Department began an antitrust investigation in 1989 and in 1991 filed an antitrust suit against these universities. While the Ivy League institutions settled, MIT contested the charges on the grounds that the practice was not anti-competitive because it ensured the availability of aid for the greatest number of students. MIT ultimately prevailed when the Justice Department dropped the case in 1994.

MIT's proximity to Harvard University[i] has created both a quasi-friendly rivalry ("the other school up the river") and a substantial number of research collaborations such as the Harvard-MIT Division of Health Sciences and Technology and Broad Institute. In addition, students at the two schools can cross-register for credits toward their own school's degrees without any additional fees. A cross-registration program with Wellesley College has existed since 1969 and a significant undergraduate exchange program with the University of Cambridge known as the Cambridge-MIT Institute was also launched in 2002. MIT has more modest cross-registration programs with Boston University, Brandeis University, Tufts University, Massachusetts College of Art, and the School of the Museum of Fine Arts, Boston. MIT maintains substantial research and faculty ties with independent research organizations in the Boston-area like the Charles Stark Draper Laboratory, Whitehead Institute for Biomedical Research, and Woods Hole Oceanographic Institution as well as international research and educational collaborations through the Singapore-MIT Alliance, MIT-Zaragoza International Logistics Program, and other countries through the MIT International Science and Technology Initiatives (MISTI) program.

The mass-market magazine *Technology Review* is published by MIT through a subsidiary company, as is a special edition that also serves as the Institute's official alumni magazine. The MIT Press is a major university press, publishing over 200 books and 40 journals annually emphasizing science and technology as well as arts, architecture, new media, current events, and social issues.

Academics

University rankings (overall)	
ARWU World	4
ARWU National	4
Forbes	11
QS World	5
Times Higher Education	3
USNWR National University	7
WM National University	12

MIT is a large, highly residential, research university with a majority of enrollments in graduate and professional programs. The university has been accredited by the New England Association of Schools and Colleges since 1929. MIT operates on a 4-1-4 academic calendar with the fall semester beginning after Labor Day and ending in mid-December, a 4-week "Independent Activities Period" in the month of January, and the spring semester beginning in early February and ending in late May.

MIT students refer to both their majors and classes using numbers or acronyms alone. Departments and their corresponding majors are numbered in the approximate order their foundation; for example, Civil and Environmental Engineering is Course I, while Nuclear Science & Engineering is Course XXII. Students majoring in Electrical Engineering and Computer Science, the most popular department, collectively identify themselves as "Course VI." MIT students use a combination of the department's course number and the number assigned to the class to identify their subjects; the course which many American universities would designate as "Physics 101" is, at MIT, simply "8.01."[f]

The School of Engineering has been ranked first among graduate and undergraduate programs by *U.S. News & World Report* since first published results in 1994. A 1995 National Research Council study of US research universities ranked MIT first in "reputation" and fourth in "citations and faculty awards" and a 2005 NBER study of high school students' revealed preferences found MIT to be the 4th most preferred college in the nation.

Undergraduate program

The four year, full-time undergraduate instructional program is classified as "balanced arts & sciences/professions" and admission is characterized as "more selective, lower transfer in." MIT offers 44 undergraduate degrees across its five schools. 1,146 bachelor of science (SB) degrees were granted in 2009, the only type of undergraduate degree MIT awards. The School of Engineering is the most popular division enrolling 44.5% of students in its 19 degree programs, followed by the School of Science (20.2%), School of Humanities, Arts, & Social Sciences (3.5%), Sloan School of Management (3.5%), and the School of Architecture and Planning (1.8%). The largest undergraduate degree programs are in Electrical Engineering and Computer Science (Course VI-2), Mechanical Engineering (Course II), Computer Science and Engineering (Course VI-3), Physics (Course VIII), Biology (Course VII), and Mathematics (Course XVIII).

Undergraduates are required to complete an extensive core curriculum called the General Institute Requirements (GIRs). The science requirement, generally completed during freshman year as prerequisites for classes in science and engineering majors, comprises two semesters of physics, two semesters of calculus, one semester of chemistry, one semester of biology, and a laboratory class in their major. The humanities, arts, and social sciences (HASS) requirement, consisting of eight semesters, includes a distribution of three classes across each of the humanities, arts, and social sciences as well as a concentration. The communication requirement consists of two communication-intensive HASS classes and two classes in their major program. Finally, all students are required to complete a swimming test and non-varsity athletes must also take four physical education classes.

The Infinite Corridor is the primary passageway through campus

Although the difficulty of MIT coursework has been characterized as "drinking from a fire hose," the freshmen retention rate at MIT are similar to other national research universities. Some of the pressure for first-year undergraduates is lessened by the existence of the "pass/no-record" grading system. In the first (fall) term, freshmen transcripts only report if a class was passed while no external record exists if a class was not passed. In the second (spring) term, passing grades (ABC) appear on the transcript while non-passing grades are again rendered "no-record". The system had previously been "Pass/No Record" all freshman year, but was amended for the Class of 2006 to prevent students from gaming the system by completing required major classes on a pass/fail basis.

Most classes rely upon a combination of faculty led lectures, graduate student led recitations, weekly problem sets (p-sets), and tests to teach material, though alternative curricula exist, e.g. Experimental Study Group, Concourse, and Terrascope. Over time, students compile "bibles", collections of problem set and examination questions and answers used as references for later students. In 1970, the then-Dean of Institute Relations, Benson R. Snyder, published *The Hidden Curriculum*, arguing that unwritten regulations, like the implicit curricula of the bibles, are often counterproductive; they fool professors into believing that their teaching is effective and students into believing they have learned the material.

In 1969, MIT began the Undergraduate Research Opportunities Program (UROP) to enable undergraduates to collaborate directly with faculty members and researchers. The program, founded by Margaret MacVicar, builds upon the MIT philosophy of "learning by doing". Students obtain research projects, colloquially called "UROPs", through postings on the UROP website or by contacting faculty members directly. Over 2,800 undergraduates, 70% of the student body, participate every year for academic credit, pay, or on a volunteer basis. Students often become published, file patent applications, and/or launch start-up companies based upon their experience in UROPs.

Graduate program

MIT's graduate program is a comprehensive doctoral program having high coexistence with undergraduate programs in the humanities, social sciences, and STEM fields as well as offering professional degrees. The Institute offers graduate programs leading to academic degrees such as the Master of Science, Doctor of Philosophy, and Doctor of Science; professional degrees such as Master of Business Administration, Master of Finance, Master of Architecture, Master of Engineering, and Engineer's Degree; and interdisciplinary graduate programs such as the M.D.-Ph.D. Admission to graduate programs is decentralized; applicants apply directly to the department or degree program. Doctoral students are supported by fellowships (30%), research assistantships (49%), and teaching assistantships (13%).

MIT awarded 1,474 master's degrees and 607 doctoral degrees in 2009. The School of Engineering is the most popular academic division enrolling 45.4% of graduate students, followed by the Sloan School of Management (17.3%), School of Science (17.3%), School of Architecture and Planning (9.5%), School of Humanities, Arts, and Social Sciences (4.9%), and Whitaker College of Health Sciences (2.5%). The largest graduate degree programs are the Sloan M.B.A, Electrical Engineering and Computer Science, Mechanical Engineering, and Chemical Engineering.

Libraries and museums

The MIT library system consists of five subject libraries for each of the academic divisions of the Institute as well as specialized libraries and archives. The libraries contain more than 2.8 million printed volumes, 2.2 million microforms, 43,000 print or electronic journal subscriptions, and 570 databases. Notable collections include the Lewis Music Library with an emphasis on 20th and 21st-century music and electronic music, the List Visual Arts Center's rotating exhibitions of contemporary art, and the Compton Gallery's cross-disciplinary exhibitions. MIT allocates a percentage of the budget for all new construction and renovation to commission and support its extensive public art and outdoor sculpture collection. The MIT Museum was founded in 1971 and collects, preserves, and exhibits artifacts significant to the life and history of MIT as well as collaborating with the nearby Museum of Science.

Research

MIT was elected to the Association of American Universities in 1934 and remains a research university with a very high level of research activity; research expenditures totaled $718.2 million in 2009. The federal government was the largest source of sponsored research, with the Department of Health and Human Services granting $255.9 million, Department of Defense $97.5 million, Department of Energy $65.8 million, National Science Foundation $61.4 million, and NASA $27.4 million. MIT employs approximately 3,500 researchers in addition to faculty.[citation needed] In 2009, MIT faculty and researchers disclosed 530 inventions, filed 184 patent applications, received 166 patents, and earned $136.3 million in royalties and other income.

In electronics, magnetic core memory, radar, single electron transistors, and inertial guidance controls were invented or substantially developed by MIT researchers. Harold Eugene Edgerton was a pioneer in high speed photography. Claude E. Shannon developed much of modern information theory and discovered the application of Boolean logic to digital circuit design theory. In the domain of computer science, MIT faculty and researchers made fundamental contributions to cybernetics, artificial intelligence, computer languages, machine learning, robotics, and cryptography.

The GNU project and free software movement originated at MIT

Current and previous physics faculty have won eight Nobel Prizes, four Dirac Medals, and three Wolf Prizes predominantly for their contributions to subatomic and quantum theory. Members of the chemistry department have been awarded three Nobel Prizes and one Wolf Prize for the discovery of novel syntheses and methods. MIT biologists have been awarded six Nobel Prizes for their contributions to genetics, immunology, oncology, and molecular biology. Professor Eric Lander was one of the principal leaders of the Human Genome Project. Positronium atoms, synthetic Penicillin, synthetic self-replicating molecules, and the genetic bases for Lou Gehrig's disease and Huntington's disease were first discovered at MIT. Jerome Lettvin transformed the study of cognitive science with his paper "What the frog's eye tells the frog's brain".

In the domain of humanities, arts, and social sciences, MIT economists have been awarded five Nobel Prizes and nine John Bates Clark Medals. Linguists Noam Chomsky and Morris Halle authored seminal texts on generative grammar and phonology. The MIT Media Lab, founded in 1985 and known for its unconventional research, has been home to influential researchers such as constructivist educator and Logo creator Seymour Papert.

Given MIT's prominence, allegations of research misconduct or improprieties have received substantial press coverage. Professor David Baltimore, a Nobel Laureate, became embroiled in a misconduct investigation starting in 1986 that led to Congressional hearings in 1991. Professor Ted Postol has accused the MIT administration since 2000 of attempting to whitewash potential research misconduct at the Lincoln Lab facility involving a ballistic missile defense test, though a final investigation into the matter has not been completed. Associate Professor Luk Van Parijs was dismissed in 2005 following allegations of scientific misconduct and found guilty of the same by the United States Office of Research Integrity in 2009.

Traditions and student activities

Main articles: Traditions and student activities at MIT and MIT class ring

The faculty and student body highly value meritocracy and technical proficiency. MIT has never awarded an honorary degree, nor does it award athletic scholarships, ad eundem degrees, or Latin honors upon graduation. However, MIT has twice awarded honorary professorships; to Winston Churchill in 1949 and Salman Rushdie in 1993.

Current students and alumni wear a large, heavy, distinctive class ring known as the "Brass Rat". Originally created in 1929, the ring's official name is the "Standard Technology Ring." The undergraduate ring design (a separate graduate student version exists as well) varies slightly from year to year to reflect the unique character of the MIT experience for that class, but always features a three-piece design, with the MIT seal and the class year each appearing on a separate face, flanking a large rectangular bezel bearing an image of a beaver. The initialism IHTFP, representing the informal school motto "I hate this fucking place" and jocularly euphemized as "I have truly found paradise," "Institute has the finest professors," and other variations, is featured on the ring given its historical prominence in student culture.

Activities

Main article: Student activities at MIT

See also: MIT hacks

MIT has over 380 recognized student activity groups, including a campus radio station, *The Tech* student newspaper, an annual entrepreneurship competition, and weekly screenings of popular films by the Lecture Series Committee. Less traditional activities include the "world's largest open-shelf collection of science fiction" in English, a model railroad club, and a vibrant folk dance scene. Students, faculty, and staff are involved in over 50 educational outreach and public service programs through the MIT Museum, Edgerton Center, and MIT Public Service Center.

The Independent Activities Period is a four-week long "term" offering hundreds of optional classes, lectures, demonstrations, and other activities throughout the month of January between the Fall and Spring semesters. Some of the most popular recurring IAP activities are the 6.270, 6.370, and MasLab competitions, the annual "mystery hunt", and Charm School. Students also have the opportunity of pursuing externships at companies in the U.S. and abroad. Many MIT students also engage in "hacking," which encompasses both the physical exploration of areas that are generally off-limits (such as rooftops and steam tunnels), as well as elaborate practical jokes. Recent hacks have included the theft of Caltech's cannon, reconstructing a Wright Flyer atop the Great Dome, and adorning the John Harvard statue with the Master Chief's Spartan Helmet.

Athletics

The student athletics program offers 33 varsity-level sports, one of the largest programs in the U.S. MIT participates in the NCAA's Division III, the New England Women's and Men's Athletic Conference, the New England Football Conference, and NCAA's Division I and Eastern Association of Rowing Colleges (EARC) for crew. In April 2009, budget cuts lead to MIT eliminating eight of its 41 sports, including the mixed men's and women's teams in alpine skiing and pistol; separate teams for men and women in ice hockey and gymnastics; and men's programs in golf and wrestling.

The Zesiger sports and fitness center houses a two-story fitness center as well as swimming and diving pools

The Institute's sports teams are called the Engineers, their mascot since 1914 being a beaver, "nature's engineer." Lester Gardner, a member of the Class of 1898, provided the following justification:

> The beaver not only typifies the Tech, but his habits are particularly our own. The beaver is noted for his engineering and mechanical skills and habits of industry. His habits are nocturnal. He does his best work in the dark.

MIT fielded several dominant intercollegiate Tiddlywinks teams through 1980, winning national and world championships. The Engineers have won or placed highly in national championships in pistol, taekwondo, track and field, swimming and diving, cross country, crew, fencing, and water polo.[citation needed] MIT has produced 128 Academic All-Americans, the third largest membership in the country for any division and the highest number of members for Division III.

The Zesiger sports and fitness center (Z-Center) which opened in 2002, significantly expanded the capacity and quality of MIT's athletics, physical education, and recreation offerings to 10 buildings and 26 acres (110000 m^2) of playing fields.[citation needed] The 124000-square-foot (11500 m^2) facility features an Olympic-class swimming pool, international-scale squash courts, and a two-story fitness center.

People

Students

Demographics of MIT student body

	Undergraduate	Graduate
Caucasian American	42.5%	40.8%
Asian American	25.6%	9.4%
Hispanic American	13.2%	3.3%
African American	8.5%	2.1%
Native American	1.0%	0.4%
Other/International	9.2%	44.0%

MIT enrolled 4,232 undergraduates and 6,152 graduate students in 2009–2010. Women constituted 45.3 percent of undergraduates and 31.1 percent of graduate students. Undergraduate and graduate students are drawn from all 50 states as well as 118 foreign countries.

MIT received 15,661 applications for admission to the Class of 2014; 1675 were admitted (10.7%) and 1078 enrolled (63.9%). 19,446 applications were received for advanced degree program across all departments; 2,991 were admitted (15.4%) and 1,880 enrolled (62.8%). The interquartile range on the SAT was 2030–2320 and 95% of students ranked in the top tenth of their high school graduating class. 97% of the Class of 2012 returned as sophomores; 82.3% of the Class of 2007 graduated within 4 years, and 91.3% (92% of the men and 96% of the women) graduated within 6 years.

Undergraduate tuition and fees total $37,782 and annual expenses are estimated at $50,100. 61% of students received need-based financial aid in the form of scholarships and grants from federal, state, institutional, and external sources averaging $35,202 per student. MIT awarded $87.6 million in scholarships and grants, the vast majority ($73.4 million) coming from institutional support. The annual increase in expenses has led to a student tradition (dating back to the 1960s) of tongue-in-cheek "tuition riots".

MIT has been nominally coeducational since admitting Ellen Swallow Richards in 1870. Richards also became the first female member of MIT's faculty, specializing in sanitary chemistry. Female students remained a very small minority (less than 3 percent) prior to the completion of the first wing of a women's dormitory, McCormick Hall, in 1962. Between 1993 and 2009, the proportion of women rose from 34 percent to 45 percent of undergraduates and from 20 percent to 31 percent of graduate students. Women currently outnumber men in Biology, Brain & Cognitive Sciences, Architecture, Urban Planning, and Biological Engineering.

A number of student deaths in the late 1990s and early 2000s resulted in considerable media attention to MIT's culture and student life. After the alcohol-related death of Scott Krueger in September 1997 as a new member at the Phi Gamma Delta fraternity, MIT began requiring all freshmen to live in the dormitory system. The 2000 suicide of MIT undergraduate Elizabeth Shin drew attention to suicides at

MIT and created a controversy over whether MIT had an unusually high suicide rate. In late 2001 a task force's recommended improvements in student mental health services were implemented, including expanding staff and operating hours at the mental health center. These and later cases were significant as well because they sought to prove the negligence and liability of university administrators *in loco parentis*.

Faculty

Main article: List of Massachusetts Institute of Technology faculty

MIT has 1,009 faculty members, of whom 198 are women. Faculty are responsible for lecturing classes, advising both graduate and undergraduate students, and sitting on academic committees, as well as conducting original research. Between 1964 and 2009, a total of 17 faculty and staff members affiliated with MIT were awarded Nobel Prizes (14 during the last quarter century). MIT faculty members past or present have won a total of 27 Nobel Prizes, the majority in Economics or Physics. Among current faculty and teaching staff, there are 80 Guggenheim Fellows, 6 Fulbright Scholars, and 29 MacArthur Fellows. Faculty members who have made extraordinary contributions to their research field as well

Institute Professors Emeriti and Nobel Laureates (from left to right) Franco Modigliani (now deceased), Paul Samuelson (also deceased), and Robert Solow

as the MIT community are granted appointments as Institute Professors for the remainder of their tenures.

A 1998 MIT study concluded that a systemic bias against female faculty existed in its college of science, although the study's methods were controversial. Since the study, though, women have headed departments within the Schools of Science and Engineering, and MIT has appointed several female vice presidents, although allegations of sexism continue to be made. Susan Hockfield, a molecular neurobiologist, became MIT's 16th president in 2004 and is the first woman to hold the post.

Tenure outcomes have vaulted MIT into the national spotlight on several occasions. The 1984 dismissal of David F. Noble, a historian of technology, became a *cause célèbre* about the extent to which academics are granted freedom of speech after he published several books and papers critical of MIT's and other research universities' reliance upon financial support from corporations and the military. Former materials science professor Gretchen Kalonji sued MIT in 1994 alleging that she was denied tenure because of sexual discrimination. In 1997, the Massachusetts Commission Against Discrimination issued a probable cause finding supporting James Jennings' allegations of racial discrimination after a senior faculty search committee in the Department of Urban Studies and Planning did not offer him reciprocal tenure. In 2006–2007, MIT's denial of tenure to African-American biological engineering professor James Sherley reignited accusations of racism in the tenure process, eventually leading to a protracted public dispute with the administration, a brief hunger strike, and the resignation of Professor Frank L. Douglas in protest.

MIT faculty members have often been recruited to lead other colleges and universities; former Provost Robert A. Brown is President of Boston University, former Provost Mark Wrighton is Chancellor of Washington University in St. Louis, former Associate Provost Alice Gast is president of Lehigh University, former Dean of the School of Science Robert J. Birgeneau is the Chancellor of the University of California, Berkeley, and former professor David Baltimore was President of Caltech. In addition, faculty members have been recruited to lead governmental agencies; for example, former professor Marcia McNutt is the director of the United States Geological Survey, urban studies professor Xavier de Souza Briggs is currently the associate director of the White House Office of Management and Budget, and biology professor Eric Lander is a co-chair of the President's Council of Advisors on Science and Technology.

Alumni

Main article: List of Massachusetts Institute of Technology alumni

Many of MIT's over 110,000 alumni and alumnae have had considerable success in scientific research, public service, education, and business. Seventy-six MIT alumni have won the Nobel Prize, forty-four have been selected as Rhodes Scholars, and fifty-five have been selected as Marshall Scholars.

Alumni in American politics and public service include Chairman of the Federal Reserve Ben Bernanke, MA-1 Representative John Olver, CA-13 Representative Pete Stark, former National Economic Council chairman Lawrence H. Summers, and former Council of Economic Advisors chairwoman Christina Romer. MIT alumni in international politics include British Foreign Minister David Miliband, Israeli Prime Minister Benjamin Netanyahu, former U.N. Secretary General Kofi Annan, and former Iraqi Deputy Prime Minister Ahmed Chalabi.

MIT alumni founded or co-founded many notable companies, such as Intel, McDonnell Douglas, Texas Instruments, 3Com, Qualcomm, Bose, Raytheon, Koch Industries, Rockwell International, Genentech, and Campbell Soup. The annual Entrepreneurship Competition has led to the creation of over 85 companies that have, in aggregate, generated 2,500 jobs, received $600 million in venture capital funding, and have a market capitalization of over $10 billion. A 2009 study claimed that the combined revenues of companies founded by MIT affiliates would make it the seventeenth largest economy in the world.

Prominent institutions of higher education have been led by MIT alumni, including the University of California system, Harvard University, Johns Hopkins University, Carnegie Mellon University, Tufts University, Rochester Institute of Technology, Northeastern University, Rensselaer Polytechnic Institute, Tecnológico de Monterrey, Purdue University, Virginia Polytechnic Institute and Quaid-e-Azam University.

More than one third of the United States' manned spaceflights have included MIT-educated astronauts (among them Apollo 11 Lunar Module Pilot Buzz Aldrin), more than any university excluding the United States service academies.

Noted alumni in non-scientific fields include author Hugh Lofting, Boston guitarist Tom Scholz, *The New York Times* columnist and Nobel Prize Winning economist Paul Krugman, *The Bell Curve* author Charles Murray, United States Supreme Court building architect Cass Gilbert, Pritzker Prize-winning architects I.M. Pei and Gordon Bunshaft.

Apollo 11 astronaut Buzz Aldrin, ScD '63 (Course XVI)

Former UN Secretary-General Kofi Annan, SM '72 (Course XV)

Federal Reserve Bank Chairman Ben Bernanke, PhD '79 (Course XIV)

Israeli Prime Minister Benjamin Netanyahu, SB '76 (Course IV), SM '78 (Course XV)

Notes

a. "We examined and discussed many colors. We all desired cardinal red; it has stood for a thousand years on land and sea in England's emblem; it makes one-half of the stripes on America's flag; it has always stirred the heart and mind of man; it stands for 'red blood' and all that 'red blood' stands for in life. But we were not unanimous for the gray; some wanted blue, I recall. But it (the gray) seemed to me to stand for those quiet virtues of modesty and persistency and gentleness, which appealed to my mind as powerful; and I have come to believe, from observation and experience, to really be the most lasting influences in life and history....We recommended 'cardinal and steel gray.'" (Alfred T. Waite, Chairman of School Color Committee, Class of 1879)

b. The other privately owned Land Grant institution is Cornell University.

d. The University of Massachusetts was founded as the Massachusetts Agricultural College in 1863.

e. The Harvard-MIT Division of Health Sciences and Technology (HST) offers joint MD, MD-PhD, or Medical Engineering degrees in collaboration with Harvard Medical School.

f. Course numbers are traditionally presented in Roman numerals, e.g. Course XVIII for mathematics. Starting in 2002, the Bulletin (MIT's course catalog) started to use Arabic numerals. Usage outside of the Bulletin varies, both Roman and Arabic numerals being used.

h. MIT's Building 7 and Harvard's Johnston Gate, the traditional entrances to each school, are 1.72 miles (2.77 km) apart along Massachusetts Avenue.

i. Vannevar Bush was the director of the Office of Scientific Research and Development and general advisor to Franklin D. Roosevelt and Harry Truman, James Rhyne Killian was Special Assistant for Science and Technology for Dwight D. Eisenhower, and Jerome Wiesner advised John F. Kennedy and Lyndon Johnson.

j. The friezes of the marble-clad buildings surrounding Killian Court are carved in large Roman letters with the names of Aristotle, Newton, Pasteur, Lavoisier, Faraday, Archimedes, da Vinci, Darwin, and Copernicus; each of these names is surmounted by a cluster of appropriately related names in smaller letters. Lavoisier, for example, is placed in the company of Boyle, Cavendish, Priestley, Dalton, Gay Lussac, Berzelius, Woehler, Liebig, Bunsen, Mendelejeff [sic], Perkin, and van't Hoff.

References

- Abelmann, Walter H., ed. *The Harvard-MIT Division of Health Sciences and Technology: The First 25 Years, 1970-1995* (2004). 346 pp

- Angulo, A. J., "The Initial Reception of MIT, 1860s−1880s," *History of Higher Education Annual,* 26 (2007), 1−28.

- Etzkowitz, Henry. *MIT and the Rise of Entrepreneurial Science* Series: Studies in Global Competition. (2002). 173 pp.

- Hapgood, Fred. *Up the Infinite Corridor: MIT and the Technical Imagination* (1993). 203 pp

- Jarzombek, Mark (2003). *Designing MIT: Bosworth's New Tech* [2]. Northeastern University Press. ISBN 1-55553-619-0. on William Welles Bosworth 164pp

- Lecuyer, Christophe. "The Making of a Science Based Technological University: Karl Compton, James Killian, and the Reform of MIT, 1930-1957," *Historical Studies in the Physical & Biological Sciences* 1992 23(1): 153-180

- Leslie, Stuart W. (1994). *The Cold War and American Science: The Military-Industrial-Academic Complex at MIT and Stanford.* Columbia University Press. ISBN 0-231-07959-1.

- Mitchell, William J. (2007). *Imagining MIT: Designing a Campus for the Twenty-First Century.* The MIT Press. ISBN 978-0-262-13479-8.

- Peterson, T. F. (2003). *Nightwork: A History of Hacks and Pranks at MIT.* The MIT Press. ISBN 978-0-262-66137-9.

- Prescott, Samuel C. (1954). *When M.I.T. Was "Boston Tech", 1861−1916.* Technology Press. ISBN 978-0-262-66139-3.

- Servos, John W. (December 1980). "The Industrial Relations of Science: Chemical Engineering at MIT, 1900-1939" [3]. *Isis* (The University of Chicago Press on behalf of The History of Science Society) **71** (4): 531–549.
- Shrock, Robert Rakes. *Geology at MIT 1865-1965: A History of the First Hundred Years of Geology at Massachusetts Institute of Technology. Vol. 1, The Faculty and Supporting Staff* (1977). 1032 pp.
- Simha, O. Robert (2003). *MIT Campus Planning,: An Annotated Chronology.* The MIT Press. ISBN 978-0-262-69294-6.
- Snyder, Benson R. (1973). *The Hidden Curriculum.* The MIT Press. ISBN 978-0-262-69043-0.
- Stratton, Julius Adams; Loretta H. Mannix (2005). *Mind and Hand: The Birth of MIT.* The MIT Press. ISBN 978-0-262-19524-9.
- Vest, Charles M. *Pursuing the Endless Frontier: Essays on MIT and the Role of Research Universities* (2004). 292 pp.
- Wildes, Karl L. and Lindgren, Nilo A. *A Century of Electrical Engineering and Computer Science at MIT, 1882-1984* (1985). 423 pp.

  Also see the bibliography [4] *maintained by MIT's Institute Archives & Special Collections* [5], *and Written Works in MIT in popular culture.*

External links

- Official website [1]

Geographical coordinates: 42°21′35″N 71°05′32″W

یجولانکیﻥ فآ ﻥوﻯﻯﻥسنا سﻥسوﻯچﺍسﻯم:pnb

Traditions and student activities at MIT

The **traditions and student activities at the Massachusetts Institute of Technology** encompass hundreds of student activities, organizations, and athletics that contribute to MIT's distinct culture.

Events

Independent Activities Period

Independent Activities Period [1] is a four-week long "term" offering hundreds of optional classes, lectures, demonstrations, and other activities throughout the month of January between the Fall and Spring terms.

Steer Roast

Steer Roast is an annual bacchanal hosted by Senior House.

Spring Weekend

Spring Weekend is an annual event that includes performances by local as well as major recording artists as well as picnics, parties, home varsity games, and other celebrations.

Sodium Drop

The Sodium Drop usually consists of a bar of metal sodium dropped into the Charles River, producing explosions due to the rapid conversion of sodium metal to sodium hydroxide and the ignition of the resulting hydrogen gas.

Time Traveler Convention

The **Time Traveler Convention** was a convention held at MIT on May 7, 2005, in the hopes of making contact with time travelers from the future. The convention was organized by Amal Dorai with help from current and former residents of the MIT living group Putz, one of the halls in the East Campus dorm. As of the date of the event, it was the most significantly publicized Time Traveler Convention, including front page coverage in the New York Times, *Wired*, and Slashdot. It was presumed time travelers would have the capability to visit any particular time if they could travel to that general time period at all. The idea originated in a Cat and Girl strip by Dorothy Gambrell.

The convention was held at 22:45 EDT on May 7, 2005 (May 8, 02:00 UTC) in the East Campus courtyard and Walker Memorial at MIT. That location is 42.360007 degrees north latitude, 71.087870 degrees west longitude. The Convention was announced in advance (that is, before the event) and over 300 contemporary people attended. (For fire safety reasons, a handful of attendees watched the convention via a closed circuit broadcast.) The spacetime coordinates continue to be publicized prominently and indefinitely, so that future time travelers will be aware and have the opportunity to have attended.

The convention featured lectures on various aspects of time travel from MIT professors and faculty, including Erik Demaine, a MacArthur "genius grant" winner, Alan Guth, an Eddington Medal winner for theoretical astrophysics, and Edward Farhi, winner of numerous MIT teaching awards. A De Lorean DMC-12, the car featured in the *Back to the Future* trilogy, was also on display, near the "landing pad" located at the exact coordinates advertised.

The convention inspired a full-length musical entitled The Time Travelers Convention, in which three college students, who all want to change their pasts, hold a convention in the hopes that they will be able to borrow an attendee's time machine. Although the school in the musical is not MIT, MIT is mentioned twice, once by name and once in the coordinates, which are the same as the coordinates given in the original convention.

Geographical coordinates: 42°21′36″N 71°05′16″W

- Official website [2]
- The Time Travelers Convention musical [3]

Brass rat

"Brass rat" refers to the MIT class ring, which prominently features the school mascot beaver on the top surface. The ring is made of gold, the beaver is the largest North American rodent, hence "gold beaver" becomes "brass rat" in student lingo.

Hacking

MIT hacks

Main article: MIT hacks

Roof and tunnel hacking

Main article: Roof and tunnel hacking

Activities

MIT has over 380 recognized student activity groups,. These are generally governed by the MIT Association of Student Activities.

Monarch B and Daedelus

The **Monarch B** was a human-powered aircraft built by a team at MIT in 1983 which won a Kremer Prize of £20,000 for sustaining a speed of over 30 km/h over a 1.5 km triangular course. It was a precursor to the MIT Daedalus effort to fly from Crete to the Greek mainland in 1988.

MIT Blackjack Team

Main article: MIT Blackjack Team

MIT Educational Studies Program

The Education Studies Program, or ESP, was created by MIT students in 1957 to make a difference in the community by sharing MIT's knowledge and creativity with local high school students. Since then, its programs have grown to support well over three thousand students each year. ESP classes are developed and taught by MIT undergraduates, graduate students, alumni, and members of the community. ESP's students are given the chance to learn from passionate and knowledgeable teachers; ESP's teachers can gain experience developing their own curricula with access to students with the strongest desire to learn. MIT ESP is the largest student-run program of its kind in the United States.

Competitions

Mystery Hunt

Main article: MIT Mystery Hunt

Entrepreneurship Competition

- The annual MIT Entrepreneurship Competition [4] has supported the creation of at least 60 companies worth a combined $10.5 billion since it started in 1990.

IAP Competitions

BattleCode (6.370)

6.370, also known previously as "RoboCraft" and now as "BattleCode", is the MIT ACM/IEEE Programming Competition. (See http://battlecode.mit.edu/) It is held every year during the Independent Activities Period at MIT, and the competition is changed annually. The game consists of armies of autonomous virtual robots battling each other, controlled solely by the AIs written by competition participants. BattleCode is programmed in Java, and the AIs (called "players") are written as extensions of a base robot class.

The competition has been roughly doubling in size every year since 2007. As of 2008, BattleCode has been opened up to virtually anyone interested in participating outside of MIT. The competition is a class at MIT and its software has been used for several other classes and projects.

- MIT 6.370 Competition [5]
- Video of 2004 final tournament [6]
- Video of 2005 final tournament [7]
- Video of 2007 final tournament [8]
- Further videos can be found on the current year's website.

Lego Robotics Competition (6.270)

- 6.270 [9]

Mobile Autonomous Systems Laboratory competition (Maslab)

Main article: Mobile Autonomous Systems Laboratory

- Maslab [10] competition

Web Programming Competition (6.470)

- 6.470 [11]

IDEAS Competition

The **MIT IDEAS Competition** encourages teams to develop and implement projects that make a positive change in the world. Entries are judged on their innovation, feasibility, and community impact. One component of the competition is the Yunus Challenge, named in honor of 2006 Nobel Prize winner Dr. Muhammad Yunus, where teams are invited to tackle a specific development need. Previous topics include increasing adherence to tuberculosis drug regimens and affordable small-scale energy storage.

The competition was developed in part by Amy Smith, who has developed a number of inventions useful to poor communities.

- The IDEAS Competition website [12]

Other Competitions

- 2.007 Design & Manufacturing [13] competition

Lecture Series Committee

- The Lecture Series Committee [14] (LSC) has weekly screenings of popular films as well as lectures by prominent speakers.

Miscellaneous

- MIT EMS [15] - student-run ambulance
- Pi Tau Sigma
- Eta Kappa Nu
- The MIT Science Fiction Society claims to have the "world's largest open-shelf collection of science fiction" in English.
- Smoot

Tim the Beaver

Tim the Beaver is the mascot at MIT [16]. His name is Tim because it is MIT backwards. A beaver was selected as the mascot because beavers are nature's engineers. This decision was made at the Technology Club of New York's annual dinner on January 17, 1914. President Maclaurin proposed the beaver. The sports teams at MIT either choose to have Tim as their mascot, or to be the Engineers.

MIT THINK Competition

THINK stands for Technology for Humanity guided by Innovation, Networking, and Knowledge. The competition challenges high school students across the United States to take a refreshing approach to designing a technological solution to a social problem. Its founding vision is that applicants will learn how to be resourceful in society, which makes networking a core component of the competition.

- The MIT THINK Competition Website [17]

Performing arts

Marching Band

The **MIT Marching Band** is purely student run, and is open to the entire MIT community. There is no audition and no prior experience is required.

The band plays at all types of events year-round. In its recent history, it has performed at football, basketball, lacrosse, field hockey, women's rugby, water polo, and hockey games. The band has also played for events such as the re-opening of the MIT Museum and the Cambridge Science Festival.

During MIT's Campus Preview Weekend in April, the band leads the prospective freshmen from the keynote address in Rockwell Cage to an activities fair in Johnson Ice Rink. Every December, the band tours downtown Boston playing holiday music.

- MIT Marching Band website [18]

Symphony Orchestra

The **MIT Symphony Orchestra** is the symphony orchestra of the Massachusetts Institute of Technology.

The origins of the MIT Symphony Orchestra (MITSO) date back as far as 1884 when the first MIT Tech Orchestra appeared on campus along with the Banjo and Glee Clubs. The orchestra disbanded and re-appeared several times over the years that followed until 1947, when Klaus Liepmann (1907-1990), MIT's first full-time professor of music and founder of the music program, became director of the MIT Glee Club, the Symphony and the Choral Society.

Nine years later John Corley (1919-2000) took over the direction of the Symphony until 1966, when David Epstein (1931-2002) became the Symphony Orchestra's music director. Under Prof. Epstein, the orchestra performed at Carnegie Hall and made several LP recordings. David Epstein's tenure ended in the spring of 1998 upon his retirement from the Institute. The MITSO has also performed with artists such as Peter Schickele, when he performed works of P.D.Q. Bach as a dog chained to the concertmaster. After an international search, Dante Anzolini became Music Director of the Orchestra and Associate Professor of Music at MIT in September 1998. For the 2006-2007 season, Paul Biss from Indiana State University served as interim conductor for MITSO, and in the fall of 2007, Adam Boyles began his tenure as the current music director.

- Official MIT website [19]
- MIT Symphony Orchestra [20]
- Bach Double Violin Concerto Hu/MCall 1981 [21] on YouTube

Chamber Chorus

- MIT Chamber Chorus [22]

Concert Choir

- MIT Concert Choir [23]

Concert Band

- MIT Concert Band [24]

MIT Live Music Connection (LMC)

- A co-op of MIT's bands on campus, the LMC provides a venue for artists to play as well as open jam sessions for students. Started in 2009 by MIT student band, The Guitar Knives, the LMC is now an official student group that holds concerts about once every 2 weeks in the Student Center, usually featuring 2 MIT bands. The LMC recently put out the first official CD of MIT bands that can be found on their website, as well as below. This sets a precedent at the school in that the CD is offered for Free Download, publicizing MIT's up and coming artists that also play the LMC's Concert Series. The LMC is also responsible for holding MIT's Battle of the Bands at Campus Preview Weekend, which it has recently taken over and established as a competitive ground for solely MIT bands.
- MIT LMC's Website [25]
- MIT LMC's Concert Review Blog [26]
- Like Never Before: The First Season (2009-2010) LMC CD - Available for Free Download [27]

Wind Ensemble

The **MIT Wind Ensemble** (or **MITWE** or **21M.426**) is a group of instrumental performers who are students at the Massachusetts Institute of Technology. The group performs classic (such as Holst and Grainger) and contemporary wind ensemble repertoire. It also commissions many new works.

The ensemble was formed in 1999 by Dr. Frederick Harris Jr.. It is led by him and Kenneth Amis, tuba player in the Empire Brass.

The ensemble performs 4 concerts per year in Kresge Auditorium. The concerts are open to the public. The ensemble also has performed with local middle school and high school bands, as part of an outreach program.

Admission to the MIT Wind Ensemble is by audition only. Current players must re-audition at the beginning of every year to remain in the ensemble. The audition consists of a short piece of the student's choice, a sight reading exercise, and a chromatic scale. Undergraduate students in the ensemble may choose to take MITWE for academic credit. In this case, the student must take a short playing exam at the end of each term.

In 2002 and 2003, the ensemble recorded its first CD ("Waking Winds") featuring 4 works by Boston area composers:

- Concertino for Violin and Chamber Winds, by Peter Child
- The Congress of the Insomniacs, by Brian Robison
- Song and Dance, by Gunther Schuller
- Drill, by Evan Ziporyn

The recording sessions took place in Jordan Hall, Kresge Auditorium, and Killian Hall.

The ensemble's second CD ("Solo Eclipse") was released in 2008, featuring new works by:

- Kenneth Amis

- Ran Blake
- Guillermo Klein

The ensemble has commissioned many works for Wind Band, including pieces by Kenneth Amis, Kenny Werner, Erica Foin, Forrest Larson, Ran Blake, Guillermo Klein, Evan Ziporyn, and others.

- MIT Wind Ensemble Homepage [28]
- Documentary about MITWE, part 1 [29]
- Documentary about MITWE, part 2 [30]
- MITWE CD: Waking Winds [31]
- MITWE CD: Solo Eclipse [32]

Musical Theater Guild

The Musical Theatre Guild is an entirely student-run theater group which performs four musicals per year (spring term, summer, fall term, and IAP). Membership is open to anyone, but preference is given to MIT students and MIT community members for cast and production roles. Performances are open to the general public.

In IAP 2003, MTG produced Star Wars: Musical Edition, a musical version of the original Star Wars movie, featuring musical numbers from existing musicals with the lyrics changed to fit the plot. In April 2005, part of the group performed selections from the show at Celebration III, a Star Wars convention for which George Lucas was present. In the fall of 2005, MTG produced Star Wars Trilogy: Musical Edition, which encompassed the entire original trilogy.

- Musical Theater Guild [33]

DanceTroupe

- DanceTroupe [34]

MIT Asian Dance Team

- MIT Asian Dance Team [35]

Tech Squares

- Tech Squares

Folk Dance Club

The MIT Folk Dance Club, founded in 1959, sponsors 3 public dance sessions every week: international folk dancing, contra dancing, and Israeli dancing.

- MIT Folk Dance Club [36]

In the 1960's it sponsored four Folk Dance Festivals. Folk Dance Festivals [37]

Ballroom Dance Club

- MIT Ballroom Dance Club [38]

MIT Shakespeare Ensemble

- A student-run theater group that puts on plays by Shakespeare during the year and non-Shakespeare during the summer.
- MIT Shakespeare Ensemble Website [39]

MIT Dramashop

- MIT's only co-curricular theater group.
- MIT Dramashop's Website [40]

A cappella

Toons

The **MIT/Wellesley Toons** are a cross-campus, co-ed college a cappella singing group. Founded in 1990, the group takes its members from both the undergraduate and graduate students of the Massachusetts Institute of Technology and the undergraduates of Wellesley College. The Toons are known for their diverse, eclectic repertoire - ranging from alternative rock to soul to Disney songs - and lively performances. The group performs several times each year at free concerts on both campuses, as well as at a variety of other venues both nearby and out-of-state.

The Toons host an annual *Concert for a Cure* in support of Multiple Sclerosis research, which draws large crowds from around the Boston area to enjoy music, dance, and other performing arts from a diverse array of groups from New England colleges and universities. The fourth annual concert - held in November 2009 - raised nearly $3000 in audience donations, which was donated to the Accelerated Cure Project.

The Toons have released five albums:

- *Part of This Complete Breakfast* (2007)
- *All Jokes Aside* (2003)
- *Holding Our Own* (2001)
- *59th Street Bridge* (1998)
- *Target Practice* (1995)
- Official homepage of The MIT/Wellesley Toons [41]

Chorallaries

The **Chorallaries of MIT** is the first co-ed a cappella performing group at The Massachusetts Institute of Technology. Founded in the winter of 1976-77, the group is typically composed of undergraduates, graduates, and occasionally faculty. They perform several free public concerts a year on the MIT campus, as well as at a number of other events on- and off-campus, including the MIT President's House and the MIT Graduation Ceremony.

Their signature song, the Engineer's Drinking Song, is a traditional tech favorite.

The Chorallaries have competed in the International Championship of Collegiate A Cappella numerous times, winning the quarter-finals in 2000, 2003, and 2006, as well as the semi-finals in 1996 and 2006. In 2010 the Chorallaries of MIT released their album "Stereophony". The track "Hot Air Balloon" is on Voices Only 2010

The group is known for its humor and creativity, culminating in "The Nth Annual **Concert in Bad Taste**".

Bad Taste is a concert devoted solely to off-color, nerdy, controversial, offensive, and often humorous material; a good-faith effort is made to offend everybody equally, but no quarter is given. Popular topics include: offensive sexual references; mocking the MIT administration; lambasting Harvard University, Wellesley College, Simmons College and other colleges in the region; excruciatingly hilarious science puns; and disgusting sexual references. The concert is usually about 2 1/2 hours long, with a mixture of skits, songs, and general hilarity.

- Chorallaries of MIT website [42]
- International Championship of College A Cappella [43]
- Review: Bad Taste 2003 in MIT newspaper, *The Tech* [44]

Resonance

The Resonance of MIT is a student rock/pop a cappella group from MIT. Founded in the 2000-2001 school year, the group is co-ed and typically consists of sixteen undergraduate and graduate students (though its size varies). It is one of seven a cappella groups at the school, and is known across campus for its frequent free performances and its funny, edgy interludes [45] used to keep audiences amused between songs.

Nationally, Resonance is perhaps best known for its recognition [46] through CASA [47], the Contemporary A Cappella Society, having received a 2004 and 2008 Contemporary A Cappella Recording Award (CARA) nomination for Best Mixed Collegiate Arrangement, a 2008 CARA award for Best Scholastic Original, as well as a berth on the 2006 Best of College A Cappella compilation CD. The group is also known for regularly hosting [48] the International Championship of College A Cappella New England Semifinals.

The group has produced three albums, its latest being the self-titled "Resonance" released in Fall 2007.

Resonance was envisioned by Sara Jo Elice who, with her friend (and eventual co-founder) Jessica Hinel, fleshed out the original idea while waiting to audition for an MIT Musical Theatre Guild production. Jay Humphries was auditioning for the same production and ended up becoming an inaugural Resonance member as well. In 2001, the MIT Association of Student Activities recognized Resonance as its seventh a cappella group on campus at the time.

The name Resonance follows an established joke among MIT a cappella groups of using a science or math-based pun to name the group. In science, resonance has to do with vibration and harmony. Specifically, resonant frequencies are the frequencies that cause natural amplification of signal - a commonly cited example being the singer who can, at the right frequency, break glass with their voice. Keeping with the theme, the resonance name is often formatted as **"res(((o)))nance."** and displayed alongside a logo of a shattered wine glass.

Resonance regularly performs on the MIT campus, at the minimum presenting a single full-length concert per term. Each concert is primarily composed of a collection of songs, both covers and originals, selected and arranged for a cappella by members of the group. Over 100 different songs have been performed by the group since 2001.

Resonance, like many a cappella groups, has a single "alum" song, taught to all members and used to close almost all performances. Group alumni are invited to join the current members on stage to finish the night. Resonance's alum song is "Easy People" by the Nields.

Resonance has released three albums:

- *Resonance* (2007)
- *Left On Red* (2005)
- *First Harmonic* (2003)

Resonance is also featured on two a cappella collections:

- *acaTunes Awards 2007* [49] (2007) - Collection, features "So Little Notice" by Sarah Dupuis as performed by Resonance
- *Best of College A Cappella 2006* (2006) - Collection, features "Mystify (Atrévete)" by Chenoa as performed by Resonance

All three Resonance full-length albums are available only through the group directly. Best of College A Cappella is produced and distributed to various retail sources by Varsity Vocals [50]. acaTunes awards are produced by acaTunes [51].

- MIT Resonance official homepage [52]
- The Contemporary A Cappella Society (CASA) reivew of Left On Red [53]
- WERS:88.9FM:: Emerson College Radio Article [54]
- The Recorded A Cappella Review Board (RARB) review of Left on Red [55]
- "Left On Red" review and review of Fall 2005 concert, Dec. 13th, 2005 [45]
- Review of Fall 2003 concert, Dec. 9th, 2003 [56]

- Review of Fall 2002 concert, Dec. 10th, 2002 [57]
- Review of second concert, Dec. 7th, 2001 [58]

Logarhythms

Founded in 1949, the **MIT Logarhythms** is an all-male a cappella performance group at the Massachusetts Institute of Technology. Initially a barbershop double quartet, the Logs (as their name is often foreshortened) have in recent years migrated to a more popular medium. Their current repertoire consists primarily of modern pop, hip hop, and classic rock, though their barbershop roots live on in a few tunes.

The Logs perform throughout Massachusetts and the New England area. Recent biannual tours have included performances around Washington DC, California, Michigan, and Texas. The group has earned songs on the Best of College A Cappella (BOCA) compilation albums from 2003, 2004, 2005, and 2009, and their album *Soundproof* received near-perfect marks in its review from the Recorded A Cappella Review Board.

In March 2007, the Logs participated in and took first place in WERS' All A Cappella Live competition at the Majestic Theatre in Boston, competing against the Tufts Beelzebubs, Brandeis VoiceMale, and the Harvard Low Keys.

- *Give Us Back Our Spyplane* (2008)
- *Natural* (2006)
- *Soundproof* (2004)
- *Superlogs* (2002)
- *Mind the Logs* (1999)
- *Redwood* (1997)
- *Songs From The Bagel* (1994)

Natural features cover songs performed and recorded by the '04-05 and '05-06 members of the MIT Logarhythms. The tracks were recorded at MIT at the Logarhythms' studio. Tracks were subsequently mixed by producer John Clark.

"Part-Time Lover" soloist Chris Vu won a 2007 CARA award as Best Male Collegiate Soloist. "Such Great Heights" received a 2007 CARA nomination for Best Male Collegiate Song.

Soundproof features cover songs performed and recorded by the '02-03 and '03-04 members of the MIT Logarhythms. The tracks were recorded at MIT at the Logarhythms' newly-built studio. Track one was mixed by Viktor Kray. All remaining tracks were mixed by John Clark.

"The Kids Aren't Alright" was featured as the first track on the Best of College A Cappella 2005 compilation. "No Such Thing" appeared as track nine on the Best of College A Cappella 2004 compilation. "Learn to Fly" was Runner Up for Best Male Collegiate Arrangement in the 2005 CARA awards.

- MIT Logarhythms Official Website [59]
- Contemporary A Cappella Society of America (CASA) [60]
- Recorded A Cappella Review Board (RARB) [61]
- Varsity Vocals (releases Best of College A Cappella Compilations) [62] The Logarhythms

Cross Products

The Cross Products [63] are MIT's Christian co-ed a cappella singing group.

Muses

MIT's only all-female a cappella group.

Techiya

Techiya is MIT's Jewish, Hebrew, Israeli a cappella group. Founded in 1994, the group released its first album in 2002, entitled Half-Life.

- Techiya official homepage [64]

Asymptones

The Asymptones [65] are MIT's low-time-commitment a capella group. Founded in 2007, they have infrequent concerts and just sing for fun.

Syncopasian

Founded in 2008, Syncopasian promotes the awareness of Asian pop culture at MIT and the surrounding community through performances of Asian a cappella music. Unlike other a cappella groups on campus, its repertoire includes songs in not only English, but also Mandarin, Cantonese, Japanese, Korean, and other languages that are East Asian in origin.

- Syncopasian official homepage [66]

Publications and media

WMBR

- campus radio station

MIT International Review

The *MIT International Review* (*MITIR*) is an interdisciplinary journal of international affairs published by the Massachusetts Institute of Technology. The aim of the publication is to "foster solution-oriented discourse about international problems.

Technique, the Yearbook and Photography Club of MIT

- *Technique* [67]

The Tech

- The Tech is MIT's student newspaper. It's published twice a week during the school year.

Counterpoint

- *Counterpoint* [68]

VooDoo

- *VooDoo* [69]

MIT Technology Insider

- MIT Technology Insider

Student government

MIT's student body has several governing organizations. The Undergraduate Association is the primary representative body for undergraduate students while the Graduate Student Council represents the interests of graduate students. Organizations like the Interfraternity Council (IFC), Panhellenic Council (Panhel), Living Group Council (LGC), and Dormitory Council (Dormcon) are independent bodies that represent the interests of fraternities, sororities, independent living groups, and undergraduate dormitories respectively.

Athletics

MIT has 33 varsity sports teams. Of the previous 41 varsity sports, eight (Alpine Skiing, Golf, Men's Ice Hockey, Women's Ice Hockey, Men's Gymnastics, Women's Gymnastics, Pistol, and Wrestling) were cut in 2009 for budget reasons. MIT also has an extensive club and intramural sports team. MIT undergraduates must complete physical education classes as well as a swim test in order to graduate.

Course numbering

MIT students refer to both their majors and classes using numbers alone. Majors are numbered in the approximate order of when the department was founded; for example, Civil and Environmental Engineering is Course I, while Nuclear Science & Engineering is Course XXII. Students majoring in Electrical Engineering and Computer Science, the most popular department, collectively identify themselves as "Course VI." MIT students use a combination of the department's course number and the number assigned to the class number to identify their subjects; the course which many universities would designate as "Physics 101" is, at MIT, "8.01." For brevity, course number designations are pronounced without the decimal point and by replacing "oh" for zero (unless zero is the last number). Thus, "8.01" is pronounced *eight oh one*, "6.001" is pronounced *six double oh one*, and "7.20" would be pronounced *seven twenty*.

External links

- MIT World [70]

Things to See and Do

Longfellow Bridge

Longfellow Bridge	
Carries	Route 3, MBTA Red Line
Crosses	Charles River
Locale	Boston, Massachusetts to Cambridge, Massachusetts
Maintained by	Massachusetts Department of Transportation
Design	steel rib Arch bridge
Total length	1,768 feet (539 m)
Beginning date of construction	July 1900
Opened	August 3, 1906
Daily traffic	28,600 cars and 90,000 mass-transit passengers
Coordinates	42°21′42″N 71°04′31″W

The **Longfellow Bridge**, also known to locals as the "Salt-and-Pepper Bridge" or the "Salt-and-Pepper-Shaker Bridge" due to the shape of its central towers, carries Route 3 and the Massachusetts Bay Transportation Authority's Red Line across the Charles River to connect Boston's Beacon Hill neighborhood with the Kendall Square area of Cambridge, Massachusetts.

Longfellow Bridge is a combination railway and highway bridge. It is 105 feet (32 m) feet wide, 1767 feet 6 inches (538.73 m) long between abutments, and nearly one-half mile in length, including abutments and approaches. It consists of eleven steel arch spans supported on ten masonry piers and two massive abutments. The arches vary in length from 101 feet 6 inches (30.94 m) feet at the abutments to 188 feet 6 inches (57.45 m) at the center, and in rise from 8 feet 6 inches (2.59 m) to 26 feet 6 inches (8.08 m). Headroom under the central arch is 26 feet (7.9 m) at mean high water. Its two large central piers, 188 feet (57 m) long and 53 feet 6 inches (16.31 m) wide, feature carved, ornamental stone towers that provide stairway access to pedestrian passageways beneath the bridge. Its sidewalks were originally both 10 feet (3.0 m) wide, but now, for unknown reasons, the upstream sidewalks are narrower than the downstream ones.

The bridge falls under the jurisdiction and oversight of Massachusetts Department of Transportation. The bridge carries approximately 28,600 cars and 90,000 mass-transit passengers every weekday. A portion of the elevated Charles/Massachusetts General Hospital train station lies at the eastern end of the bridge.

History

The first river crossing at this site was a ferry, first run in the 1630s. The West Boston Bridge (a toll bridge) was constructed in 1793 by a group of private investors with a charter from the Commonwealth. At the time, there were only a handful of buildings in East Cambridge. The opening of the bridge caused a building boom along Main Street, which connected the bridge to Old Cambridge. New streets were laid out, and land reclaimed from the swamps along the Charles River. The Cambridge and Concord Turnpike (now Broadway) was connected to the bridge's western approach around 1812. The bridge became toll-free on January 30, 1858.

In 1898 the Cambridge Bridge Commission was created to construct "a new bridge across Charles River, to be known as Cambridge Bridge, at, upon, or near the site of the so-called West Boston Bridge... suitable for all the purposes of ordinary travel between said cities, and for the use of the elevated and surface cars of the Boston Elevated Railway Company." At its first meeting on June 16, 1898, Willam Jackson was appointed Chief Engineer; shortly afterward Edmund M. Wheelwright was appointed Consulting Architect. Both then traveled to Europe, where they made a thorough inspection of notable bridges in France, Germany, Austria and Russia. Upon their return, they prepared studies of various types of bridges, including bridges of stone and steel arch spans. Although both state and national regulations required a draw bridge, it became evident that a bridge without a draw would be cheaper and better-looking. The state altered its regulations accordingly, and after the War Department declined to follow suit, the United States Congress drew up an act permitting the bridge, which the President signed on March 29, 1900. Construction began in July 1900; the bridge opened on August 3, 1906, and was formally dedicated on July 31, 1907.

The new Cambridge Bridge. Note the lack of MIT in the distance.

Longfellow Bridge was originally known as the Cambridge Bridge, but was renamed in 1927[citation needed] by the Massachusetts General Court for Henry Wadsworth Longfellow, who wrote about the West Boston Bridge in the poem "The Bridge", in 1845.

Wheelwright was inspired by the 1893 Columbian Exposition and was attempting to emulate the great bridges of Europe. Its four large piers are ornamented with the prows of Viking ships, carved in granite, which refer to a hypothetical voyage by Leif Eriksson up the Charles River circa 1000 AD, as promoted by Harvard professor Eben Horsford. It is also decorated with the city seals of Boston and Cambridge.

Until 1952, the centermost traffic lanes of the bridge also contained tracks which connected what is now known as the Blue Line, running from crossovers at the Cambridge end to the subway tracks, across the bridge and into Boston to the North Russell Street Incline of the Blue Line subway. Before the Orient Heights Blue Line yards were built, major repairs to that line's trains were performed at the Eliot Square carbarns in Cambridge.

On May 1, 2007, a fire broke out under the bridge. Ignited by a cigarette left by vagrants who sometimes stay in the covered crawlspace under the bridge deck, the fire caused the bridge to be shut down to vehicle and train traffic. This fire also severed Internet2 connectivity to Boston, causing problems with the Chicago-New York OC-192 route, according to the Internet2 blog [1].

Past neglect and future rehabilitation

The Longfellow Bridge, like many bridges in the Commonwealth, is in a state of disrepair. "Since 1907, the only major maintenance conducted on the bridge has been a small 1959 rehabilitiation project and some lesser repairs done in 2002."

In the summer of 2008, the western sidewalk and inner traffic lane were closed, the Red Line was limited to 10 mph, and Fourth-of-July fireworks-watchers were banned from the bridge, all because of concerns that the bridge might collapse under the weight and vibration. The speed restriction was lifted in August 2008, and the lane and sidewalk were opened later on.

On August 4, 2008 Governor Deval Patrick signed into law a $3 billion Massachusetts bridge repair funding package he had sponsored. Bond funds will be used to pay for the rehabilitation of the Longfellow, with a preliminary cost estimate of $267.5 million. If maintenance had been performed regularly, the total historical cost is estimated to have been about $81 million. Design began in spring 2005; construction is expected to begin in spring 2011 and end in fall 2015.

Ownership and management of the overhaul was transferred from the Department of Conservation and Recreation (DCR) to the new Massachusetts Department of Transportation on November 1, 2009, along with other DCR bridges.

Ironwork theft

In the summer of 2008, two state employees stole 2347 feet (715 m) (linear) of decorative iron trim that had been removed from the bridge for refurbishment and sold it for scrap. The men, one a Department of Conservation and Recreation district manager, were charged with receiving $12,147 for the historic original parapet coping. The estimated cost to remake the pieces, scheduled for replication by 2012, was over $500,000. The men were convicted in September 2009.

Gallery

The MBTA's Red Line trains cross the Longfellow Bridge.

As seen from the Prudential Tower observatory

View of the Bridge from East Cambridge

Further reading

- Jackson, William (1909). *Report of the Cambridge bridge commission and report of the chief engineer upon the construction of Cambridge bridge*. Printing department.
- Freeman, Dale H. (2000). *A changing bridge for changing times : the history of the West Boston Bridge, 1793-1907 ; a thesis*. University of Massachusetts Boston. ISBN B0006RH37A.
- Seitinger, Susanne (2002). "Lookin' Good, Feelin' Good: the transformation of Charles Circle" [2] (PDF). Retrieved 2008-09-12.
- Moskowitz, Eric (July 25, 2010). "Linking cities and eras" [3]. *Boston Globe*: pp. Pgs. 1–4. Retrieved August 7, 2010.

External links

- Longfellow Bridge [4] at *Structurae*
- Restoration of the Longfellow Bridge [5]
- Daniel, Mac (January 22, 2006). "Longfellow Bridge lane to close" [6]. The Boston Globe.
- "Defects lead to closure of a Longfellow Bridge sidewalk" [7]. The Boston Globe. June 6, 2008.
- Ebbert, Stephanie (June 7, 2008). "Longfellow Bridge is off-limits July 4th" [8]. The Boston Globe.
- Ebbert, Stephanie (June 26, 2008). "Two lanes closed on Longfellow Bridge" [9]. The Boston Globe.
- "The Bridge", poem by Henry Wadsworth Longfellow [10]
- Longfellow Bridge project page [11]
- http://hdl.loc.gov/loc.pnp/hhh.ma1225

Charles River

Geographical coordinates: 42°22′14″N 71°3′13″W

Charles River	
 The Longfellow Bridge crossing over the Charles River, in the winter.	
Country	United States
State	Massachusetts
Cities	Hopkinton, Boston
Source	Echo Lake
- location	Hopkinton, Massachusetts, United States
- elevation	350 ft (107 m)
- coordinates	42°11′34″N 71°30′43″W
Mouth	Boston Harbor
- location	Boston, Massachusetts, United States
- elevation	0 ft (0 m)
- coordinates	42°22′14″N 71°3′13″W
Length	80 mi (129 km)
Basin	308 sq mi (798 km²)

Charles, Mystic and Neponset river watersheds

The **Charles River** is an 80 mi (129 km) long river that flows in an overall northeasterly direction in eastern Massachusetts, USA. From its source in Hopkinton, the river travels through 22 cities and towns until reaching the Atlantic Ocean at Boston. It is also sometimes called the **River Charles**.

Route

The Charles River is fed by about 80 brooks and streams and several major aquifers as it flows snakelike for 80 miles (129 km), starting at Echo Lake (42°11′35″N 71°30′43″W) in Hopkinton, through 22 cities and towns in eastern Massachusetts before emptying into Boston Harbor. 33 lakes and ponds, and 35 communities are entirely or partially part of the Charles River watershed. Despite the river's length and relatively large drainage area (308 square miles; 798 km²), its source is only 26 miles (42 km) from its mouth, and the river drops only 350 feet (107 m) from source to sea. It is the most densely populated river basin in New England.[*citation needed*]

Brandeis University, Harvard University, Boston University, and the Massachusetts Institute of Technology are all located along the Charles River. Near its mouth, it forms the border between downtown Boston and Cambridge and Charlestown (a neighborhood of Boston). Here, the river opens out into a broad basin and is lined by the parks of the Charles River Reservation. On the Charles River Esplanade stands the Hatch Shell, where concerts are given in summer evenings. The basin is especially known for its Independence Day celebration. The middle section of the river, between the Watertown Dam and Wellesley is partially protected by the properties of the Upper Charles River Reservation and other state parks, including the Hemlock Gorge Reservation, Cutler Park, and the Elm Bank Reservation.

Recreation

The river is well known for its rowing, sculling, dragonboating, and sailing, both recreational and competitive. The "Lower Basin" between the Longfellow and Harvard bridges is home to Community Boating, the Harvard University Sailing Center, and the MIT Sailing Pavilion. The Head of the Charles Regatta is held here every October. In early June, the annual Hong Kong Boston Dragon boat Festival is held in Cambridge, near the Weeks Footbridge.

The Charles River Bike Path runs 23 miles (37 km) along the banks of the Charles, starting at the Museum of Science and passing the campuses of MIT, Harvard and Boston University. The path is popular with runners and bikers. Many runners gauge their distance and speed by keeping track of the mileage between the bridges [1] along the route.

History

The river's name, preceding the English version, was once thought to be **Quinobequin** (meandering), though that attribution has been discredited by, among others, the Harvard University Librarian in 1850.[citation needed] The river was used by Native Americans for local transportation and fishing, and as part of the passage from southeastern Massachusetts to northern New England.

View of the Charles River and Boston at night

Captain John Smith explored and mapped the coast of New England, naming many features including the Charles River, which he gave the Native American name, Massachusetts River. When Smith presented his map to Charles I he suggested that the king should feel free to change any of the "barbarous names" for "English" ones. The king made many such changes, but only four survive today, one of which is the Charles River, which Charles named for himself.

In portions of its length, the Charles drops slowly in elevation and has relatively little current. Despite this, early settlers in Dedham, Massachusetts, found a way to use the Charles to power mills. In 1639, the town dug a canal from the Charles to a nearby brook that drained to the Neponset River. By this action, a portion of the Charles's flow was diverted, providing enough current for several mills. The new canal and the brook together are now called Mother Brook. The canal is regarded as the first industrial canal in North America. Today it remains in use for flood control.

Waltham was the site of the first fully integrated textile factory in America, built by Francis Cabot Lowell in 1814[citation needed], and by the 19th century, the Charles River was one of the most industrialized areas in the United States. Its hydropower soon fueled many mills and factories. By the century's end, 20 dams had been built across the river, mostly to generate power for industry. An 1875 government report listed 43 mills along the 9.5-mile (15 km) tidal estuary from Watertown Dam to Boston Harbor. From 1816 to 1968, the U.S. Army operated a gun and ammunition storage and later production facility known as the Watertown Arsenal. While it was key to many of the nation's war efforts over its several decades in operation, not the least of which being the American Civil War and World War I, its location in Watertown so near the Charles did great environmental harm. The old arsenal itself was declared a Super Fund site and, after its closure by the government, had to be cleaned at significant expense before it could be safely used again for other purposes. Likewise, the many factories and mills along the banks of the Charles supported a buoyant economy in their time but left a legacy of massive pollution.

Creation of modern Boston-Cambridge basin

Today's Charles River basin between Boston and Cambridge is almost entirely a work of human design. Owen A. Galvin was appointed head of the Charles River Improvement Commission by Governor William E. Russell in 1891. Their work led to the design initiatives of noted landscape architects Charles Eliot and Arthur Shurcliff, both of whom had apprenticed with Frederick Law Olmsted, and by the architect and landscape architect Guy Lowell. This designed landscape now includes over 20 parks and natural areas along 19 miles (31 km) of shoreline, from the New Dam at the Charlestown Bridge to the dam near Watertown Square.

A sunny day on the Charles River Esplanade

Eliot first envisioned today's river design in the 1890s, an important model being the layout of the Alster basin in Hamburg, but major construction began only after Eliot's death with the damming of the river's mouth at today's Museum of Science, an effort led in by James Jackson Storrow. The new dam, completed in 1910, stabilized the water level from Boston to Watertown, eliminating the existing mud flats, and a narrow embankment was built between Leverett Circle and Charlesgate. After Storrow's death, his widow Mrs. James Jackson Storrow donated $1 million toward the creation of a more generously landscaped park along the Esplanade; it was dedicated in 1936 as the Storrow Memorial Embankment. This also enabled the construction of many public docks in the Charles River Basin. In the 1950s a highway (Storrow Drive) was built along the edge of the Esplanade to connect Charles Circle with Soldiers Field Road, and the Esplanade was enlarged on the water side of the new highway.

The Inner Belt highway was proposed to cross the Charles River at the Boston University Bridge, but its construction was canceled in the 1970s.

Pollution and remediation efforts

As sewage, industrial wastewater and urban runoff flowed freely into the river from the surrounding city, the Charles River became well known for its high level of pollutants, gaining such notoriety that by 1955, Bernard DeVoto wrote in *Harper's Magazine* that the Charles was "foul and noisome, polluted by offal and industrious wastes, scummy with oil, unlikely to be mistaken for water." It was not an uncommon sight to see toxins coloring the river pink and orange in spots, fish kills and submerged cars.

Once popular with swimmers, awareness of the river's high pollution levels forced the state to shut down several popular swimming areas, including Cambridge's Magazine Beach and Gerry Landing public beaches. Until very recently, rowers and sailors who fell into the water were advised to go to the hospital for tetanus shots.

Efforts to clean up the river and restore it to a state where swimming and fishing would be acceptable began as early as the 1960s and the program to clean up the Charles for good took shape in 1965 with the creation of the Charles River Watershed Association. In 1995, the United States Environmental Protection Agency declared a goal of making the river swimmable by 2005. In 1996, then governor William Weld plunged, fully clothed, into the river to prove his commitment to cleaning up the river. In July 2007, the river hosted the Charles River Masters Swim Race, the first sanctioned race in the Charles in over five decades.

Sailboats moored on the Charlestown side of the Charles River with Bunker Hill Monument in the distance

A combination of public and private initiatives helped dramatically lower levels of pollutants by focusing on eliminating combined sewer overflows and storm water runoff. A new Charles River Dam was constructed downstream from the Science Museum site to keep salt water out of the basin. Since Weld's stunt, the river's condition has improved dramatically, although it was not deemed entirely swimmable by 2005. In 1995 the EPA rated the river's quality as a "D" compared to the most recent ranking of a "B+" and most days of the year, the river now meets swimming standards below the Harvard Bridge. With the improved water quality, swimming and fishing are progressively re-emerging as about 90% of the length of the river is now considered safe for swimming. Health risks remain, however, particularly after rainstorms and when walking in certain riverbeds stirs up toxic sediment.[citation needed]

During the period September 2004 to September 2006, the City of Cambridge and the state's Department of Conservation and Recreation introduced vegetation at Magazine Beach just west of the BU Bridge on the Cambridge side of the river. This introduced vegetation had significant trouble living there because it was not native to the Charles River.[citation needed] The vegetation installed created a wall preventing the reintroduction of swimming at Magazine Beach.Wikipedia:Neutral point of view#

The Conservation Law Foundation opposes the permit given to Mirant for the Mirant Kendall Generating Station, an electricity plant near Kendall Square, charging that the water it releases causes blooms of hazardous microorganisms, due to its warm temperature.

It is a common belief that the water quality of the Charles River is at its worst after a large rainfall because of pollutants carried by runoff. However, a study, published in the Journal of the American Water Resources Association (April 2008), completed by researchers at Northeastern University, found high concentrations of E. coli bacteria in the Charles River after a long period of no rain. Using a mathematical model, the researchers then determined that two major tributaries, the Stony Brook and Muddy River, are the predominant sources of E. coli in the lower Charles River.

Oysters have been used to filter and clean Charles River water.

In popular culture

- The Charles River is an icon for Boston and is featured in the song "Dirty Water" by The Standells:

    Down by the River...

    Down by the banks of the River Charles

- Todd Rundgren's song "Boat on the Charles" from *Runt: The Ballad of Todd Rundgren* is written from the point of view of someone contemplating suicide in the Charles because of an unrequited love.

Looking towards Boston across the Charles in winter

- In William Faulkner's *The Sound and the Fury*, the tormented Quentin character commits suicide by drowning himself in the Charles.
- The 1994 film *The River Wild* opens with Meryl Streep rowing under the Watertown Bridge (Galen Street, Rt. 16) proceeding east past the Perkins School for the Blind Chapel tower and on to Boston.
- In the novel *The Bell Jar* by Sylvia Plath, the protagonist, Esther, briefly considers committing suicide by jumping into the Charles off of a bridge.
- In the short story "The Other" by Jorge Luis Borges a mature Borges sits on the bank of the river Charles and comes faces to face with a younger version of himself. He determines that in the past he must have had the encounter during a dream and dismissed it as fantasy, though later accepting it as real.
- In the film "Eternal Sunshine Of The Spotless Mind" directed by Michel Gondry, characters Joel and Clementine go, by her initiative, to make a picnic to the frozen Charles River. From that scene comes the famous image of both lying on broken ice.

Gallery

The Charles River from the Boston side, facing Weld Boathouse and the main campus of Harvard University in Cambridge.

See also

- List of crossings of the Charles River
- List of Charles River boathouses
- List of Massachusetts rivers
- Sudbury Aqueduct Linear District which crosses the river from Needham to Newton on the Echo Bridge

John W. Weeks Bridge

References

- *Inventing the Charles River*, by Karl Haglund, MIT Press, 2003, in collaboration with the Charles River Conservancy.
- *Gaining Ground: A History of Landmaking in Boston*, by Nancy S. Seasholes, MIT Press, 2003.
- *Omeros*, by Derek Walcott, Faber and Faber (London), 1990. (Repeated references to the Charles river in descriptions of Boston life.)
- Benet, Steven Vincent & Carmer, Carly, *The Charles, Rivers of America* Series, New York: Farrar & Rinehart, 1941

External links

- The Esplanade Association [2]
- Charles River Watershed Association [3]
- Charles River Conservancy [4]
- Department of Conservation and Recreation - Charles River [5]
- "Swimmable by 2005" EPA Effort [6]
- Charles River Swimming Club [7]
- Charles River Museum of Industry [8]
- US Geological Survey data on flow in Charles River at Waltham with links to data for other measurement sites [9]

MIT Museum

MIT Museum, founded in 1971, is the museum of the Massachusetts Institute of Technology, located in Cambridge, Massachusetts. It hosts collections of holography, artificial intelligence, robotics, maritime history, and the history of MIT. Its holography collection of 1800 pieces is the largest in the world, though not all of it is exhibited. Currently works of Harold Edgerton and Arthur Ganson are the two largest displays ongoing for a long time. Occasionally, there are various exhibitions, usually on the intersection of art and technology.

Hologram Artwork from MIT Museum

Since 2005 the official mission of the museum has been, "to engage the wider community with MIT's science, technology and other areas of scholarship in ways that will best serve the nation and the world in the 21st century."

For a long time, it used to house the "Hall of Hacks" showcasing some of the famous MIT hacks, but the section was closed in 2001.[1]

External links

- Museum website [2]

Geographical coordinates: 42°21′46″N 71°5′57″W

Harvard Art Museums

Harvard Art Museums	
Established	1895
Location	Cambridge, Massachusetts
Director	Thomas W. Lentz
Website	harvardartmuseums.org [1]

The **Harvard Art Museums**, part of Harvard University, comprise three museums (the Fogg Museum, the Busch-Reisinger Museum, and the Arthur M. Sackler Museum) and four research centers (Straus Center for Conservation and Technical Studies, the Center for the Technical Study of Modern Art, the Harvard Art Museums Archives, and the Archaeological Exploration of Sardis).

The Harvard Art Museums are distinguished by the range and depth of their collections, their exhibitions, and the original research of their staff. The collections include approximately 250,000 objects in all media, ranging in date from antiquity to the present and originating in Europe, North America, North Africa, the Middle East, South Asia, East Asia, and Southeast Asia.

In 2008, the 32 Quincy Street building that formerly housed the Fogg Museum and the Busch-Reisinger Museum closed for a major renovation project to create a new museum building designed by architect Renzo Piano that will house all three museums one facility. During the renovation, selected works from all three museums are on display at the Arthur M. Sackler Museum, located at 485 Broadway.

The Harvard Art Museum's online Collection Search features 250,000 works of art.

Representative works

See also

- Fogg Museum
- Busch-Reisinger Museum
- Arthur M. Sackler Museum

External links

- Harvard Art Museums website [2]
- Fogg Museum website [3]

- Busch-Reisinger Museum website [4]
- Arthur M. Sackler Museum website [5]
- Archaeological Exploration of Sardis, Turkey website [6]
- Center for the Technical Study of Modern Art website [7]
- Harvard Art Museums Archives website [8]
- The Straus Center for Conservation and Technical Studies website [9]
- Harvard Art Museums Collection Search website [10]
- Harvard University website [11]

Harvard Museum of Natural History

The **Harvard Museum of Natural History** is a natural history museum on the grounds of Harvard University in Cambridge, Massachusetts. It has three parts:

- the Harvard University Herbaria
- the Museum of Comparative Zoology
- the Harvard Mineralogical Museum.

The museum is physically connected to the Peabody Museum of Archaeology and Ethnology and one admission grants visitors access to both museums.

Harvard Museum of Natural History complex

Museum contents

The Harvard Museum of Natural History was created in 1998 as the "public face" of three research museums — the Museum of Comparative Zoology, the Geological Museum, and the Herbaria—with a mission to enhance public understanding and appreciation of the natural world and the human place in it. Museum exhibitions draw on Harvard University's natural history collections; Harvard's research faculty provides unparalleled expertise; and an array of programs for members and the general public sparks a lively exchange of information and ideas, founded in the spirit of discovery. With more than 180,000 visitors annually, the Harvard Museum of Natural History is the University's most-visited museum.

In the Museum's permanent galleries, visitors encounter the rich diversity of life on earth, from dinosaurs to fossil invertebrates and reptiles, to large mammals, birds and fish, and the only mounted Kronosaurus. The mineralogical galleries present a systematic display of meteorites, minerals and gemstones. The galleries also house the historic Blaschka glass models of plants, popularly known as the Glass Flowers. In addition, a series of changing exhibitions bring focus to timely subjects, often featuring the work of world-renowned nature photographers.

The Museum's educational programs encourage a hands-on, observation-based approach. With a growing reputation as a source of unique and effective science education and a successful partnership with Cambridge public schools, the Museum welcomes increasing numbers of school children and their families to its programs each year.

Public lectures are another of the Museum's primary activities. Each year, over twenty free presentations by Harvard biologists, international conservationists, and popular authors lead their audiences to a closer look at current issues in the world of science and nature.

A robust travel program complements the museum's mission to enhance awareness of the natural world. Traveling in small groups often led by Harvard science faculty, Museum travelers experience exotic destinations that are of particular importance as recognized hotspots of biodiversity.

The museum is member-based, with over 3,200 current members, primarily from the Boston metropolitan area. While the Museum is affiliated with the Harvard's Faculty of Arts and Sciences and receives important support from the University, it derives most of its operating income from admissions, membership, gifts, and programmatic revenues. Geographical coordinates: 42°22′42.29″N 71°6′55.99″W

External links

- Harvard Museum of Natural History [1]
- Harvard Museum of Natural History Travel Program [2]

Harvard University Herbaria

The **Harvard University Herbaria** and Botanical Museum are institutions located on the grounds of Harvard University at 22 Divinity Avenue, Cambridge, Massachusetts. The Botanical Museum [1] is one of three which comprise the Harvard Museum of Natural History.

The Herbaria, founded in 1842 by Asa Gray, are one of the 10 largest in the world with over 5 million specimens, and including the Botany Libraries, form the world's largest university

Harvard University Herbaria

owned herbarium. HUH hosts the Gray Herbarium Index (GCI) [2] as well as an extensive specimen, botanist, and publications database [2]. HUH was the center for botanical research in the United States of America by the time of its founder's retirement in the 1870s. The materials deposited there are one of the three major sources for the International Plant Names Index.

The Botanical museum [1] was founded in 1858. It was originally called the *Museum of Vegetable Products* and was predominantly focused on an interdisciplinary study of useful plants (i.e. economic botany and horticulture). The nucleus of materials for this museum was donated by Sir William Hooker, the Director of the Royal Botanic Garden at Kew. George Lincoln Goodalle became the museum's first director in 1888; under his direction the building was completed in 1890 and provided both research facilities and public exhibit space, which were the botanical compliment to the "Agassiz" Museum of Comparative Zoology. Three successive directors substantially enlarged the collections of economic products, medicinal plants, artifacts, archeological materials, pollen, and photographs.

Faculty and students continue to add significantly to the extensive paleobotanical collections, particularly Precambrian material containing early life forms.

The Oakes Ames Collection of Economic Botany, the Paleobotanical Collection [3] (including the Pollen Collection), and the Margaret Towle Collection of Archaeological Plant Remains are housed in the Botanical Museum building. The Botany libraries [4] and various herbaria are located in the Harvard University Herbaria [5] building.

The Ware Collection of Glass Models of Plants [6], popularly known as the "Glass Flowers," are considered one of the University's great treasures. Commissioned by Goodale and created by Leopold and Rudolf Blaschka from 1887 through 1936, the collection comprises over 3,000 models including life-size and enlarged parts for over 840 species. This is the only collection of its type in the world.

The Botanical Museum of Harvard University and the other museums that comprise the Harvard Museum of Natural History are physically connected to the Peabody Museum of Archaeology and Ethnology and one admission grants visitors access to all museums.

References

- Harvard University Herbaria [5]
- Harvard Museum of Natural History [1]

Harvard Mineralogical Museum

The **Mineralogical and Geological Museum at Harvard** (**Harvard Mineralogical Museum** being the accepted short form of the name) is located on the grounds of Harvard University in Cambridge, Massachusetts and is one of three museums which collectively comprise the Harvard Museum of Natural History.

References

- Mineralogical and Geological Museum at Harvard [1]

Museum of Comparative Zoology

The **Museum of Comparative Zoology**, full name "The Louis Agassiz Museum of Comparative Zoology", often abbreviated simply to "MCZ", is a zoology museum located on the grounds of Harvard University in Cambridge, Massachusetts. It is one of three museums which collectively comprise the Harvard Museum of Natural History. The current director of the museum is James Hanken, the Louis Agassiz Professor of Zoology at Harvard University.

Many of the exhibits in the museum have not only zoological interest but also historical significance. These include a fossil sand dollar which was found by Charles Darwin in 1834, Captain Cook's mamo, and two pheasants which once belonged to George Washington.

This museum and the other institutions that comprise the Harvard Museum of Natural History are physically connected to the Peabody Museum of Archaeology and Ethnology; for visitors, one admission ticket grants access to both museums.

History

The Museum of Comparative Zoology was founded in 1859 through the efforts of Louis Agassiz, the zoologist, and the museum is sometimes referred to as "The Agassiz" after its founder. Agassiz designed the collection to illustrate the variety and comparative relationships of animal life.

Departments

The museum comprises twelve departments: Biological Oceanography, Entomology, Herpetology, Ichthyology, Invertebrate Paleontology, Invertebrate Zoology, Mammalogy, Marine invertebrates, Malacology, Ornithology, Population Genetics, and Vertebrate Paleontology. The Ernst Mayr Library and its archives join in supporting the work of the museum. The Ernst Mayr Library is a founding member of the Biodiversity Heritage Library [1].

Displays

In contrast to more modern museums, the Harvard Museum of Natural History has many hundreds of stuffed animals on display, from the collections of the Museum of Comparative Zoology. Notable exhibits include whale skeletons, the largest turtle shell ever found (eight feet long), "the Harvard mastodon", a 50-foot (15 m) long Kronosaurus skeleton, the remains of a Dodo, and a Coelacanth preserved in fluid.

Prehistoric and extinct animals

The collection of prehistoric and extinct animals on display, considered to be one of the largest in the northeast United States, includes (note that some are casts and models):

Canis dirus- Dire Wolf

Smilodon

Eryops

Tiktaalik

Ophiacodon

Probelesodon

Probainognathus

Vincelestes

Gobiconodon

Australopithecus

Homo

Menoceras

Mesohippus

Teleoceras

Equus

Lestodon

Panochthus

Toxodon

Moropus

Mammut americanum- American mastodon

Coryphodon

Merycoidodontidae- Oreodonts

Stenomylus

Hypertragulus

Platygonus

Latimeria chalumnae- Coelacanth

Dinodontosaurus

Pteranodon

Exaeretodon

Massetognathus

Thrinaxodon

Belesodon(?)

Dinnebitodon

Stupendemys

Tylosaurus

Megalania

Hyperodapedon

Homeosaurus

Toxochelys

Platychelys

Eurysternum

Xiphactinus

Paleothyris

Edops

Diploceraspis

Greererpeton

Bothriolepis

Osteolepis

Eusthenopteron

Cephalaspis

Edaphosaurus

Dimetrodon

Xenacanthus

Pantylus

Tremalops

Acheloma

Seymouria

Diplocaulus

Diadectes

Deinonychus

Ceratosaurus

Stegoceras

Tenontosaurus

Protoceratops

Coelophysis

Heterodontosaurus

Corythosaurus

Triceratops

Kronosaurus

Steneosaurus

Temnodontosaurus

Plateosaurus

Gualosuchus

Chanaresuchus

Gracilisuchus

Mesorhinosaurus(?)

Aepyornis- Elephant Bird

Raphus cucullatus- Dodo

Alca impennis- Great Auk

Dinornis- Giant Moa

Monachus tropicalis- Caribbean Monk Seal

Hydrodamalis gigas- Steller's Sea Cow

Meganeura

Eryon

Menippe

Potamon

Isotelus

Mecochirus

Bumastis

Eurypterus

Paradoxides

Image gallery

 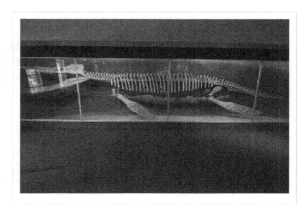

References

- The Museum of Comparative Zoology (homepage) [2]
- Boston Phoenix [3]; "Best Freak Show (Other than the Subway)"
- *The Rarest of the Rare* by Nancy Pick [4]

Geographical coordinates: 42°22′42.50″N 71°06′56.00″W

Busch–Reisinger Museum

Harvard Art Museums/Busch-Reisinger Museum	
Established	1903
Location	Cambridge, Massachusetts
Director	Thomas W. Lentz
Website	harvardartmuseums.org [1]

The **Busch-Reisinger Museum**, opened to the public in 1903, is one of two museums in North America dedicated to the study of art from the German-speaking countries of Europe. The other museum is the Neue Galerie, located in New York City. The Busch-Reisinger joins the Fogg Museum and the Arthur M. Sackler Museum as part of the Harvard Art Museums.

From 1921-1991, the Busch-Reisinger was located in Adolphus Busch Hall at 29 Kirkland Street. The hall continues to house the Busch-Reisinger's founding collection of medieval plaster casts and an exhibition on the history of the Busch-Reisinger Museum; it also hosts concerts on its world-renowned Flentrop pipe organ. In 1991, the Busch-Reisinger moved to the new Werner Otto Hall, designed by Gwathmey Siegel & Associates, at 32 Quincy Street.

In 2008, Otto Hall closed and is being demolished as part of a major renovation project to create a new museum building designed by architect Renzo Piano that will house all three museums one facility. During the renovation, selected works from all three museums are on display at the Arthur M. Sackler Museum, located at 485 Broadway.

Collection

The Busch-Reisinger's holdings include Vienna Secession art, German Expressionism, 1920s abstract art, and material related to the Bauhaus. Other strengths include late medieval sculpture and 18th-century art. The museum also holds noteworthy postwar and contemporary art from German-speaking Europe, including works by Georg Baselitz, Anselm Kiefer, Gerhard Richter, and one of the world's most comprehensive collections of works by Joseph Beuys. Many of the works in the Busch-Reisinger collection can be accessed as part of the Harvard Art Museums' online Collection Search, which features 250,000 works of art.

See also

- Harvard Art Museum
- Fogg Museum
- Arthur M. Sackler Museum

External links

- Harvard Art Museums website [2]
- Fogg Museum website [3]
- Busch-Reisinger Museum website [4]
- Arthur M. Sackler Museum website [5]
- Archaeological Exploration of Sardis, Turkey website [6]
- Center for the Technical Study of Modern Art website [7]
- Harvard Art Museums Archives website [8]
- The Straus Center for Conservation and Technical Studies website [9]
- Harvard Art Museums Collection Search website [10]
- Harvard University website [11]

Fogg Museum

Harvard Art Museums/Fogg Museum	
U.S. National Register of Historic Places	
Location:	Cambridge, Massachusetts
Built/Founded:	1925/1896
Architect:	Coolidge, Shepley, Bulfinch & Abbott
Architectural style(s):	Georgian Revival
Governing body:	Harvard University
Added to NRHP:	May 19, 1986
NRHP Reference#:	86001282

The **Fogg Museum**, opened to the public in 1896, is the oldest of Harvard University's art museums. The Fogg joins the Busch-Reisinger Museum and the Arthur M. Sackler Museum as part of the Harvard Art Museums.

The museum was originally housed in an Italian Renaissance-style building designed by Richard Morris Hunt. In 1925, the building was demolished and replaced by a Georgian Revival-style structure designed by Coolidge, Shepley, Bulfinch, and Abbott. In 2008, the building closed for a major renovation project to create a new museum building designed by architect Renzo Piano that will house all three Harvard art museums in one facility. During the renovation, selected works from all three museums are on display at the Arthur M. Sackler Museum.

Collection

The Fogg Museum is renowned for its holdings of Western paintings, sculpture, decorative arts, photographs, prints, and drawings from the Middle Ages to the present. Particular strengths include Italian Renaissance, British Pre-Raphaelite, and French art of the 19th century, as well as 19th- and 20th-century American paintings and drawings.

The museum's Maurice Wertheim Collection is a notable group of impressionist and postimpressionist works that contains many famous masterworks, including paintings and sculpture by Paul Cézanne, Edgar Degas, Édouard Manet, Henri Matisse, Pablo Picasso, and Vincent van Gogh. Central to the Fogg's holdings is the Grenville L. Winthrop Collection, with more than 4,000 works of art. Bequeathed to Harvard in 1943, the collection continues to play a pivotal role in shaping the legacy of the Harvard Art Museums, serving as a foundation for teaching, research, and professional training programs. It includes important 19th-century paintings, sculpture, and drawings by William Blake, Edward Burne-Jones, Jacques-Louis David, Honoré Daumier, Winslow Homer, Jean Auguste Dominique Ingres, Pierre-Auguste Renoir, Auguste Rodin, John Singer Sargent, Henri de Toulouse-Lautrec, and James Abbott McNeill Whistler.

Many of the works in the Fogg Museum can be accessed as part of the Harvard Art Museums' online Collection Search, which 250,000 works of art.

Gallery

See also

- Harvard Art Museums
- Busch-Reisinger Museum
- Arthur M. Sackler Museum

External links

- Harvard Art Museums website [2]
- Fogg Museum website [3]
- Busch-Reisinger Museum website [4]
- Arthur M. Sackler Museum website [5]
- Archaeological Exploration of Sardis, Turkey website [6]
- Center for the Technical Study of Modern Art website [7]
- Harvard Art Museums Archives website [8]
- The Straus Center for Conservation and Technical Studies website [9]
- Harvard Art Museums Collection Search website [10]
- Harvard University website [11]

Arthur M. Sackler Museum

Harvard Art Museums/Arthur M. Sackler Museum	
Established	1985
Location	485 Broadway, Cambridge, Massachusetts 02138
Director	Thomas W. Lentz
Website	harvardartmuseums.org [1]

The **Arthur M. Sackler Museum** joins the Fogg Museum and the Busch-Reisinger Museum as part of the Harvard Art Museums. Its postmodern building was designed by British architect James Stirling and opened to the public in October 1985.

In 2008, the 32 Quincy Street building that formerly housed the Fogg and Busch-Reisinger collections closed for a major renovation project to create a new museum building designed by architect Renzo Piano that will house all three museums in one facility. During the renovation, selected works from all three museums are on display at the Sackler.

Collection

The Sackler holds world-renowned collections of archaic Chinese jades and Japanese *surimono*, as well as Chinese bronzes, ancient ceremonial weapons, and Buddhist cave-temple sculptures; Chinese and Korean ceramics; and Japanese woodblock prints, calligraphy, narrative paintings, and lacquer boxes.

The Sackler's collections of ancient and Byzantine art include notable works in all media from Greece, Rome, Egypt, and the Near East. They are especially strong in the pottery of ancient Greece, and in small bronzes and coins from throughout the ancient Mediterranean world.

The museum also holds works on paper from Islamic lands and India, including paintings, drawings, calligraphy, and manuscript illustrations, with particular strength in Rajput art, as well as significant Islamic ceramics from the 8th through 19th century, including Samanid epigraphic wares, luster wares from Iraq, Iran, and Spain, and İznik Ottoman wares.

Many of the works in the Sackler Museum can be accessed as part of the Harvard Art Museums' online Collection Search, which features 250,000 works of art.

Gallery

See also

- Harvard Art Museums
- Fogg Museum
- Busch-Reisinger Museum

External links

- Harvard Art Museums website [1]
- Arthur M. Sackler Museum website [1]
- Harvard Art Museums Collection Search website [10]
- Harvard University website [11]

Glass Flowers

The **Glass Flowers**, formally **The Ware Collection of Blaschka Glass Models of Plants,** is a famous collection of highly-realistic glass botanical models at the Harvard Museum of Natural History at Harvard University in Cambridge, Massachusetts.

They were made by Leopold and Rudolf Blaschka from 1887 through 1936 at their studio in Hosterwitz, Germany, near Dresden. They were commissioned by Professor George Lincoln Goodale, founder of Harvard's Botanical Museum, for the purpose of teaching botany, and financed by Goodale's former student, Mary Lee Ware and her mother, Elizabeth Ware. Over 3000 models, of 847 different plant species, were made.

A Blaschka glass model of part of a cashew tree at the Harvard Museum of Natural History

The models

In an article for the *Journal of American Conservation* authors McNally and Buschini note that "the Glass Flowers are not made simply of glass. Many are painted (particularly models made in the years 1886–95) and varnished; some parts are glued together, and some of the models contain wire armatures within the glass stems. Coloring of the models ranges from paint to colored glass to enameling." To this day, no one has been able to duplicate the Blaschka's fine artistry.

Botanist Donald Schnell gives testimony to the astonishing accuracy of the models. He writes of a plant, *Pinguicula,* the details of whose pollination were unknown. By painstaking analysis of its structures, he worked out the probable mechanism of pollination. On visiting the glass flowers exhibit for the first time in 1997, he was enjoying the "enchanting and very accurate" models, when he was astonished to see a panel showing *Pinguicula* and a pollinating bee: "one sculpture showed a bee entering the flower and a second showed the bee exiting, lifting the stigma apron as it did so," precisely as Schnell had hypothesized. "As far as I know Professor Goodale never published this information, nor did it seem to have been published by anyone back then, but the process was faithfully executed."

In the "Journal of American Conservation" authors Whitehouse and Small state that "the superiority in design and construction of the Blaschka models surpasses all modern model making to date and the skill and art of the Blaschkas rests in peace for eternity.

Restoration

The flowers have suffered deterioration and are undergoing restoration. In a 1999 article about the collection in the journal *ResearchPennState* curatorial associate Susan Rossi-Wilcox is quoted as saying "It took a long time for the faculty here to go from thinking about the Glass Flowers as a teaching collection to thinking about them as art objects." Rossi-Wilcox went on "See the white powdery stuff on the leaves? This is glass corrosion. The majority of these models are affected. That's the great irony. The models showing plant diseases are also showing glass diseases." Others have acquired breaks or hairline cracks due to vibrations in the building. In 2000 Harvard began a restoration program, estimated to take at least six years. A *Boston Globe* story described the elaborate measures taken and the painstaking effort required merely to move some of the flowers one flight of stairs upward to a conservation area.

Public response

The Glass Flowers are one of the most famous attractions of the Boston area. More than 175,000 visitors view the collection annually. In 1936, when Harvard invited the public to tour the campus in honor of its tercentenary, a *New York Times* reporter taking the tour commented "Tercentenary or no, the chief focus of interest remains the famous glass flowers, the first of which was put on exhibition in 1893, and which with additions at intervals since, have never failed to draw exclamations of wonder or disbelief from visitors."

A visitor returning to Back Bay in 1951 after a ten-year absence wrote "I was told the two sights above all others that visiting salesmen from the country wish to see when in Boston are the glass flowers at the Harvard Museum of Natural History in Harvard Square and the Mapparium at the Christian Science Church building."

Marianne Moore wrote in a poem, "Silence,"

> My father used to say,
>
> "Superior people never make long visits,
>
> have to be shown Longfellow's grave,
>
> or the glass flowers at Harvard."

According to Rossi-Wilcox, the question people most often ask after seeing them is, "'Where are the *glass* flowers?' Because nobody can believe these are made of glass.".

Glass Invertebrates

The Blaschkas also made glass models of invertebrates. Cornell University has some on display[1][2]; however, most are stored for safekeeping at the Corning Museum of Glass in Corning, New York[3]. Other locations exhibiting the Blaschka invertebrates include the Boston Museum of Science, the Harvard Museum of Natural History, the National Museum of Ireland [4], and the Redpath Museum of McGill University.

See also

- Artificial flowers
- Glassblowing
- Glass museums and galleries
- Lampworking

External links

- The Ware Collection of Blaschka Glass Models of Plants [5] Harvard website
- Invertebrate Models at Cornell University [6]
- "Glass Flowers bloom again at HMNH" [7], Harvard University Gazette
- "'Glass Flowers' gallery to close for renovations" [8], Harvard University Gazette
- "Care for Glass Flowers branches out: Natural History Museum's fragile flowers get needed cleaning and repair" [9], Harvard University Gazette
- "These creatures see dusty duty: Obscure cousins of the Glass Flowers depict denizens of the deep" [10], Harvard University Gazette
- "Eclipsed for decades, Harvard's glass animals step out" [11], Harvard University Gazette
- Corning Museum of Glass [12]

Peabody Museum of Archaeology and Ethnology

The **Peabody Museum of Archaeology and Ethnology** is a museum affiliated with Harvard University in Cambridge, Massachusetts.

Founded in 1866, it is one of the oldest and most renowned museums focusing on anthropological material, and is particularly strong in New World and Mesoamerican ethnography and archaeology. The Museum also houses an archive of over 500,000 images relating to the collection. The Peabody Museum of Archaeology and Ethnology shares a building with the Harvard Museum of Natural History, and is under the direction of William T. Fash.

Main entrance to the Peabody Museum

Permanent exhibits

In its exhibit halls the museum displays artifacts from its vast collection of casts from Mesoamerican monuments. It also devotes exhibits to the history of indigenous peoples of North America as well as a diverse array of objects from the Pacific Islands.

External links

- Peabody Museum homepage [1]

Geographical coordinates: 42°22′41.50″N 71°06′53.30″W

Semitic Museum

The **Semitic Museum** at Harvard University was founded in 1889, and moved into its present location at 6 Divinity Avenue in Cambridge, Massachusetts in 1903.

The Harvard Semitic Mvsevm

From the beginning, it was the home of the Department of Near Eastern Languages and Civilizations, a departmental library, a repository for research collections, a public educational institute, and a center for archaeological exploration. Among the Museum's early achievements were the first scientific excavations in the Holy Land (at Samaria in 1907-1912) and excavations at Nuzi and Tell el-Khaleifeh in the Sinai, where the earliest alphabet was found.

The Museum's artifacts include pottery, cylinder seals, sculpture, coins and cuneiform tablets. Many are from museum-sponsored excavations in Israel, Jordan, Iraq, Egypt, Cyprus, and Tunisia. The museum holds a replica of the Merneptah stele. The Museum is dedicated to the use of these collections for the teaching, research, and publication of Near Eastern archaeology, history, and culture.

External links

- Semitic Museum official site [1]

MIT Chapel

The **MIT Chapel** (dedicated 1955) is a non-denominational chapel designed by noted architect Eero Saarinen. It is located on the campus of the Massachusetts Institute of Technology, next to Kresge Auditorium and Kresge Oval, which Saarinen also designed, in Cambridge, Massachusetts. Though a small building, it is often noted as a successful example of mid-Century modern architecture in the US. Saarinen also designed the landscaping surrounding all three.

Leland M. Roth included the building in his *History of American Architecture*, using it to illustrate the contrast between Saarinen's approach and that of Mies (who designed a chapel for IIT). Roth said that "through the sheer manipulation of light and the its focus on a blazingly white marble altar block, Saarinen created a place of mystic quiet."

Exterior.

From the outside the chapel is a simple, windowless brick cylinder set inside a very shallow concrete moat. It is 50 feet (15 m) in diameter and 30 feet (9.1 m) high, and topped by an aluminum spire. The brick is supported by a series of low arches. Saarinen chose bricks that were rough and imperfect to create a textured effect. The whole is set in two groves of birch trees, with a long wall to the east, all designed by Saarinen. The wall and trees provide a uniform background for the chapel, and isolate the site from the noise and bustle of adjacent buildings.

Within is a remarkably intimate space, stunning in its immediate visual impact. Windowless interior walls are undulating brick. Like a cascade of light, a full-height metal sculpture by Harry Bertoia glitters from the circular skylight down to a small, unadorned marble altar. Natural light filters upward from shallow slits in the walls catching reflected light from the moat; this dim ambient light is complemented by artificial lighting. The chapel's curving spire and bell tower was designed by the sculptor Theodore Roszak and was added in 1956.

The chapel has an excellent organ that was custom-designed for the space by Walter Holtkamp of the Holtkamp Organ Company, located in Cleveland, Ohio. Holtkamp was instrumental in the 1950s, in the revival of the classic school of organ-building.

Interior.

See also

- Architecture of the Massachusetts Institute of Technology

References

Geographical coordinates: 42°21′29.94″N 71°05′38.94″W

St. John's Roman Catholic Church

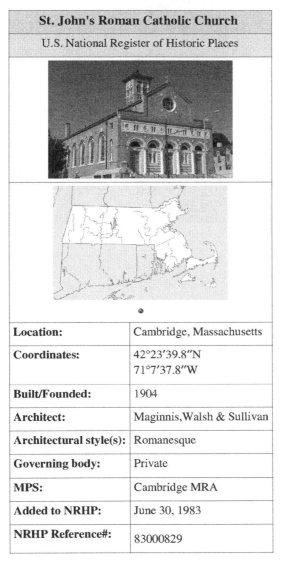

St. John's Roman Catholic Church	
U.S. National Register of Historic Places	
Location:	Cambridge, Massachusetts
Coordinates:	42°23′39.8″N 71°7′37.8″W
Built/Founded:	1904
Architect:	Maginnis,Walsh & Sullivan
Architectural style(s):	Romanesque
Governing body:	Private
MPS:	Cambridge MRA
Added to NRHP:	June 30, 1983
NRHP Reference#:	83000829

St. John's Roman Catholic Church is an historic church at 2270 Massachusetts Avenue in Cambridge, Massachusetts. This was the church attended by the late Speaker of the House, "Tip" O'Neill.

The church was built in 1904 and added to the National Register of Historic Places in 1983.

A Christ statue in front of the church

Christ Church (Cambridge, Massachusetts)

Christ Church	
U.S. National Register of Historic Places	
U.S. National Historic Landmark	
Christ Church in 1792.	
Location:	Garden Street, Cambridge, Massachusetts
Coordinates:	42°22′30.95″N 71°7′16.09″W
Area:	0.5-acre (2000 m^2)
Built/Founded:	1761
Architect:	Harrison,Peter
Governing body:	Private
Added to NRHP:	October 15, 1966
Designated NHL:	October 9, 1960
NRHP Reference#:	66000140

For other churches with this name, please see Christ Church (disambiguation)

Christ Church, at Zero Garden Street in Cambridge, Massachusetts, U.S.A., is a parish of the Episcopal Diocese of Massachusetts, and is a National Historic Landmark.

History

The congregation was founded in 1759 by members of the King's Chapel who lived in Cambridge to have a church closer to their homes and to provide Church of England services to students at Harvard College across Cambridge Common. The church's first Rector was East Apthorp, and most of the founding members lived along the near-by 'Tory Row', now called Brattle Street.

The church was designed by noted colonial era architect Peter Harrison, who also designed the King's Chapel in Boston. Its wooden frame rests on a granite foundation built from ballast stones from ships arriving at Boston Harbor. The church was originally finished in a sanded paint treatment to give the appearance of a traditional English stone church.

During the American Revolution Christ Church was attacked by dissenting colonials for its Tory leanings, but it was also the site of a prayer service which George and Martha Washington attended while quartered in the nearby mansion now known as the Longfellow National Historic Site. The church was closed, and its organ melted down for bullets during the Revolution.

For several years after the American Revolution, the church stood empty. In the later years of the eighteenth century the church was re-opened as an Episcopal Church and has remained so. The original chapel was expanded in 1857 to accommodate a larger congregation and to help raise funds for the church by expanding pew rental income. The church was dramatically redecorated in 1883, but it was restored to its original simplicity in 1920 [1].

Generations of Harvard students from Richard Henry Dana, Jr., author of *Two Years Before the Mast*, to Teddy Roosevelt, who was asked not to continue as a Sunday School teacher because he would not become an Episcopalian, have made Christ Church their parish home during their studies.

It was declared a National Historic Landmark in 1960.

Christ Church has a long history of social activism, supporting the civil rights movement, the peace movement, and ministries of social justice. In April 1967 the Reverend Martin Luther King and Doctor Benjamin Spock were denied access to a building at Harvard University to hold a press conference denouncing the Vietnam War, but the Reverend Murray Kenney welcomed them to Christ Church; a plaque in the parish hall commemorates the event. Another activist to speak at Christ Church was Jesse Louis Jackson, who spoke as part of a Martin Luther King, Jr. celebration in 2004.

Gallery

Church Interior.

View of the Cambridge Common, ca. 1808-9, with Harvard
College on the left and Christ Church on the right.

External links

- Christ Church Website [2]

First Church of Christ, Scientist (Cambridge, Massachusetts)

First Church of Christ, Scientist 13 Waterhouse Street Cambridge, Massachusetts	
15 March 2009	
Architectural style	Classical Revival
Structural system	6 story (including basement) redbrick with copper clad dome
Town	13 Waterhouse Street Cambridge, Massachusetts
Country	United States
Started	1924
Completed	1930
Architect	Giles M. Smith of Bigelow and Wadsworth, later Bigelow, Wadsworth, Hubbard and Smith
Engineer	Guastavino Fireproof Construction Company, dome

First Church of Christ, Scientist is an historic redbrick 6-story domed Christian Science church building located at 13 Waterhouse Street, in Cambridge, Massachusetts. It was designed in 1917 by church member Giles M. Smith of the noted Boston architectural firm of Bigelow and Wadsworth (later Bigelow, Wadsworth, Hubbard and Smith), who patterned it after Thomas Jefferson's The Rotunda at the University of Virginia and the Pantheon in Rome. Due to cost constraints it was built in two phases between 1924 and 1930. The basement and ground floor levels topped by a belt course comprised the first phase, while the additional four stories and the massive dome comprised the second and final phase. The dome itself was designed and built by the noted Guastavino Fireproof Construction Company, which in 1898 had done the reconstruction of the dome in The Rotunda at UVA and the construction in 1906 of the dome of the Mother Church Extension in Boston. Guastavino used its patented tile arch system consisting of Akoustolith, a porous ceramic material resembling stone, on the interior, with limestone on the exterior. The tile was manufactured at its plant in nearby Woburn. In 1933 copper flashing was added to the exterior of the dome in order correct a leakage problem. An oculus provided light to the interior. The first services in the completed building were held on April 30, 1930, and after becoming debt free, it was dedicated on May 23, 1937.

First Church of Christ, Scientist is still located in the building and is still an active branch of the Christian Science Mother Church.

The First Parish in Cambridge

The First Parish in Cambridge, a Unitarian Universalist church, is located in Harvard Square in Cambridge, Massachusetts. The church is notable for its almost 400 year history, which includes pivotal roles in the development of the early Massachusetts government, the creation of Harvard College, and the refinement of current liberal religious thought.

The current site of the First Parish in Harvard Square

Site history

The original First Parish, called at the time the first Meeting House, was built near the corner of Dunster and Mount Auburn Streets in 1632. The Meeting House's first minister, Thomas Hooker, stayed only a handful of years; he and most of his flock moved to Connecticut to escape religious persecution in 1636. Reverend Thomas Shepard, a significant leader of the great Puritan migration to New England at the time, gathered a new church, the First

A 1836 illustration by the daughter of Harvard President Josiah Quincy III of the September 1836 procession of Harvard alumni leaving the First Parish Meeting House and walking to the Pavilion

Church in Cambridge on February 1, 1636. One year later, Reverend Shepard used his influence with the General Court of Massachusetts to move Harvard College to Newtowne (later called Cambridge), a short distance away from his newly established church, so that the Harvard college students might 'benefit from proximity' to his evangelical preaching. The Harvard College Yard became the site for the second Meeting House, built in 1652, and the third, in 1706, and the fourth, 1756, all located in the corner now occupied by the college's Lehman Hall.

In 1833, the congregation built the fifth and final Meeting House, which stands adjacent to present-day Harvard Yard. Harvard College held its annual commencement ceremonies therein for the next forty years. Five Harvard College Presidents---Everett, Sparks, Walker, Felton, Hill, and Eliot---began their inaugural terms there as well. The Parish House was built in 1902, and the interior of the Meeting House remodeled in 1914. The Crothers chapel was dedicated in 1941.

Governmental role

In the century following the founding of the Town of Cambridge in 1630, the whole community transacted the parish affairs through town meetings. Said another way, the townspeople were responsible for governing the area and for providing financial support for the Meeting House and the ministry. In 1733, the First Parish in Cambridge moved away from its close governmental governmental role and separately organized itself as a territorial parish. Within the town (which was considered a 'parish' after 1733), the church was a relatively small, covenanted body of those admitted to full communion. Such costs as the maintenance of the meeting house and the salary of the town's "public teacher of piety, religion, and morality" (who was also the minister of the church) were met by regular assessments on all persons domiciled within the territorial limits of the parish (unless exempted because they were supporting either Baptist or Episcopal worship). The power of the parish to assess the inhabitants for ecclesiastical purposes was abolished in Massachusetts in 1833. Since then, the parish has been a poll parish, rather than a territorial parish.

Evolution of church doctrine

Throughout the 17th century, Reverend Shepard and his successors preached a Calvinistic doctrine. In the 18th century, the ministers moved the theology in a more liberal theology direction. Specifically, Reverend William Brattle and Reverend Nathaniel Appleton amended their Calvinist preaching to encourage 'free inquiry,' and they held a tolerant and catholic spirit towards those who differed on doctrinal matters. Appleton's successor, Timothy Hilliard, was Arminian rather than Calvinistic in theology.

The division between Calvinists and Arminians, which appeared in many churches of the Standing Order in the 18th century, reached a time of crisis in the period from 1805 to 1830. The minister of the Cambridge church at that time was the Reverend Abiel Holmes, the father of Oliver Wendell Holmes. Reverend Holmes held to orthodox doctrinal views, but he remained on friendly terms with the liberal or Arminian party for three decades after his installation in 1792. In 1826, however, he decided to break off relations with the liberals, specifically abolishing pulpit exchanges with the liberal or Unitarian ministers.

After vainly attempting to persuade Reverend Holmes to return to his earlier, more inclusive practices, the Parish voted to dismiss him as its public teacher of religion and morality. By 1829, most of the Parish became Unitarian. Dr. Holmes and the more conservative members of his flock departed and founded the Shepard Congregational Society. In 1899, it was agreed that the church associated with that society should be called the First Church in Cambridge (Congregational), now part of the United Church of Christ, and this church, the First Church in Cambridge (Unitarian)[now Unitarian Universalist].

The Reverend William Newell, the first avowedly Unitarian minister, led the congregation from 1830 to 1868. His immediate successor, Francis Greenwood Peabody, would become a leader of the Social Gospel movement. The fourteenth minister, Reverend Dr. Samuel McChord Crothers, an eloquent preacher and widely read essayist, managed to attract a following from both the University and the Old Cambridge communities.

Present membership

Since the early days of Dr. Crothers' ministry, the town of Cambridge has changed greatly. Instead of being a suburban community, separated from Boston by an hour's travel time, the town has become an urban center in its own right. The Cambridge church is to all intents and purposes a downtown church. Its membership fluctuates, as urban communities do, and its composition varies. The current church leadership, however, is committed to maintaining the witness of liberal religion, in keeping with the struggles of earlier generations.

Notable personages

- Thomas Hooker establishes the first Meeting House in 1633.
- The General Court of Massachusetts banished Anne Hutchinson from Massachusetts during sessions held in the first Meeting House in 1637.
- U.S. President George Washington worshiped in the fourth Meeting House in 1775.
- Edward Everett received the General Marquis de La Fayette with an address of welcome in 1825.
- Ralph Waldo Emerson gave his Phi Beta Kappa oration on "The American Scholar" in 1837.

Ministers of First Parish in Cambridge

- **1633 - 1636** Thomas Hooker
- **1633 - 1636** Samuel Stone
- **1636 - 1649** Thomas Shepard
- **1649 - 1650** Henry Dunster (interim)
- **1650 - 1668** Jonathan Mitchel
- **1671 - 1681** Urian Oakes
- **1682 - 1692** Nathaniel Gookin, son of Maj.-Gen. Daniel Gookin
- **1696 - 1717** William Brattle
- **1717 - 1784** Nathaniel Appleton
- **1783 - 1790** Timothy Hilliard
- **1792 - 1829** Abiel Holmes
- **1830 - 1868** William Newell
- **1874 - 1879** Francis G. Peabody
- **1882 - 1893** Edward H. Hall
- **1894 - 1927** Samuel M. Crothers
- **1928 - 1934** Ralph E. Bailey
- **1935 - 1944** Leslie T. Pennington
- **1945 - 1958** Wilburn B. Miller
- **1959 - 1977** Ralph N. Helverson
- **1978 - 1987** Edwin A. Lane
- **1989 - 2006** Thomas J. S. Mikelson
- **1997 - 2007** Jory Agate
- **2008–present** Fred Small

References

- Cambridge, Massachusetts. First Parish in Cambridge. Records, 1658-1993, Andover-Harvard Theological Library, Harvard Divinity School [1]

External links

- First Parish in Cambridge Official site [2]
- Harvard Square Library [3]

Geographical coordinates: 42°22′28.5″N 71°7′9.3″W

Memorial Church of Harvard University

The **Memorial Church of Harvard University**, more commonly known as the **Harvard Memorial Church** (or simply **Mem Church**) is a building on the campus of Harvard University.

History

Predecessors

The first distinct building for worship at Harvard University was Holden Chapel, built in 1744. The college soon outgrew

Memorial Church

the building, which was replaced by a chapel inside Harvard Hall in 1766, then a chapel in University Hall in 1814, and finally by Appleton Chapel, a building dedicated solely to worship sited where The Memorial Church now stands.

Standing for 73 years before the current building, Appleton Chapel was home to religious life at Harvard until 1932. Its namesake is preserved inside Memorial Church, as the Appleton Chapel portion of the main building houses the daily service of Morning Prayer. When Appleton Chapel was built in 1858, thanks to the generosity of Samuel Appleton, Morning Prayer attendance was compulsory. When attendance became voluntary in 1886, the College was left with a building that had become too large for the Morning Prayer services and too small for the Sunday services. Although there was talk of building a more suitable chapel for worship at Harvard, nothing was done until soon after World War I when Harvard University President Abbott Lawrence Lowell (1909-1933) combined the idea of a war memorial with the need for a new chapel. Appleton Chapel was torn down after the 1931 Commencement. The University Architects Coolidge, Shepley, Bulfinch & Abbott, were enlisted to design the new building, and they planned a structure that would complement the imposing edifice of Widener Library. This created an open area known as the Tercentenary Theatre, where Commencement Exercises are held.

Memorial Church

The current Memorial Church was built in 1932 in honor of the men and women of Harvard University who died in World War I. The names of 373 alumni were engraved within alongside a sculpture named *The Sacrifice* by Malvina Hoffman. It was dedicated on Armistice Day on November 11, 1932.

Since then, other memorials have been established within the building commemorating those Harvardians who later died in World War II, the Korean War, and the Vietnam War. For seventy-five years, it has stood in Harvard Yard opposite Widener Library as a physical reminder of Harvard's spiritual heritage. Since its inception, the Harvard Memorial Church has had weekly choral music provided at its Sunday services by the Harvard University Choir, which is composed of both graduate and undergraduate students in the university.

Gallery

Sanctuary in December

Bustling Harvard Yard

Winter time

World War I Memorial

World War II Memorial

External links

- The Memorial Church – Home Page [1]

Harvard-Epworth United Methodist Church

The **Harvard-Epworth United Methodist Church** is a church located beside Harvard Law School near the Cambridge, Massachusetts common. Its congregation was organized in March 1941 by the merger of Harvard Street Methodist Church and Epworth Methodist Church.

The building was designed by A. P. Cutting of Worcester, Massachusetts in Richardson Romanesque style, and constructed by Cutting and Bishop. Costs were born primarily by George Bird and philanthropist Frederick Hastings Rindge. Its cornerstone was laid on October 3, 1891 and the church dedicated on February 22, 1893. The structure is built of Southville red granite with East Longmeadow sandstone trimming, and furnished inside with fine wood. Its square, central tower is 110 feet in height and capped with a red, pyramidal roof.

Harvard-Epworth United Methodist Church

External links

- Harvard-Epworth United Methodist Church [1]

Longfellow National Historic Site

The Longfellow National Historic Site, also known as the
Vassall-Craigie-Longfellow House, in Cambridge, Massachusetts.

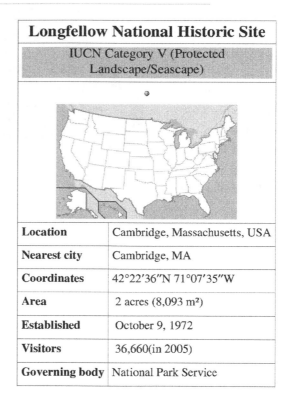

Longfellow National Historic Site	
IUCN Category V (Protected Landscape/Seascape)	
Location	Cambridge, Massachusetts, USA
Nearest city	Cambridge, MA
Coordinates	42°22′36″N 71°07′35″W
Area	2 acres (8,093 m²)
Established	October 9, 1972
Visitors	36,660(in 2005)
Governing body	National Park Service

The **Longfellow National Historic Site**, also known as the **Vassall-Craigie-Longfellow House**, is a historic site located at 105 Brattle Street in Cambridge, Massachusetts. For almost fifty years, it was the home of noted American poet Henry Wadsworth Longfellow. For a time, it had previously served as the headquarters of George Washington.

The house was built in 1759 for John Vassall, who fled the Cambridge area at the beginning of the American Revolutionary War because of his loyalty to the king of England. George Washington used the abandoned home as his first official headquarters as commander of the Continental Army; the home served as his base of operations during the Siege of Boston until he moved out in July 1776. Andrew Craigie, Washington's Apothecary General, was the next person to own the home for a significant period of time. After purchasing the house in 1791, he instigated the home's only major addition. Craigie's financial situation at the time of his death in 1819 forced his widow Elizabeth Craigie to take in boarders. It was as a boarder that Henry Wadsworth Longfellow came into the home. He became its owner in 1843, when his father-in-law Nathan Appleton purchased it as a wedding gift. He lived in the home until his death in 1882.

The last family to live in the home was the Longfellow family, who established the Longfellow Trust in 1913 for its preservation. The home was donated in 1972, along with all its furnishings, and was made part of the National Park Service. The home, which represents the mid-Georgian architectural style, is seasonally open to the public.

History

Early history

The original house was built in 1759 for Loyalist John Vassall who inherited the land along what was called the King's Highway in Cambridge when he was 21. He demolished the structure that had stood there and built a new mansion. The home became his summer residence with his wife Elizabeth (Oliver) and children until 1774. His wife's brother was Thomas Oliver, then royal lieutenant governor of Massachusetts. On the eve of the American Revolution in September 1774, they fled Boston.

1854 image of the home labeled as
"Headquarters, Cambridge 1775" in
reference to George Washington

In the days after the Battles of Lexington and Concord, the home was used as a temporary hospital. Colonel John Glover and the Marblehead Regiment occupied the house as their temporary barracks in June 1775, followed by General George Washington, Commander-in-Chief of the newly-formed Continental Army. Washington used the home as his headquarters and home while he planned the Siege of Boston between July 1775 and April 1776; he found the view of the Charles River particularly useful for that purpose. Originally, Washington had used the home of Samuel Langdon in Cambridge but decided he needed more space for his staff. The home was shared with several aide-de-camps, including colonel Robert H. Harrison. During his time there, Washington was visited by John Adams and Abigail Adams, Benedict Arnold, Henry Knox, and Nathaniel Greene. In his study, Washington also confronted Dr. Benjamin Church with evidence that he was a spy. It was in this house that Washington received a poem written by Phillis Wheatley, the first published African-American poet. "If you should ever come to Cambridge", he wrote to her, "I shall be happy to see a person so favored by the Muses".

Martha Washington joined her husband in December 1775 and stayed until March 1776. She brought with her Washington's nephew George Lewis as well as her son John Parke Custis and his wife Eleanor Calvert. On Twelfth Night in January 1776, the couple celebrated their wedding anniversary in the home. Mrs. Washington reported to a friend that "some days we have [heard] a number of cannon and shells from Boston and Bunkers Hill". She used the front parlor as her personal reception room, still furnished with the English-made furniture left behind by the Vassalls. The Washingtons also had several servants, including a tailor named Giles Alexander, and several slaves including "Billy" Lee. They also entertained very often. Surviving household accounts show that the family purchased large quantities of beef, lamb, wild ducks, geese, fresh fish, plums, peaches, barrels of cider, gallons of brandy and rum, and 217 bottles of Madeira wine purchased in a two-week period.

Washington left the house in April 1776. Nathaniel Tracy, who had made a great fortune as one of the earliest and most successful privateers under Washington, owned the house from 1781 to 1786. He then went bankrupt and sold the house to Thomas Russell, a wealthy Boston merchant, who in turn occupied it until 1791.

Craigie family and boarders

Andrew Craigie bought the house in 1791; Craigie had been the first Apothecary General of the American army. In his ballroom, Craigie hosted Prince Edward, Duke of Kent and Strathearn, the father of Queen Victoria. While living in the home, he married the daughter of a Nantucket clergyman, 22-year old Elizabeth Craigie, 17 years her elder. Craigie overspent in trying to restore the home and, when he died in 1819, he left his wife Elizabeth in great debt; Mrs. Craigie took in boarders to support herself, most often people connected to nearby Harvard University. Short-term residents of the home included Jared Sparks, Edward Everett, and Joseph Emerson Worcester.

Longfellow moved to Cambridge to take a job at Harvard College as Smith Professor of Modern Languages and of Belles Lettres. A friend, Cornelius Conway Felton, recommended that Longfellow rent a room on the third floor of the home of a Professor Stearns on Kirkland Street; Longfellow stayed there for the 1836–1837 academic year. Beginning in the summer of 1837, he rented rooms on the east side of the second floor of the home on Brattle Street, now owned by Elizabeth Craigie. At first, Mrs. Craigie thought he was a student at Harvard and refused to rent to him until he convinced her that he was a professor as well as the author of the book she was reading, *Outre-Mer*.

Longfellow's new landlady had earned a reputation for being eccentric and often wore a turban. In the 1840s, Longfellow wrote about an incident when canker-worms were devastating the elm trees on the property. Mrs. Craigie "would sit by the open window and let them crawl over her white turban. She refused to have the trees protected against them & said, Why, sir, they have as good a right to live as we—they are our fellow worms". The maid at the time, a woman named Miriam, served Longfellow his meals in his room. Longfellow called her "the giantess".

The rooms Longfellow rented were the rooms once used personally by George Washington while it was his headquarters. He proudly wrote to his friend George Washington Greene: "I live in a great house which looks like an Italian villa: have two large rooms opening into each other. They were once Gen. Washington's chambers".

The first major works Longfellow composed in the home were *Hyperion*, a prose romance likely inspired by his pursuit for the affections of Frances Appleton, and *Voices of the Night*, a poetry collection which included "A Psalm of Life". 20th-century literary scholar Edward Wagenknecht notes that it was these early years at the Craigie House which marked "the real beginning of Longfellow's literary career". His landlady, Elizabeth Craigie, died in 1841.

Longfellow family

After Elizabeth Craigie's death, the entire property was leased by Joseph Emerson Worcester from her heirs; he in turn rented the eastern half of the house to Longfellow. In 1843, the house was purchased by Nathan Appleton, who gave the house to Longfellow as a wedding gift when Longfellow married Nathan's daughter Frances. He paid $10,000 for the home. Frances wrote to her brother Thomas Gold Appleton on August 30, 1843: "We have decided to let Father purchase this grand old mansion", especially after Longfellow's friend George Washington Greene reminded them "how noble an inheritance this is — where Washington dwelt in every room". Longfellow was proud of the connection to Washington and in 1844 purchased a bust of the home's

Henry Wadsworth Longfellow with his sons Charles and Ernest and his wife Frances

former occupant, a copy of the sculpture by Jean-Antoine Houdon. Worcester and his wife became tenants under Longfellow in the western half of the house until their new home a few doors down was completed that spring. Mrs. Longfellow wrote on May 5, 1844, "Worcester family left us in complete possession [of the house], with rooms nicely cleaned, and uncarpeted stairs and entries".

Nathan Appleton also purchased the land across the street, as Longfellow's mother wrote, "so that their view of the River Charles may not be intercepted". In all, Longfellow's gift included nine acres of land.

Longfellow lived in the house for the next four decades, producing many of his most famous poems including "Paul Revere's Ride" and "The Village Blacksmith", as well as longer works such as *Evangeline*, *The Song of Hiawatha*, and *The Courtship of Miles Standish*. In all, while living in this house, Longfellow published eleven poetry collections, two novels, three epic poems, and several plays as well as a translation of Dante Alighieri's *Divine Comedy*. Even as the poet's popularity increased, Longfellow and his wife most often referred to the home as "Craigie House" or "Craigie Castle".

Longfellow oversaw the creation of a formal garden and his wife oversaw decorating the interior. Mrs. Longfellow purchased several items from Tiffany's in New York as well as $350 worth of carpets. They installed central heating in 1850 and gaslight in 1853. During their time in the house, the Longfellows hosted famous artists, writers, politicians and other luminaries who were attracted to Longfellow's hospitality and fame. Specific visitors included Charles Dickens, William Makepeace Thackeray, singer Jenny Lind, and actress Fanny Kemble. Dom Pedro II, Emperor of Brazil also visited the house privately and requested the company of Longfellow, Ralph Waldo Emerson, Oliver Wendell Holmes, Sr., and James Russell Lowell. Mr. and Mrs. Longfellow also raised their three daughters and two sons in the home. Longfellow and his wife stayed in the home until their respective deaths but spent their summers after 1850 in Nahant, Massachusetts.

Longfellow often wrote in his first-floor study, formerly Washington's office, surrounded by portraits of his friends, including charcoal portraits by Eastman Johnson of Charles Sumner, Ralph Waldo Emerson, Nathaniel Hawthorne, and Cornelius Conway Felton. Longfellow would write either at the center table, at the desk, or in the armchair by the fire.

Fanny Longfellow died in the home in June 1861 after her dress accidentally caught fire; her husband attempted to quell the flames, managing to keep her face from burning. Longfellow himself was burned on his own face and was scarred badly enough that he began growing a beard to hide it.

Preservation and current use

Longfellow died in 1882 and his daughter Alice Longfellow was the last of his children to live in the home. In 1913, the surviving Longfellow children established the Longfellow House Trust to preserve the home as well as its view to the Charles River. Their intention was to preserve the home as a memorial to Longfellow and Washington and to showcase the property as a "prime example of Georgian architecture".

Memorial by Daniel Chester French and Henry Bacon

In 1962, the trust successfully lobbied for the house to become a national historic landmark. In 1972, the Trust donated the property to the National Park Service and it became the Longfellow National Historic Site; it is now open to the public as a house museum. On display are many of the original nineteenth century furnishings, artwork, over 10,000 books owned by Longfellow, and the dining table around which many important visitors gathered. Everything on display was owned by the Longfellow family.

The site also possesses some 750,000 original documents relevant to the former occupants of the home. These archives are open to scholarly research by appointment.

Across the street from the Longfellow National Historic Site is the municipal park known as Longfellow Park. In the middle sits a memorial by sculptor Daniel Chester French dedicated in 1914. In addition to a bust of the poet, a carved bas-relief by Henry Bacon depicts the famous characters Miles Standish, Sandalphon, the village blacksmith, the Spanish student, Evangeline, and Hiawatha.

Architecture and landscape

The structure of the original house was built in the Georgian architectural style. The pair of large pilasters that frame the facade expressed John Vassall's aristocratic background. In 1791, Andrew Craigie added the two side piazzas and the two-story back ell and also expanded the library into a twenty by thirty foot ballroom with its own entrance. During the Longfellow family's time in the home, very few structural changes were made. As Frances Longfellow wrote, "we are full of plans & projects with no desire, however, to change a feature of the old countenance which Washington has rendered sacred".

Back end of the Longfellow National Historic Site, as seen from the garden

The Longfellow National Historic Site is noted for its garden on the northeast end of the property. Henry Wadsworth Longfellow oversaw the creation of the original garden, shaped as a lyre, shortly after his wedding. In 1845, he began refurbishing the garden in earnest and imported trees from England with help from Asa Gray. These trees included "a number of evergreens, among them a cedar of Lebanon and pines from the Himalayas, Norway, Switzerland and Oregon". The lyre shape proved impractical and a new design was made with the help of a landscape architect named Richard Dolben in 1847. The new design was a square surrounding a circle that was cut into four tear-shaped garden beds outlined by trimmed boxwood. Mrs. Longfellow referred to the shape as a "Persian rug".

After her father's death in 1882, Alice Longfellow commissioned two of America's first female landscape architects, Martha Brookes Hutcheson and Ellen Biddle Shipman, to redesign the formal garden in the Colonial Revival style. The garden was recently restored by an organization called Friends of the Longfellow House, which completed the final stage of its reconstruction, the historic pergola, in 2008.

Replicas

For a time, Longfellow's home was one of the most photographed and most recognizable homes in the United States. In the early twentieth century Sears, Roebuck and Company sold scaled-down blueprints of the home so that anyone could build their own version of Longfellow's home. Several replicas of Longfellow's home appear throughout the United States. One replica, simply called Longfellow House, still exists in Minneapolis, Minnesota. Originally built by businessman Robert "Fish" Jones, it currently serves as an information center for the Minneapolis Park System and is on the Grand Rounds Scenic Byway.

2/3 scale replica of the Longfellow House in Minnehaha Park in Minneapolis

See also

• Wadsworth-Longfellow House in Portland, Maine

External links

• Longfellow National Historic Site official website [1]
• National Parks Conservation Association [2]
• State of the Parks [3]

Performing Arts

List Visual Arts Center

List Visual Arts Center, established in 1985, is the contemporary art gallery of the Massachusetts Institute of Technology. The LVAC is internationally recognized for the 4-6 exhibitions it presents each year in its 6000-square-foot (560 m^2) galleries. The LVAC organized Fred Wilson's installation for the US Pavilion at the 2003 Venice Biennale. The LVAC is housed in the Wiesner building, an I.M. Pei-designed, fully accessible facility that incorporates the work of painter Kenneth Noland, sculptor Scott Burton, and environmental sculptor Richard Fleischner, commissioned through MIT's Percent-for-Art program. The Percent-for-Art program, administered by the LVAC, allocates funds for

List Visual Arts Center

the commission of art in connection with each new campus construction or major renovation project. Past commissions include Louise Nevelson's Transparent Horizon in front of the Landau Building, Sol LeWitt's polychrome floor in the Green Center for Physics, and Anish Kapoor's untitled stainless steel piece in the Stata Center.

The LVAC maintains a permanent collection primarily sited throughout campus of over 3,000 prints, photographs, drawings, paintings, sculptures, textiles, collages, and other objects of contemporary art. The public sculpture collection includes major works by such artists as Alexander Calder, Jorge Pardo, Henry Moore, Pablo Picasso, Sarah Sze, and Mark DiSuvero. An interactive map of all publicly-situated art is available here [1]. The Center also maintains the Student Loan Art Collection, consisting of 500 original works of art. Through this popular annual loan program students may borrow original works of art from the collection for their private rooms and communal spaces.

External links

- List Visual Arts Center [2]
- Map of public art on MIT campus [1]

Carpenter Center for the Visual Arts

Carpenter Center for the Visual Arts	
U.S. National Register of Historic Places	
The Carpenter Center	
Location:	Cambridge, Massachusetts
Coordinates:	42°22′23.28″N 71°6′52.66″W
Built/Founded:	1963
Architect:	Le Corbusier
Architectural style(s):	No Style Listed
Governing body:	Harvard University
Added to NRHP:	April 20, 1978
NRHP Reference#:	78000435

The **Carpenter Center for the Visual Arts** at Harvard University, in Cambridge, Massachusetts is the only building actually built by Le Corbusier in the United States, and one of only two in the Americas (the other is the Curutchet House in La Plata, Argentina). Le Corbusier designed it with the collaboration of Chilean architect Guillermo Jullian de la Fuente at his 35 rue de Sévres studio; the on-site preparation of the construction plans was handled by the office of Josep Lluís Sert, then dean of the Harvard Graduate School of Design. He had formerly worked in Le Corbusier's atelier and had been instrumental in winning him the commission. The building was completed in 1962.

The building was made possible by a $1,500,000 donation by the Carpenters, who never met the architect; in the end they had to increase their donation to meet increased building costs.[citation needed]

It houses the department of Visual and Environmental Studies of the University, as well as the Harvard Film Archive, the largest collection of 35mm films in New England. It screens a large quantity of independent, international and silent films.

Le Corbusier never actually saw the building. He was invited to the opening ceremony, but he declined the invitation on account of his poor health.

External links

- Photographs [1]
- Harvard Film Archive [2]
- Department of Visual and Environmental Studies [3]
- Research on the Carpenter Center [4]

Attractions

Walden Street Cattle Pass

Walden Street Cattle Pass	
U.S. National Register of Historic Places	

Usually nearly concealed under the Walden Street Bridge, the tunnel is seen here exposed during 2007-08 bridge reconstruction work.

Location:	Cambridge, Massachusetts
Coordinates:	42°23′21.9″N 71°7′28.8″W
Built/Founded:	1857
Architect:	Unknown
Architectural style(s):	No Style Listed
Governing body:	State
MPS:	Cambridge MRA
Added to NRHP:	June 3, 1994
NRHP Reference#:	94000554

Walden Street Cattle Pass, also referred to as the **cow path**, is an historic site adjacent to the MBTA Commuter Rail Fitchburg Line right-of-way, under the Walden Street Bridge in Cambridge, Massachusetts. It was added to the National Historic Register in 1994.

The site, a tunnel for moving cattle between the railroad and the nearby stockyards of the 19th century, was built in 1857. The cattle yards were closed in 1868 or "about 1871", but the cattle trade continued; "until the 1920s, cows were unloaded here and driven down Massachusetts Avenue, through Harvard Square, and across the river to the Brighton Abattoir".

Restoration (re-pointing) of the tunnel's brickwork was carried out during the 2007-08 replacement of the second-generation bridge dating from 1914. The third-generation bridge opened for traffic in December 2008. The Cambridge City Council has discussed creation of a vantage point for viewing the tunnel.

See also

- National Register of Historic Places listings in Cambridge, Massachusetts

Gallery

Another view of the Cattle Pass during restoration

The rebuilt bridge, looking north

The rebuilt bridge, looking south

External links

- Artists' rendition of reconstructed bridge [1]

Lexington and West Cambridge Railroad

The **Lexington and West Cambridge Railroad** was a railroad company chartered in 1845 and opened in 1846, that operated in eastern Massachusetts. It and its successors provided passenger service until 1977 and freight service until 1980 or early 1981.

History

Legend

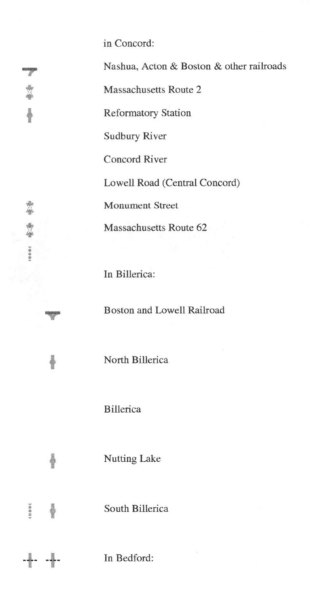

in Concord:

Nashua, Acton & Boston & other railroads

Massachusetts Route 2

Reformatory Station

Sudbury River

Concord River

Lowell Road (Central Concord)

Monument Street

Massachusetts Route 62

In Billerica:

Boston and Lowell Railroad

North Billerica

Billerica

Nutting Lake

South Billerica

In Bedford:

Bedford Springs

Great Road

Middlesex and Boston Street Railway

South Road

14.81 Bedford Depot

Elm Brook

in Lexington:

Hanscom Air Force Base

Interstate 95

Bedford St. (Routes 4, 225), M&BSt.Ry.

12.28 North Lexington

11.06 Lexington Station

10.09 Munroe Station

Pierce's Bridge (Maple Street)

9.72 Pierce's Bridge Station

9.02 East Lexington Station

in Arlington:

8.06 Arlington Heights

Park Avenue

	7.20	Brattle Station
	6.34	Arlington Centre Station
		Mass. Avenue (U.S. Route 3) and BERy
	5.47	Lake Street Station
		Lake Street
		Massachusetts Route 2
		in Cambridge:
		Alewife Brook Parkway (Routes 2, 16, U.S. 3)
	4.53	Brick Yards (Fens) Station
		Fitchburg Railroad

Mileage from Boston

A single track line was constructed in 1845-46, connecting Lexington Center to the Fitchburg Railroad (now the MBTA Fitchburg Line) in West Cambridge (near the site of the modern Alewife Station). When the separate *town* of West Cambridge changed its name to Arlington in 1867, the railroad was also renamed, as the **Lexington and Arlington Railroad**.

The Boston and Lowell Railroad purchased the line in 1870 and built a new connection (most of which would constitute a major portion of the later Fitchburg Cutoff) to their main line at Somerville Junction. The connection, from what is now the Magnolia Field-Varnum Street area

Alewife Linear Park, near the corner of Cedar Street and Massachusetts Avenue, Cambridge. When the passenger trains ran here, the North Cambridge station stood in the foreground, on the right, and the intersection was called "North Cambridge Junction".

in Arlington, ran through North Cambridge and West Somerville (Davis Square); a station was located at Somerville Junction, marked by a park near what are now Centre and Woodbine Streets. It created a subsidiary, the **Middlesex Central Railroad**, to build an extension from Lexington to Bedford and then Concord Center (Lowell Road), which opened in 1873. The Lowell Road station was adjacent to today's Minuteman National Historical Park. A 2.5-mile (4.0 km) extension from Concord Center to Concord Prison (Reformatory Station on Elm Street) would give the name **Reformatory Branch** to the Bedford-Concord segment in 1879. The branch continued another half mile further west to a junction (called "Concord Junction" or "Middlesex Junction" per different sources) with the Nashua, Acton & Boston Railroad and other rail lines.

The independent Billerica and Bedford Railroad built a connecting narrow gauge line in 1877, but went bankrupt the next year. In 1885, the Middlesex Central purchased the right-of-way and used it to build a standard gauge extension to North Billerica from Bedford. The North Billerica-Boston segment was known as the **Lexington Branch**.

The Boston and Maine Railroad purchased all of the Boston and Lowell in 1887. According to railroad historians, double-tracking from Somerville Junction to Lexington was instituted just prior to the B&M era, in 1885-86, and discontinued in 1927. Double width bridge abutments can be found in Arlington. The branch eventually ended service, as it had begun, as a single track line.

Regular service on the line used the route through Somerville Junction, via West Somerville (Davis Square) and North Cambridge, from 1870 until 1927, at which time it reverted to the original route via the Fitchburg main line. The latter route is represented in the chart at the right (with present-day highways superimposed). The branch split off from the main line about 0.4 mile west of the West Cambridge Station, located 4.16 miles from Boston at Sherman Street on the main line. The turnoff was by the once-flourishing brickyards at the site of today's Rindge Towers.

At one time, around the turn of the century, there were 38 trains a day through Arlington, a lesser number through Lexington.[citation needed] On April 24, 1926, passenger service ended on the Reformatory Branch, and on February 5, 1927, the remaining freight service was abandoned on the short segment between Concord Center and Reformatory Station. On December 31, 1931, passenger service on the outer Lexington Branch from Bedford and North Billerica was discontinued. Remaining services were converted from steam to diesel trains in 1956.

In 1962, the Boston and Maine abandoned both segments north and west of Bedford. It was noted at the time that the Bedford-Concord section had only seen 19 trains in 19 years. The town of Bedford purchased the rights of way within its boundaries in 1963.

By 1965, the Massachusetts Bay Transportation Authority was subsidizing a single daily passenger train (using Budd Rail Diesel Cars) between Boston and Bedford. On December 26, 1976, the MBTA purchased the rights of way and passenger equipment from the Boston and Maine (which retained freight trackage rights). Operation of MBTA Commuter Rail at that time was contracted to the Boston and Maine (later it was awarded to other private companies).

Beginning on January 10, 1977, a snowstorm blocked the line for a few days, after which the MBTA announced it would not resume passenger service.

In 1979, the Interstate Commerce Commission gave permission for the Boston and Maine Railroad to stop running freights on the line. Common power on the branch at that time was SW # 1227. The last freight train to ply the line was hauled by a GP9, with 23 cars. According to one source the final trip was in 1980, and the same year the tracks were severed from the main line. Another source gives the date of the final run as January 31, 1981.

In 1980, a federal judge ruled that the Lexington Branch must be restored after construction of the parking garage at Alewife Station over the right-of-way. In 1981, the MBTA and the town of Arlington signed an agreement allowing the line to be abandoned, and town land to be used temporarily for construction access, in return for support for bikeway conversion.

Rail trails

The right-of-way was railbanked in 1991. Although the rails were removed, trackage can be relaid without objection if the MBTA should find it necessary.

The **Minuteman Bikeway** opened between Alewife and Bedford in 1993. A former Boston and Maine Rail Diesel Car (RDC) of the type used on the line was purchased and is on display at the western end of the trail at Bedford Depot Park.

The **Alewife Linear Park** (portions of which are also known as the Somerville Community Path and the Cambridge Linear Park) follows the right-of-way used by the Lexington Branch from 1870 to 1927, from Somerville nearly to Alewife. One of the main access points to the Linear Park is situated where the park crosses Massachusetts Avenue, at the intersection with Cedar Street, adjacent to which the North Cambridge station was located.

The **Bedford Narrow Gauge Rail Trail** connects at Bedford Depot and heads north toward Billerica, passing Fawn Lake (also known as Hayden Pond). The current connection is indirect; the Minuteman ends at South Road, but the Narrow Gauge begins at Loomis

Heroism on the line. A 1920 railroad tragedy was memorialized in 1989 by a Cambridge City Council order. The historic marker shown here is displayed at the Cedar Street portal to the Alewife Linear Park.

Street just east of Hartford Street. The Bedford DPW is planning a more direct, 10-foot (3.0 m) sidewalk connection. It is named after the Billerica and Bedford Railroad, even though a standard-gauge railroad succeeded it. A historical recreation of the narrow-gauge predecessor has been installed near Loomis Street. The trail is paved only from Loomis Street to Great Road; after that it is improved with stone dust. The public portion of the trail ends after five miles (8 km) at the Bedford/Billerica town line (marked with a pair of gates in the middle of the woods), after which it becomes sandy (requiring a mountain bike or walking on foot) and continues on private property. Bedford plans to pave its portion of the trail and name it the "Narrow Gauge Bikeway".

The **Reformatory Branch Rail Trail** follows the old right-of-way from Railroad Avenue at Bedford Depot Park to Concord, though the bridges over the Sudbury River and Assabet River near Egg Rock no longer exist. The unimproved dirt hiking trail passes the Great Meadows National Wildlife Refuge. From Railroad Avenue, it is 4 miles (6.4 km) to Lowell Road in Concord, and then another 2.5 miles (4.0 km) on the other side of the river to the Concord State Prison.

The Narrow Gauge and Reformatory Branch Rail Trails are part of the Bay Circuit Trail and Greenway, which hopes to expand to include the private portion of the Narrow Gauge.

External links

- Masterson, Les (October 18, 2006). "Trains brought faster service" [1]. The Arlington Advocate. Retrieved 2009-05-22.

Alewife Linear Park

Geographical coordinates: 42°23′53″N 71°8′4″W

The **Linear Park** is a mixed-use path, about one mile (1.6 km) long, running through Cambridge and Somerville (Massachusetts), and connecting the Minuteman Bikeway and the Fitchburg Cutoff Path near Alewife with the Somerville Community Path at Davis Square. The path is used for bicycling, walking, jogging, and inline skating. The path runs though a long, narrow park that was built above the MBTA Red Line subway when it was extended from Davis Square to Alewife. It was established by the MBTA in 1985, and is maintained by the cities of Cambridge and Somerville.

Alewife Linear Park, Somerville, Massachusetts

The segment in Cambridge is also known as the **Cambridge Linear Park**. The Somerville segment is signed as the "Somerville Community Path: Alewife Linear Park Segment".

The Massachusetts Highway Department has designed an improved crossing of Massachusetts Avenue in Cambridge, but as of 2008, it is unclear when this will be constructed.

History

From Somerville nearly to Alewife, the park follows a right-of-way first established in 1870 and used by a succession of railroad companies. This route was used for passenger service on the Lexington Branch between 1870 and 1927, and for freight operations on the Fitchburg Cutoff for several decades longer.

See also

- Watertown Branch Railroad - Linear park initiative

External links

- Friends of the Community Paths [1]

Harvard Bridge

Harvard Bridge	

Harvard Bridge crossing the frozen Charles River from Cambridge to Boston, Massachusetts	
Carries	Route 2A
Crosses	Charles River
Locale	Boston, Massachusetts to Cambridge, Massachusetts
Maintained by	Massachusetts Department of Transportation (MassDOT)
Design	haunched girder bridge
Material	steel
Total length	659.82 meters (2164.8 ft) (roadway) 364.4 smoots ± one ear (620 m) (sidewalk from Storrow Drive to Cambridge only)
Width	21.13 meters (69.3 ft) (total width) 15.8 meters (52 ft) (roadway)
Load limit	78.4 metric tons (86.4 short tons)
Clearance below	3.7 meters (12 ft)
Beginning date of construction	1887
Completion date	1891
Opened	1891-09-01
Daily traffic	49000 as of 2005
Coordinates	42°21′16″N 71°05′29″W

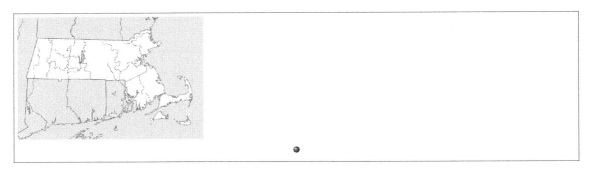

The **Harvard Bridge** (also known locally as the **MIT bridge** or the **"Mass Ave" bridge**) carries Massachusetts Avenue (Route 2A) from Back Bay, Boston to Cambridge, Massachusetts. It is the longest bridge over the Charles River.

Named for the Reverend John Harvard, it was originally built in 1891 with a swing span. The bridge was revised over the years until its superstructure was completely replaced in the late 1980s. It is locally known for being measured in the idiosyncratic unit called the smoot.

Conception

In 1874, the Massachusetts Legislature passed two acts, Chapters 175 and 314 to authorize the construction of a bridge between Boston and Cambridge. Nothing further happened until 1882, when a follow-up act (Chapter 155) with more specifics was enacted. The location was expressed as

> **Acts of 1882, Chapter 155, Section 1:** The cities of Boston and Cambridge are authorized to construct a bridge and avenue across Charles river, from a point on Beacon street, in Boston, to a point in Cambridge, west of the westerly line of the Boston and Albany railroad. ... to the limitation that the line thereof shall not be north-east of a line drawn from the junction of Beacon street and West Chester park, in Boston, to the junction of the harbor line with Front Street, extended, in Cambridge, nor south-west of a line drawn from the junction of Beacon street, Brookline avenue and Brighton avenue, in Boston, to the junction of the Boston and Albany railroad with Putnam avenue, extended, in Cambridge.

The bridge was to have a draw with an opening of at least 38 feet (12 m). Unfortunately, Boston did not like this act, mainly because it did not provide for an overhead crossing of the Grand Junction Branch of the Boston and Albany Railroad. So nothing happened until the act was amended by **Acts of 1885, Chapter 129**, which changed the draw to a clear opening of at least 36 feet (11 m) and no more, until the other bridges below the proposed location were required to have a larger opening. Still nothing happened, until the City of Cambridge petitioned the Massachusetts Legislature in 1887 to compel Boston to proceed. This resulted in **Acts of 1887, Chapter 282**, which was mandatory for both cities. It required that each city pay for half the bridge, and allowed Boston to raise up to US$250,000 (US$6.03 million in present terms) for this purpose, in excess of its debt limit. This implied an estimated cost of US$500,000 (US$12.1 million in present terms) for the bridge.

The act authorized a commission to build the bridge. The commission was to consist of the mayors of Boston and Cambridge plus one additional person to be appointed by the mayors. If the mayors failed to appoint a third commissioner, the governor was to do it for them. The mayors of Boston and Cambridge, Hugh O'Brien and William E. Russell, appointed Leander Greeley of Cambridge as the third commissioner. This changed over time.

Year(s)	Mayor of Boston	Mayor of Cambridge	Third Commissioner
1887–1888	Hugh O'Brien	William E. Russell	Leander Greeley
1889–1890	Thomas N. Hart	Henry H. Gilmore	
1891	Nathan Matthews, Jr.	Alpheus B. Alger	Leander Greeley (died 15 February 1891) George W. Gale

The bridge opened on 1 September 1891. The original cost of construction to 1 March 1892 was US$510,642.86. This is equivalent to US$12.3 million in present terms.

The expectations of having built the bridge were clear.

> The effect that the bridge will have upon both cities is obvious. The low land and marshes on the Cambridge side, formerly almost valueless, have been filled in and have become valuable; and Cambridge is now connected with the choicest residential portions of Boston. The residents of the Back Bay, South End, Roxbury, and other southern sections of Boston are now connected directly, by way of West Chester park and the bridge, with Cambridge, Belmont, Arlington, and adjacent towns; and this thoroughfare in Boston, it is believed, will ultimately be the central one of the city.

Engineering

In the Act of 1887, the bridge was to be a wooden pile structure with stone pavement for the first 200 feet (61 m) because the Charles River Embankment extension was expected to take that space, but that was changed such that the whole distance would be of iron spans on stone piers. The general plans were approved on 14 July 1887. The engineers were William Jackson (Boston City Engineer), John E. Cheney (assistant Boston City Engineer), Samuel E. Tinkham (assistant engineer), and Nathan S. Brock (assistant engineer at bridge).

The subsurface conditions at the bridge location are extreme. Much of Boston is underlain with clay, but the situation at the bridge is exacerbated by a fault which roughly follows the path of the Charles River itself. From a depth of approximately 200 to 300 feet (60 to 90 m) below existing ground, is a very dense till composed of gravel and boulders with a silt-clay matrix. Above that to approximately

30 feet (9 m) below the surface is Boston blue clay (BBC). Over this are thin layers of sand, gravel, and fill. The BBC is overconsolidated up to a depth of approximately 70 feet (20 m).

The substructure originally consisted of two masonry abutments and twenty-three masonry piers, as well as one pile foundation with a fender pier for the draw span. The superstructure was originally twenty-three cantilevered fixed spans and suspended spans, of plate girders with one swing span. The Boston abutment rests on vertical piles, while the Cambridge end is directly on gravel.

Postcard of Harvard Bridge looking toward Boston in 1910

Originally, the bridge was built across the Charles River connecting West Chester Park, in Boston, with Front Street, in Cambridge. This is now called Massachusetts Avenue on both sides of the river. As originally built, the total length between centers of bearings on abutments was 2164 feet 9 inches (659.82 m) with a draw 48 feet 4 inches (14.73 m) wide between centers. The width of the bridge was 69 feet 4 inches (21.13 m) except near and on the draw.

The bridge as built was composed of fixed and suspended spans roughly 75 feet (23 m) long and piers 90 feet (27 m) apart, center to center. The span lengths alternated between 75 and 105 feet (23 and 32 m). The longer spans were cantilevered, while the shorter spans were suspended between the cantilevers.

The original roadway contained two lanes for horse-drawn vehicles and two street car tracks, for a total width of 51.0 feet (15.5 m). There were also two 9-foot-2-inch (2.79 m) sidewalks. The original roadway and sidewalk stringers were of wood, with an approximately 1.25-inch (32 mm) thick covering of asphalt on the sidewalk.

The exception was at the swing span, which was 48 feet (15 m) wide. This span was approximately 149 feet (45 m) long, and sat on a wooden pier. It was a double-cantilevered, electrically-driven structure also carrying a bridge caretaker's house.

Naming

Postcard of Harvard Bridge and MIT between 1916 and 1924

The bridge was named for the Reverend John Harvard, for whom Harvard University is also named, rather than after the university itself. Other names suggested included Blaxton, Chester, Shawmut, and Longfellow. The structure now called the Longfellow Bridge opened 15 years later. John Harvard was an early donor to what later became the university; not, as is often assumed, its founder.

Possibly due to its proximity to the bridge, there have been a number of tales reported at MIT as to how the bridge came to be named "Harvard". According to one MIT legend,[citation needed] the bridge is so named because when it was originally constructed the state offered to name it after the Cambridge school that was most deserving. Harvard argued that their contribution to education was well-known, and thus they deserved the name. MIT concurred, having analyzed the bridge and found it structurally unsound (and thus more deserving of the Harvard name than the MIT name). Subsequently the bridge collapsed after five years of construction and was rebuilt, confirming the MIT engineers' fears.[citation needed]

The story is apocryphal. The Harvard Bridge was first constructed in 1891. MIT did not move to its current location adjacent to the bridge until 1916. However, the 1980s reconstruction actually was due to a design concern, see below.

Maintenance and updates

In 1898, 3-foot (0.91 m)-wide bicycle lanes were installed next to each curb.

The bridge was declared unsafe in 1909, requiring all of the iron and steel to be replaced. The draw was elevated slightly and the trolley rails were replaced as well.

When the Metropolitan District Commission (MDC) took control of the bridge in 1924, they rebuilt much of the bridge superstructure. They replaced the wooden stringers with steel "I" beams, topped wooden deck elements with concrete and brick, and replaced the street car rails. Structural steel hangers replaced wrought iron. The swing span was converted into two 75-foot (23 m) fixed spans the same width as the rest of the bridge. The wooden pier was heavily modified with concrete and stone to make it resemble the other piers, increasing the number of stone piers from 23 to 24.

Heavy traffic at the Mass Ave and Memorial Drive intersection on the Cambridge end of the bridge led to the construction of an underpass in 1931. The underpass eliminated the at-grade intersection.

The bridge was often known as the "Xylophone Bridge" because of the sound its wooden decking made when traffic traveled over it. This decking was replaced in 1949 with 3-inch (76 mm) concrete-filled "I-beam lok" grating topped with a 2.25-inch (57 mm) thick bituminous wearing surface. At this time, all bearings were replaced, and the trolley car tracks were removed, as were granite blocks. The trolley car poles were reused for street lights. Ramps between the bridge and the under-construction Storrow Drive were added.

The 1924 sidewalk slabs were replaced by precast, prestressed slabs in 1962.

The fifteen expansion dams were replaced or repaired in 1969.

Engineering study, 1971-1972

There was an engineering study done by the Metropolitan District Commission (later merged into the Department of Conservation and Recreation) in 1971-1972 due to complaints by bridge users of excessive vibration. The bridge was found to be understrength for its load. Before the final study was complete, the recommendation was to place a load limit of 8 short tons (7.3 t) per axle and a total of 15 short tons (14 t) per vehicle, or to restrict trucks to the interior lanes, where the bridge was stronger. A 25-short-ton (23 t) limit was imposed.

Suggestions made included strengthening the existing structure by adding either struts or plates to make the existing four beams along the length of the bridge into a stiffening truss, or to replace the superstructure with a new one, made of either steel or concrete, which would be up to current standards. The recommendation was to replace the superstructure with one weighing approximately the same in order to reuse the piers, which were in good condition.

The reasoning was that the cost of a new structure could be predicted much more easily than the cost of repairing and reinforcing the existing bridge. The resulting new bridge would be of known materials and quality, such as ductile structural steel rather than brittle wrought iron, and rated at AASHO HS-20. Repairing the existing structure would leave old wrought iron of uncertain quality and condition standing, and would not bring the design up to (then) current standards. Detailed engineering calculations were included. The price was estimated at 2.5 million to 3 million U.S. dollars (US$13 million in present terms).

The action taken based on this study was to establish load restrictions on the bridge, 15 short tons (14 t) in the outer lanes, 25 short tons (23 t) on the inner lanes. This was expanded in 1979 to a flat limit of 15 short tons (14 t) on the whole bridge.

Superstructure replacement, 1980s

After the failure of the Mianus River Bridge at Greenwich, Connecticut in 1983, the Harvard Bridge was shut down and inspected because it contained similar elements, specifically the suspended spans. Traffic was restricted to the inner two lanes due to the discovery of two failed hangers on span 14. A few days later, all trucks and buses were banned from the bridge.

In 1986, a report was published containing the plan to replace the superstructure on the existing supports. Alternatives considered were very similar to the 1972 report, and were similarly decided. Structural modifications included an upgrade from four longitudinal girders to six of the same shape, elimination of ramp "B", and replacement of a stairway with a handicapped pedestrian ramp on the Boston end of the bridge.

The historic value of the bridge was considered significant, so the plan was to make the replacement superstructure appear similar, with similar railing and lighting. In order to document the pre-existing structure, a Historic American Engineering Record (HAER) would be prepared.

Ramp "B", from southbound (Boston bound) bridge lanes to eastbound Storrow Drive, caused traffic to merge onto Storrow Drive from the left (high speed) lanes using a short acceleration lane, causing safety issues. The MDC requested elimination of this ramp. Compared to overall bridge traffic of 30,000 vehicles per day, traffic on ramp B was found to be low, approximately 1,500 vehicles per day with a peak of 120 vehicles per hour.

Pier 12 was exhibiting inappropriate movement and was scheduled for reinforcement.

The work would be done in two phases. Phase 1 would reinforce the downstream side of the bridge to allow MBTA bus traffic, and was expected to take 5 months. Most of this effort would be spent on the underside of the bridge and would not affect existing traffic. Phase 2 would replace the entire superstructure and was expected to take three construction seasons to implement. Cost was estimated to be US$20M (US$39.7 million in present terms). Phase 1 finished in 1987, and Phase 2 in 1990.

Before-and-after images

This image shows the bridge from the upstream Cambridge side in 1985. If you click on the image, you can see construction barrels restricting traffic from the outside lanes, and how the bridge was showing wear.

This is roughly the same view, in 2009. This superstructure is in much better shape, only 20 years after completion, than the 1985 image of the superstructure roughly 40 years after its most recent major work.

Underside of the bridge in 1985. Image shows how the bridge was originally built and modified later, but before the superstructure was replaced.

Underside of the bridge in 2009. Image shows how the replacement superstructure was built, with 6 longitudinal girders and a different bracing, et cetera.

Bridge length measurement

Main article: Smoot

Smoot mark 210, east side of the bridge

The Harvard Bridge is measured, locally, in *smoots*.

In 1958, members of the Lambda Chi Alpha fraternity at MIT measured the bridge's eastern sidewalk by carrying or dragging the shortest pledge that year, Oliver Smoot, end over end.

Crossing pedestrians are informed by length markers painted at 10-smoot intervals that the bridge is 364.4 smoots long, "plus one ear". The qualifier "plus or minus" was originally intended to express measurement uncertainty, but over the years the words "or minus" have gone missing in many citations, including the markings on the bridge itself. The marks are repainted twice each year by members of the fraternity.

During the reconstruction in the 1980s, the smoot markings were repainted on the new deck, and the sidewalks were divided into smoot-length slabs rather than the standard six feet.

Length discrepancy

Given that Smoot was 5 feet 7 inches (1.702 m) tall in 1958, the given measurement in smoots of 364.4 yields a "bridge length" of about 620 meters (2030 ft). Published sources give the length of the bridge as approximately 660 meters (2170 ft). The difference in length between the sidewalk markings and the published figure represents a 40-meter (130 ft) discrepancy. A possible cause is that in 1958, there were ramps to Storrow Drive on both sides of the bridge. There are smoot marks on both sidewalks, which fail to cover the entire length of the bridge. The fraternity apparently only measured the length of the sidewalk from the point where it is interrupted. It seems possible that the pledges were fooled by the apparent end of the sidewalk at the Storrow Drive ramps.

Houdini

According to a marker near the southeast end of the bridge, Harry Houdini performed one of his "well known escapes" from this bridge on 1 May 1908. Other sources have it as 30 April 1908.

Harry Houdini jumps from the bridge

Panoramic view from Harvard Bridge in the winter, looking east, with the Cambridge shore on the left and the Boston shore on the right. The Longfellow Bridge is in the middle, downstream.

See also

- List of crossings of the Charles River

Notes

a. See the following sections, especially #Maintenance and updates and following.

External links

- Harvard Bridge [1] at *Structurae*

Harvard Yard

Old Harvard Yard	
U.S. National Register of Historic Places	
U.S. National Historic Landmark District	
Harvard Yard with freshman dorms in the background	
Location:	Cambridge, Massachusetts
Coordinates:	42°22′28.3″N 71°7′1.9″W
Built/Founded:	1718
Architect:	Multiple
Architectural style(s):	Georgian, Other, Federal
Governing body:	Private
Added to NRHP:	February 6, 1973
NRHP Reference#:	73000287

Harvard Yard is a grassy area of about twenty-five acres (0.1 km²), adjacent to Harvard Square in Cambridge, Massachusetts, that constitutes the oldest part and the center of the campus of Harvard University. Geographically the yard area is bordered to the west by Massachusetts Avenue and Peabody Street, the north by Cambridge Street, the northeast by Broadway, the east by Quincy Street, and the south by Harvard Street and Massachusetts Avenue. It contains thirteen of Harvard College's seventeen freshman dormitories, as well as four libraries, five buildings of classrooms and academic departments, and the central administrative offices of the Faculty of Arts and Sciences and the university, located in University Hall and Massachusetts Hall, respectively.

The western third of Harvard Yard, which opens onto Massachusetts Avenue at Johnston Gate, is known as the Old Yard, and around it cluster most of the freshman dormitories. Among these is Massachusetts Hall, which, having been constructed in 1720, is the oldest still-standing building on Harvard's campus and one of the two oldest academic buildings in the United States. The lower floors of Massachusetts Hall house the offices of the President of Harvard University.

Also located in the Old Yard is the statue of the university's first benefactor, John Harvard. This monument is a frequent target of pranks, hacks, and humorous decorations, such as the colorful lei shown at right, below. Moreover, Harvard students urinate on the very foot that tourists rub for good luck. Facing Massachusetts Hall is Harvard Hall. The original Harvard Hall on this site housed the College library, including the books donated by John Harvard, after whom the college and the building were named—all but one of which were destroyed when the building burned in 1764. Rebuilt in 1766, Harvard Hall now houses classrooms.

Across the Old Yard from Johnston Gate stands University Hall, and the now-famous statue of John Harvard by Daniel Chester French. The statue has earned the nickname "the statue of three lies" from its inscription, "John Harvard, Founder, 1638". In truth, the statue is not modeled after John Harvard, Mr. Harvard did not found the university, and the founding was in 1636. University Hall was the site of the now-famous sit-in and teach-in protests during the late 1960s, while Massachusetts Hall was the site of the more recent 2001 living-wage campaign sit-in.

Other buildings

The center of Harvard Yard is a wide grassy area known as Tercentenary Theater, framed by the monumental Widener Library and Memorial Church. Harvard's annual commencement exercises, as well as occasional special convocations, take place in Tercentenary Theater.

The libraries located in Harvard Yard are Widener Library, its connected Pusey Library annex, Houghton Library for rare books and manuscripts, and Lamont Library, the main undergraduate library. Classroom and departmental buildings include Emerson Hall, Sever Hall, Robinson Hall, and Boylston Hall.

The freshman dormitories of Harvard Yard include the upper levels of Massachusetts Hall, and Wigglesworth Hall, Weld Hall, Grays Hall, Matthews Hall, Straus Hall, Mower Hall, Hollis Hall, Stoughton Hall, Lionel Hall, Holworthy Hall, Canaday Hall, and Thayer Hall.

Nestled among Mower, Hollis, Lionel, and Stoughton Halls is the Holden Chapel, home of the Holden Choirs. Also in this section of the yard stands the Phillips Brooks House, designed by Alexander Wadsworth Longfellow, Jr., and home of the Phillips Brooks House Association (PBHA), Harvard

University's center for service activities. At the southwest corner of the Yard is Lehman Hall, or Dudley House, the administrative unit for non-resident and off-campus students. Next to Lehman Hall is Wadsworth House, a canary-yellow building that houses the headquarters of the Harvard Alumni Association and the university library system. Finally, Loeb House sits on the east side; it is the site of Harvard's governing bodies, the Harvard Corporation and the Board of Overseers.

Below ground facilities

Harvard Yard is underpinned by a network of subterranean tunnels carrying people, steam heating and cooling, utilities, and other services across the Harvard campus. Observant students have taken notice of the effects these tunnels have had on the above-ground surface areas of the yard during winter.

External links

• Map of Harvard Yard [1]

Mount Auburn Cemetery

Mount Auburn Cemetery	
U.S. National Register of Historic Places	
U.S. National Historic Landmark District	
Mount Auburn Cemetery	
Location:	Cambridge and Watertown, Massachusetts
Coordinates:	42°22′14″N 71°8′45″W
Built/Founded:	1831
Architect:	Alexander Wadsworth; Dr. Jacob Bigelow
Architectural style(s):	Exotic Revival, Other, Gothic Revival
Governing body:	Private
Added to NRHP:	April 21, 1975
Designated NHLD:	May 27, 2003
NRHP Reference#:	75000254

Mount Auburn Cemetery was founded in 1831 as "America's first garden cemetery", or the first "rural cemetery", with classical monuments set in a rolling landscaped terrain. The appearance of this type of landscape coincides with the rising popularity of the term "cemetery," which etymologically traces its roots back to the Greek for "a sleeping place." This language and outlook eclipsed the previous harsh view of death and the afterlife, pictorialized in old graveyards and church burial plots. The 174 acre (70 ha) cemetery is important both for its historical aspects and for its role as an arboretum. Most of the cemetery is located in Watertown, Massachusetts, though the 1843 granite Egyptian revival entrance lies in neighboring Cambridge, adjacent to the Cambridge City and Sand Banks Cemeteries.

History

The land that would eventually become Mount Auburn Cemetery was originally named Stone's Farm, though locals referred to it as "Sweet Auburn" after the 1770 poem "The Deserted Village" by Oliver Goldsmith. Mount Auburn Cemetery was inspired by Père Lachaise cemetery in Paris and was itself an inspiration to cemetery designers, most notably at Abney Park in London. Mount Auburn Cemetery was designed largely by Henry Alexander Scammell Dearborn with assistance from Dr. Jacob Bigelow and Alexander Wadsworth.

Bigelow came up with the idea for Mount Auburn as early as 1825, though a site was not acquired until five years later. Bigelow, a medical doctor, was concerned about the unhealthiness of burials under churches as well as the possibility of running out of space. With help from the Massachusetts Horticultural Society, Mount Auburn Cemetery was founded on 70 acres of land authorized by the Massachusetts Legislature for use as a garden or rural cemetery. The purchase of the original land cost $6,000; it later extended to 170 acres. The main gate was built based in the Egyptian Revival architecture style and cost $10,000. The cemetery was dedicated in 1831 by Joseph Story, first president of the Mount Auburn Association.

The cemetery is credited as the beginning of the American public parks and gardens movement. It set the style for other suburban American cemeteries such as Laurel Hill Cemetery (Philadelphia, 1836), Mt. Hope Cemetery, America's first municipal rural cemetery (Rochester, New York, 1838), Green-Wood Cemetery (Brooklyn, 1838), The Green Mount Cemetery, Baltimore, Maryland 1838, Albany Rural Cemetery (Menands, New York, 1844) and Forest Hills Cemetery (Jamaica Plain, 1848) as well as Oakwood Cemetery in Syracuse, New York. It can be considered the link between Capability Brown's English landscape gardens and Frederick Law Olmsted's Central Park in New York (1850s).

Mount Auburn was established at a time when Americans had a sentimental interest in rural cemeteries. It is still well known for its tranquil atmosphere and accepting attitude toward death. Many of the more traditional monuments feature poppy flowers, symbols of blissful sleep. In the late 1830s, its first unofficial guide, *Picturesque Pocket Companion and Visitor's Guide Through Mt. Auburn*, was published and featured descriptions of some of the more interesting monuments as well as a collection of prose and poetry about death by writers including Nathaniel Hawthorne and Willis Gaylord Clark. Because of the number of visitors, the cemetery's developers carefully regulated the grounds: They had a policy to remove "offensive and improper" monuments and only "proprietors" (i.e., plot owners) could have vehicles on the grounds and were allowed within the gates on Sundays and holidays.

The main tower in the Cemetery

Cemetery today

More than 93,000 people are buried in the cemetery as of 2003. A number of historically significant people have been interred there since its inception, particularly members of the Boston Brahmins and the Boston elite associated with Harvard University as well as a number of prominent Unitarians.

The cemetery is nondenominational and continues to make space available for new plots. The area is well known for its beautiful environs and is a favorite location for Cambridge bird-watchers. Guided tours of the cemetery's historic, artistic, and horticultural points of interest are available.

Mount Auburn's collection of over 5,500 trees includes nearly 700 species and varieties. Thousands of very well-kept shrubs and herbaceous plants weave through the cemetery's hills, ponds, woodlands, and clearings. The cemetery contains more than 10 miles (17 km) of roads and many paths. Landscaping styles range from Victorian-era plantings to contemporary gardens, from natural woodlands to formal ornamental gardens, and from sweeping vistas through majestic trees to small enclosed spaces. Many trees, shrubs, and herbaceous plants are tagged with botanic labels containing their scientific and common names.

The cemetery was among those profiled in the 2005 PBS documentary *A Cemetery Special*.

Notable burials

- Hannah Adams, (1755–1831), author.
- Louis Agassiz (1807–1873), scientist
- Elizabeth Cary Agassiz (1822–1907), scientist, author
- Nathan Appleton (1779–1861), congressman
- William Appleton (1786–1862), congressman
- Benjamin E. Bates (1808–1878), industrialist, founder of Bates College
- Jacob Bigelow (1787–1879), designer of Mt. Auburn Cemetery
- J.W. Black (1825-1896), photographer
- Edwin Booth (1833–1893), actor
- Nathaniel Bowditch (1773–1838), mathematician, seaman, author; his monument was the first life size bronze to be cast in America

Bigelow Chapel

- Phillips Brooks (1835–1893), American Episcopal bishop
- William Brewster (1851–1919), ornithologist
- Charles Bulfinch (1763–1844), architect
- McGeorge Bundy (1919–1996), presidential cabinet official
- George Cabot (1752–1823), statesman
- James Henry Carleton (1814–1873), United States Army officer
- William Ellery Channing (1780–1842), Unitarian theologian
- John Ciardi (1916–1986), Poet, translator
- Alvan Clark (1804–1887), astronomer and telescope maker
- Robert Creeley (1926–2005), poet
- Benjamin Williams Crowninshield (1772–1851), statesman, U.S. Secretary of the Navy
- Frank Crowninshield (1872–1947), creator & editor of "Vanity Fair" Magazine
- Benjamin Robbins Curtis (1809–1874), Supreme Court justice
- Charlotte Cushman (1816–1876), actress
- Felix Octavius Carr Darley (1821–1888), artist
- Samuel Dexter (1761–1816), congressman
- Dorothea Dix (1802–1887), nurse, hospital reformer
- Mary Baker Eddy (1821–1910), religious leader

- Harold "Doc" Edgerton (1903–1990), engineer, scientist
- Charles William Eliot (1834–1926), Harvard University president
- Edward Everett (1794–1865), Governor of Massachusetts, President of Harvard University, United States Secretary of State, speaker at the Gettysburg Address
- William Everett (1839–1910), congressman
- Achilles Fang (1910–1995), sinologist, comparatist, and friend of Ezra Pound

Mary Baker Eddy Memorial

- Fannie Farmer (1857–1915), cookbook author
- Fanny Fern (1811–1872), feminist author
- Felix Frankfurter (1882–1965), United States Supreme Court Justice
- Buckminster Fuller (1895–1983), architect
- Isabella Stewart Gardner (1840–1924), art collector, museum founder
- Charles Dana Gibson, (1867–1944), illustrator
- Curt Gowdy (1919–2006), sportscaster
- Asa Gray (1810–1888), 19th century American botanist
- Horace Gray (1828–1902), Supreme Court justice
- Horatio Greenough (1805–1852), sculptor
- Charles Hale (1831–1882), journalist, statesman
- Charles Hayden (1870–1937), financier and philanthropist
- Oliver Wendell Holmes, Sr. (1809–1894), physician/author
- Winslow Homer (1836–1910), artist
- Albion P. Howe (1818–1897), Union army general
- Julia Ward Howe (1819–1910), activist, poet
- Dr. Harriot Kezia Hunt (1805–1875) early female physician - her monument, a statue of Hygieia, was carved by Edmonia Lewis.
- Harriet Jacobs (1813–1897), escaped slave and author of Incidents in the Life of a Slave Girl.
- Edward F. Jones (1828–1913), NY Lt. Gov. 1886-1891
- Edwin H. Land (1909–1991), scientist
- Abbott Lawrence (1792–1855), politician, philanthropist
- Henry Cabot Lodge (1850–1924), politician
- Henry Cabot Lodge, Jr. (1902–1985) politician
- Henry Wadsworth Longfellow (1807–1882), poet
- A. Lawrence Lowell (1856–1943), Harvard University president
- Amy Lowell (1874–1925), poet
- Charles Russell Lowell (1835–1864), Civil War General and casualty of the Battle of Cedar Creek
- Francis Cabot Lowell (1855–1911), U.S. Congressman and Federal Judge

- James Russell Lowell (1819–1891), poet and foreign diplomat
- Josephine Shaw Lowell (1843–1905), Wife of Gen. Charles Russell Lowell, sister of Col. Robert Gould Shaw
- Maria White Lowell (1821–1853), poet and wife of James Russell
- Bernard Malamud (1914–1986), writer
- Jules Marcou (1824–1898), geologist
- William T.G. Morton (1819–1868), demonstrator of ether anesthesia
- Stephen P. Mugar (1901–1982), Armenian-American businessman and philanthropist
- Shahan Natalie (1884–1983), principal organizer of Operation Nemesis, Armenian national philosophy writer
- Charles Eliot Norton (1827–1908), scholar and author
- Robert Nozick (1938–2002), philosopher
- Richard Olney (1835–1917), statesman
- Harrison Gray Otis (1765–1848), U.S. Representative, mayor of Boston
- Maribel Vinson-Owen (1911–1961), 9 time U.S. skating champion and coach
- Maribel Y. Owen (1940–1961), U.S. pairs figure skating champion
- Laurence R. Owen (1944–1961), U.S. ladies skating champion
- Harvey D. Parker (1805–1884), hotelier
- Josiah Quincy III (1772–1864), statesman, educator
- John Rawls (1921–2002), philosopher
- Anne Revere (1903–1990), actress
- William Eustis Russell (1857–1896), Governor of Massachusetts
- Julian Seymour Schwinger, theoretical physicist, Nobel laureate
- Lemuel Shaw (1781–1861), Chief Justice of the Massachusetts Supreme Judicial Court
- B.F. Skinner (1904–1990), psychologist
- Franklin W. Smith (1826-1911), promoter of historical architecture
- Johann Gaspar Spurzheim (1776–1832), phrenologist
- Daniel C. Stillson (1830–1899)[1], Inventor of the Stillson pipe wrench
- Joseph Story (1779–1845), US Supreme Court Justice
- Charles Sumner (1811–1874), statesman
- Frank William Taussig (1859–1940), economist
- Randall Thompson (1899–1984), composer
- William S. Tilton, (1828–1889), Civil War brigade commander
- Charles Tufts (1781–1876), businessman who donated the land for Tufts University

Charles Sumner's grave

- Benjamin Waterhouse (1754–1846), physician
- Nathaniel Parker Willis (1806–1867), publisher
- Robert Charles Winthrop (1809–1894), statesman
- Roger Wolcott (1847–1900), Governor of Massachusetts

See also

- List of United States cemeteries
- List of botanical gardens in the United States
- Massachusetts Horticultural Society
- Poets' Graves

Further reading

- Nathaniel Dearborn. A concise history of, and guide through Mount Auburn [2]: with a catalogue of lots laid out in that cemetery; a map of the grounds, and terms of subscription, regulations concerning visitors, interments, &c., &c. Boston: N. Dearborn, 1843. 1857 ed. [3]
- Moses King. Mount Auburn cemetery [4]: including also a brief history and description of Cambridge, Harvard University, and the Union Railway Company. Cambridge, Mass.: Moses King, 1883.

External links

- Mount Auburn Cemetery official site [5]
- *Mount Auburn Cemetery: A New American Landscape,* a National Park Service Teaching with Historic Places (TwHP) lesson plan [6]

Alewife Brook Reservation

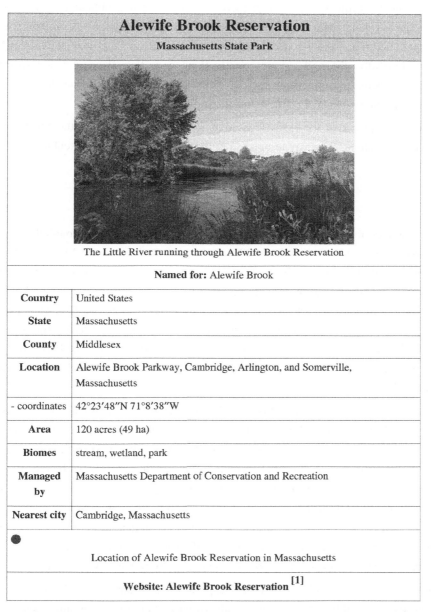

Alewife Brook Reservation	
Massachusetts State Park	
The Little River running through Alewife Brook Reservation	
Named for: Alewife Brook	
Country	United States
State	Massachusetts
County	Middlesex
Location	Alewife Brook Parkway, Cambridge, Arlington, and Somerville, Massachusetts
- coordinates	42°23′48″N 71°8′38″W
Area	120 acres (49 ha)
Biomes	stream, wetland, park
Managed by	Massachusetts Department of Conservation and Recreation
Nearest city	Cambridge, Massachusetts
Location of Alewife Brook Reservation in Massachusetts	
Website: Alewife Brook Reservation [1]	

Alewife Brook Reservation is a Massachusetts state park located in Cambridge, Arlington, and Somerville. The park is managed by the Department of Conservation and Recreation.

Description

Alewife Brook Reservation is a 120-acre (0.49 km^2) urban wild. A large proportion of the park is wetland, including the Little River, though there is also a wooded upland and meadow area. The reservation serves as a habitat for numerous indigenous and migratory birds. Common species include osprey, great blue heron and the woodcock, whose unusual mating ritual may sometimes be observed by visitors. Additionally, the park's ponds (Little Pond and Blair Pond) provide spring spawning grounds for anadromous herring, which migrate from the Atlantic Ocean via the Mystic River and Alewife Brook, a tributary which, in turn, drains the Little River.

The reservation is adjacent to the Alewife Station at the northern end of the MBTA Red Line in Cambridge. The Minuteman Bikeway terminates at the reservation and the Fitchburg Cutoff Path runs through it.

History

The Fitchburg Railroad main line in 1843 was the first rail link constructed through the swampy area in western Cambridge. It still serves as the MBTA Commuter Rail Fitchburg Line. The Lexington and West Cambridge Railroad was branched off in 1846, with the curving connection still visible today, passing under Alewife Brook Parkway, along the west side of the Alewife Station parking garage, and proceeding northwest along the right-of-way of the present-day Minuteman Bikeway. The Watertown Branch Railroad was opened in 1851, branching from the Fitchburg and curving south behind what is now the Fresh Pond Shopping Center on the east side of Alewife Brook Parkway (then merely swampland). By 1852, several spurs were serving local freight customers, including ice houses on the south side of Spy Pond.

In 1870, the Boston and Lowell Railroad bought the Lexington and constructed a connection from the Alewife area through what is now Davis Square to Somerville Junction. Most of this connection is now the Somerville Community Path and Alewife Linear Park, but at the west end passed through what is now Alewife Center, and met up with the Lexington after curving past the stub ends of Fairmont and Lafayette Streets. This new connection also had a southerly fork known as the Fitchburg Cutoff, passing just north of the present-day Alewife Station, crossing the now-removed Fitchburg-Lexington connection, and joining the Fitchburg mainline. A pre-reservation map from 1903 shows these railroads criss-crossing the reservation, as well as Alewife Brook proceeding farther south to drain Fresh Pond. The swampy area is largely undeveloped, compared to the surrounding neighborhoods.

The reservation was originally planned by landscape designer Charles Eliot in conjunction with the Alewife Brook Parkway, although it has been substantially altered since its initial set-aside. It forms part of Boston's Metropolitan Park District, established in 1893. The Alewife Brook was straightened and channelized next to the parkway between 1909 and 1912, with road construction completed by 1916. Landscaping was performed by the famed Olmsted Brothers firm.[citation needed]

Recreational opportunities

- Birding
- Hiking
- Running
- Playing Fields
- Playground

Bike path

A bike path project for the Reservation has received $4.5M from the American Recovery and Reinvestment Act of 2009. The "Minuteman Bike Path connector" will link the Mystic River bike path to the Minuteman Bikeway and Alewife Station.

See also

- List of Massachusetts State Parks

External links

- Official website [1]
- Friends of Alewife Reservation website [2]
- Water quality data [3]
- Combined sewer outflow reduction - annual update [4]

Fresh Pond (Cambridge, Massachusetts)

Fresh Pond	
 The pond in winter	
General plan for Fresh Pond Park, by the Olmsted Brothers landscape design firm (1897). "[A]lmost none of the plans to relocate the carriage drive [to the route shown] were ever implemented."	
Location	Cambridge, Massachusetts
Coordinates	42°23′N 71°9′W
Lake type	reservoir
Basin countries	United States
Surface area	155 acres (63 ha)

Fresh Pond is a reservoir and park in Cambridge, Massachusetts. Prior to the Pond's use exclusively as a reservoir, its ice had been harvested by Boston's "Ice King", Frederic Tudor, and others, for shipment to North American cities and to tropical areas around the world.

Fresh Pond Reservation consists of a 155 acre (627,000 m²) kettle hole lake, and 162 acres (656,000 m²) of surrounding land, with a 2.25 mile (3.6 km) perimeter road popular with walkers, runners and cyclists, and a 9 hole golf course. On the northern outskirts of the Fresh Pond Reservation lies a nursing home called the Neville Center (formerly Neville Manor).

Water and ice

In the mid 1800s, the Pond was privately owned and home to a flourishing ice-harvesting industry, with ice shipped as far as Europe, China, and India. In 1856, a private company began supplying its customers with drinking water from the Pond. In 1865 the business came under city ownership. By the end of the century the Pond and the land surrounding it was entirely city-owned, and an elaborate public water supply system had been developed.

Fresh Pond is part of the overall Cambridge water system. Its water is fed to the pond via an aqueduct from the Hobbs Brook and Stony Brook Reservoirs, located in Lexington, Lincoln, Waltham and Weston, Massachusetts. After purification at the Walter J. Sullivan Water Treatment Facility adjacent to Fresh Pond, the water is pumped upwards to the underground Payson Park Reservoir in Belmont. From there it flows back to Cambridge, with gravity providing the pressure to distribute drinking water to residents and businesses.

Transportation

Fresh Pond is bordered by Fresh Pond Parkway, Huron Avenue, Grove Street, Blanchard Road, and Concord Avenue. The Reservation can be reached via the Minuteman Bikeway or MBTA 72, 74, 75, and 78 buses. It is a 10 minute walk from Alewife Station on the MBTA Red line.

Proposed Watertown Branch trail

Main article: Watertown Branch Railroad

A portion of the nearly abandoned Watertown Branch Railroad is situated between Fresh Pond Parkway and the water treatment facility. Currently overgrown in parts, this single track line enters the Fresh Pond reservation at its northeastern edge, near the Concord Avenue—Fresh Pond Parkway rotary. The line continues in a southerly direction along much of the eastern boundary of the reservation until it reaches the Huron Avenue overpass to the south. The branch terminates in the nearby town of Watertown. There have been some past proposals to have this rail line, disused since 2001, converted into a rail trail and linear park.

See also

- Fresh Pond Hotel
- Nathaniel Jarvis Wyeth

General references

- City of Cambridge Water Department [1]
- Fresh Pond reservation history [2]
- Sinclair, Jill (April 2009). *Fresh Pond: The History of a Cambridge Landscape*. Cambridge, Mass.: MIT Press. ISBN 978-0-262-19591-1.
- Weightman, Gavin (2003). *The Frozen-Water Trade: A True Story*. New York: Hyperion

External links

- "Fresh Pond Reservation" [3]. Friends of Fresh Pond Reservation. February 2006. Retrieved 3 February 2010.

Minuteman Bikeway

The **Minuteman Bikeway** is a 10 mile (16 km) paved multi-use rail trail located in the Greater Boston area of Massachusetts.

Route

Legend

The Minuteman Commuter Bikeway in Bedford, near Wiggins Avenue

In Bedford:

Railbanked line to Concord Reformatory

South Road

Bedford Depot Park

to Billerica

Elm Brook

Wiggins Avenue

in Lexington:

Hartwell Avenue

to Hanscom Air Force Base

Interstate 95

Bedford Street (Routes 4, 225)

Revere Street

Hancock Street

Lexington B&M Station

Woburn Street

Site of B&M's Munroe Station

Pierce's Bridge (Maple Street)

Arlington's Great Meadows

Site of B&M's East Lexington Station

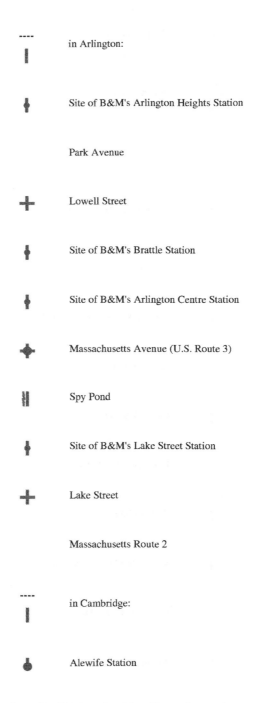

in Arlington:

Site of B&M's Arlington Heights Station

Park Avenue

Lowell Street

Site of B&M's Brattle Station

Site of B&M's Arlington Centre Station

Massachusetts Avenue (U.S. Route 3)

Spy Pond

Site of B&M's Lake Street Station

Lake Street

Massachusetts Route 2

in Cambridge:

Alewife Station

The Minuteman Bikeway runs from Bedford to the Alewife station at the northern end of the Red Line in Cambridge. It passes through the towns of Lexington and Arlington on the way. Also along the route are several notable regional sites, including Alewife Brook Reservation, Spy Pond and "Arlington's Great Meadows" (actually located in Lexington).

At its Cambridge terminus, the bikeway connects with two other bike paths: the Fitchburg Cutoff Path and the Cambridge Linear Park which, in turn, leads to the Somerville Community Path. Plans are underway to extend the Somerville Community Path to downtown Boston, which would create a much larger continuous bikeway accessible from the Minuteman.

At the Bedford end, the Minuteman Bikeway connects with the Narrow Gauge Rail Trail and the Reformatory Branch Rail Trail.

History

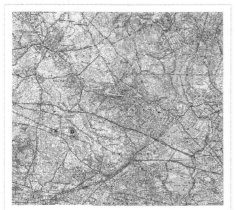

Map from 1946, where Boston & Maine Railway passes along the route of today's Minuteman Bikeway.

The path comprising the current Minuteman Bikeway has a long history. The trail closely approximates the route that Paul Revere took on his famous ride in 1775, which heralded the beginning of the American Revolution.

Along the way to becoming a railroad, the path's right-of-way was laid out east of Lexington in 1846 by the Lexington and West Cambridge Railroad and west of Lexington in 1873 by the Middlesex Central Railroad.

Railbanking of the line was first proposed in 1974, three years before passenger rail service was discontinued, and a full seven years before rail service was discontinued altogether (in 1981). In 1991, the final plan for the conversion was approved, and construction started on the original section of the bikeway. The path was dedicated in 1992 and completed the following year.

In 1998 the bikeway was extended from East Arlington to Alewife station (in Cambridge). In 2002 it was entirely repaved and in 2004 the Bedford Depot Park Enhancement Project was completed at its west terminus.

The property is currently owned by the Massachusetts Bay Transportation Authority and leased to the municipalities through which it passes on an interim basis.[citation needed]

Uses

Area residents use the bikeway for a host of activities, including bicycling, walking, jogging, and inline skating. The main use of the path, however, is for casual biking. In the winter there is often enough snow on the bikeway for cross-country skiing, as the bikeway is largely unplowed. In 2007, Arlington began plowing from the Lexington border to Alewife Station. No motorized vehicles are allowed except for powered wheelchairs and emergency vehicles.

Future possibilities

New connections under contemplation include one from Lexington to the Battle Road Trail, one to the Charles River bike path via the abandoned Watertown Branch Railroad, and one to the Mystic River bike path following Alewife Brook. The Alewife Brook extension has received $4M from the American Recovery and Reinvestment Act of 2009 as the "Minuteman Bikepath Connector" project.

Artwork posted on the Minuteman Bikeway by local artist Sonik

See also

- Minutemen

- Uncle Sam Memorial Statue

External links

- Friends of the Community Paths [1]
- Depot Park at the Bedford terminus [1]
- Rails-to-Trails Conservancy [2]
- Video of entire trail south to north [3]
- 1870s railroad maps of what is now the Minuteman Bikeway [4]
- Clear the Trail advocacy organization [5]
- Friends of Lexington Bikeways Blog [6]
- Map with popups of old maps from the 1870s showing each section of the bikeway [7]
- On a Google map [8]

Harvard Lampoon

The *Harvard Lampoon* is an undergraduate humor publication and social organization founded in 1876 at Harvard University in Cambridge, Massachusetts.

Overview

Published since 1876, *The Harvard Lampoon* is the second longest-running English-language humor magazine, after the Yale Record. The organization also produces occasional humor books (the best known being the 1969 J.R.R. Tolkien parody *Bored of the Rings*) and parodies of national magazines such as *Entertainment Weekly* and *Sports Illustrated*. Much of the organization's capital is provided by the licensing of the "Lampoon" name to *National Lampoon*, begun by *Harvard Lampoon* graduates in 1970.

The organization is housed a few blocks from Harvard Square in a small mock-Flemish castle with a copper statue of an ibis on the roof. The *Lampoon* is known for its bacchanalian parties, which can result in smashed plates and furniture. The Lampoon's affairs are administered by Harvard Lampoon, Inc., whose Board of Graduate Trustees includes such people as James Murdoch and Bill Oakley. Robert K. Hoffman, co-founder of the National Lampoon and major donor to the Dallas Museum of Art was a Trustee until his death in 2006, and was declared a Trustee "Ad-Infinitum" a year later. The bone of his pinky finger is said to be encased in a block of lucite in the Harvard Lampoon Social Club's "Brainatorium Crypt."

History

The Harvard Lampoon began in 1876, three years after the founding of *The Harvard Crimson*. However, the *Lampoon* and its sensibility have been an especially important expression of American humor and comedy since the late 1960s. An important line of demarcation came when *Lampoon* editors Douglas Kenney and Henry Beard wrote the Tolkien parody *Bored of the Rings*. The success of this book and the attention it brought its authors led directly to the creation of the *National Lampoon* magazine, which spun off a live show *Lemmings*, and then a radio show in the early 1970s, *The National Lampoon Radio Hour* introducing such performers as Christopher Guest, Harry Shearer and Chevy Chase. *Lampoon* writers from these shows were subsequently hired to help create *Saturday Night Live*. This was the first in a line of many TV shows that *Lampoon* graduates went on to write for, including *The Simpsons, Futurama, Saturday Night Live, Late Night with David Letterman, Seinfeld, NewsRadio, The Office, 30 Rock*, and dozens of others. Lampoon alumni include such famous comedians as Conan O'Brien, Andy Borowitz, and B.J. Novak. Etan Cohen wrote for *Beavis and Butthead* as an undergraduate member. In 1986 former editor Kurt Andersen co-founded the satirical magazine *Spy*, which employed *Lampoon* writers Paul Simms and Eric Kaplan, and published the work of *Lampoon* alumni Patricia Marx, Lawrence O'Donnell and Mark O'Donnell.

In 2006, the *Lampoon* began regularly releasing content on their website, including pieces from the magazine and web-only content. In October 2007, the *Lampoon* launched a new design for its website: www.harvardlampoon.com. In 2009, the *Lampoon* published a parody of *Twilight* called *Nightlight*, which is a *New York Times* bestseller.

See also

- Harvard Lampoon Building

External links

- *The Harvard Lampoon* [1]

Harvard Lampoon Building

Harvard Lampoon Building	
U.S. National Register of Historic Places	
Location:	Cambridge, Massachusetts
Coordinates:	42°22′17.8″N 71°7′2.5″W
Built/Founded:	1909
Architect:	Wheelwright,Edmund M.
Architectural style(s):	Mock Flemish
Governing body:	Private
Added to NRHP:	March 30, 1978
NRHP Reference#:	78000440

Harvard Lampoon Building (or "The Lampoon Castle") is an historic building at 44 Bow Street in Cambridge, Massachusetts and is home to the Harvard Lampoon.

The Harvard University building was constructed in 1909 by Edmund M. Wheelwright and added to the National Historic Register in 1978.

Transportation In and Around Cambridge

Logan International Airport

IATA: BOS – ICAO: KBOS – FAA LID: BOS

BOS

Location of the Logan International Airport

Summary	
Airport type	Public
Owner	Massachusetts Port Authority (Massport)
Serves	Boston, Massachusetts
Location	East Boston, Mass.

Hub for	{{{hub}}}
Elevation AMSL	20 ft / 6 m
Coordinates	42°21′47″N 071°00′23″W
Website	www.massport.com/logan/ [1]

Runways			
Direction	**Length**		**Surface**
	ft	**m**	
4L/22R	7,861	2,396	Asphalt
4R/22L	10,005	3,050	Asphalt
9/27	7,000	2,134	Asphalt
14/32	5,000	1,524	Asphalt
15L/33R	2,557	779	Asphalt
15R/33L	10,083	3,073	Asphalt

Statistics (2009)	
Aircraft operations	345,306
Passengers	25,512,086

Source: FAA, Massport.

FAA Airport Diagram

General Edward Lawrence Logan International Airport (IATA: **BOS**, ICAO: **KBOS**, FAA LID: **BOS**) in the East Boston neighborhood of Boston, Massachusetts, United States (and partly in the Town of Winthrop, Massachusetts). It covers 2384 acres (965 ha), has six runways, and employs an estimated 16,000 people.

Though Boston is the largest metropolitan area in the United States which does not serve as a hub for any full service airline, Logan Airport serves as a focus city for AirTran Airways, American Airlines, and JetBlue Airways. US Airways also carries out many operations from the airport, and all major airlines fly to Boston from all or the majority of their primary and secondary hubs. It is also a destination of many major European airlines. The airport has service to destinations in the United States, as well as Canada, the Caribbean, Europe, and Mexico.

The largest airport in New England, Logan Airport is one of the 20 busiest airports in the U.S., with over 25 million passengers a year, and is 19th in flight movements. The airport is also the 12th busiest airport in the U.S. based on international traffic. This is mainly because of the lack of variety of international departures throughout other New England airports. In 2007, it handled 3,808,000 international passengers. Logan Airport stimulates the New England regional economy by approximately $7.6 billion per year, generating $559.4 million in state and local tax receipts.

History

Boston's Logan International Airport from the airside lounge of Terminal E, illustrating how the airport is largely surrounded by water. In the foreground is an Aer Lingus Airbus A330-200.

Originally called **Boston Airport**, Logan opened on September 8, 1923, and was used primarily by the Massachusetts Air Guard and the Army Air Corps. At that time, it was known as **Jeffery Field**. The first scheduled commercial passenger flights were initiated by Colonial Air Transport between Boston and New York City in 1927.

The airport has expanded over the years, including the addition of 1800 acres (730 ha) built on landfill in Boston Harbor and the incorporation of the former Governors, Noddle's and Apple Islands. As a consequence the airport is almost entirely surrounded by water. In 1952, the airport became the first in the United States with an indirect rapid transit connection. In 1956, the state renamed the airport as General Edward Lawrence Logan International Airport after a Spanish-American War officer from South Boston.

The era of the jumbo jet began at Logan during the summer of 1970 when Pan Am inaugurated daily Boeing 747 service to London Heathrow Airport. Non-stop flights to London now are scheduled by British Airways, American Airlines, and Virgin Atlantic.

When Terminal E opened in 1974, it was the second largest international arrivals facility in the United States.[citation needed] Since that time the number of international travelers using Logan has tripled. International long-haul travel has been the fastest growing market sector at Logan. Increased passenger traffic had led the Massachusetts Port Authority (Massport) to embark on a major airport renewal project called the "Logan Modernization Project" from 1994 to 2006. The project included a new parking garage, a new hotel, moving walkways, terminal expansions and improvements, and a two-tiered roadway system that separates arrival from departure road traffic.

Massport's relationship with neighboring communities has been highly strained since the mid-1960s, when the agency took control of a significant parcel of residential land and popular fishing area adjacent to the northwest side of the airfield. This project was undertaken to extend Runway 15R/33L, which would later become Logan's longest runway. Residents of the affected neighborhood, known as Wood Island, were bought out of their homes and forced to relocate. Public opposition came to a head when residents lay down in the streets in an attempt to block bulldozers and supply trucks from reaching the intended construction zone.

Construction has been completed on an additional runway, 14-32, which officially opened to air traffic on November 23, 2006. Runway 14-32 is Logan's first major runway addition in more than forty years. This runway was first proposed in 1973, but had been delayed by court action.

In April 2007, the FAA issued a green light for construction of a new center field taxiway long-sought by Massport to alleviate airfield congestion. The 9300-foot (2830 m) taxiway is located between, and parallel to, Runways 4R-22L and 4L-22R. News of the project angered Logan's neighboring residents. In 2009, the new taxiway became operational, ahead of schedule and under budget.

Baggage loading of a Lufthansa Boeing 747-400 during a temporary closure due to heavy snowfall

A scene from the 2006 film *The Departed* was filmed on location at Logan, inside the connector bridge between Terminal E and the Central Parking Garage. Terminal C and several United Airlines aircraft can be seen in the background.

Parts of the recent Delta Air Lines 2007 "Anthem" commercial were filmed inside Terminal A as well as the connector bridge between Terminal A and Central Parking.

On April 9, 2008, Massport announced that Grand China Airlines had formally applied to the Civil Aviation Administration of China for approval to operate daily non-stop passenger flights to Boston from Beijing using Boeing 787 aircraft. According to Massport, due to delays in production of the 787, the service did not begin before 2010. This is also consistent with government regulations on Chinese route approval, which has allocated all Chinese routes up through 2009. Logan last had service to Asia in July 2001, when Korean Air discontinued service to Seoul, Korea, which operated with a stop in Washington, D.C.

In October 2009, US Airways announced that the airline will close its Boston crew base in May 2010. The airline cites an "operations realignment" as the reason for the closure. Over 400 employees were transferred or terminated.

Statistics

For 12-month period ending September 30, 2006, the airport had 409,066 aircraft operations, an average of 1,120 per day: 60% scheduled commercial, 32% air taxi and 8% general aviation.

In 2009, Logan Airport handled about 25,512,000 passengers, with 3,696,000 being international passengers. The largest mainline airline at Logan Airport is JetBlue carrying 18.59% of all arriving and departing passengers combined, followed by American Airlines (14.21%), US Airways (12.98%), Delta Air Lines (12.09%), and United Airlines (9.74%). However, these figures may be misleading, since they do not include American Eagle, US Airways Express, or Delta Connection, each of which has significant operations at Logan Airport. Logan Airport also handled over of cargo and mail.

As of August 2010, Logan ranks 9th for on-time domestic departures with 82% of domestic flights departing on time. The airport ranks 20th in on-time domestic arrivals with 78% of domestic flights arriving on time.

Busiest Domestic Routes from Logan (2009-2010)

Rank	City	Passengers	Top Carriers
1	Chicago (O'Hare), Illinois	762,000	American, JetBlue, United
2	Atlanta, Georgia	726,000	AirTran, Delta
3	Baltimore, Maryland	523,000	AirTran, JetBlue, Southwest
4	New York (LaGuardia), New York	521,000	American, Delta, US Airways
5	San Francisco, California	502,000	American, JetBlue, United, Virgin America
6	Los Angeles, California	474,000	American, JetBlue, United, Virgin America
7	New York (JFK), New York	439,000	American, Delta, JetBlue
8	Charlotte, North Carolina	436,000	JetBlue, US Airways
9	Washington (National), DC	425,000	American, Delta, US Airways
10	Washington (Dulles), DC	390,000	JetBlue, United

Facilities and infrastructure

Logan International Airport covers an area of 2384 acres (965 ha) which contains six runways:

Logan's distinctive central control tower

- Runway 4L/22R: 7,861 × 150 ft (2,396 × 46 m), Surface: Asphalt
- Runway 4R/22L: 10,005 × 150 ft (3,050 × 46 m), Surface: Asphalt
- Runway 9/27: 7,000 × 150 ft (2,134 × 46 m), Surface: Asphalt
- Runway 14/32: 5,000 × 100 ft (1,524 × 30 m), Surface: Asphalt
- Runway 15L/33R: 2,557 × 100 ft (779 × 30 m), Surface: Asphalt
- Runway 15R/33L: 10,083 × 150 ft (3,073 × 46 m), Surface: Asphalt

The distinctive central control tower, nearly a dozen stories high, is a local landmark with its pair of segmented elliptical pylons and a six-story platform trussed between them.

New runway - 14-32

Runway 14-32, which officially opened to air traffic on November 23, 2006, is unidirectional. Runway 32 is used for landings and 14 is used for takeoffs. Massport is barred by a court order from using the runway for overland landings or takeoffs, except in emergencies. [citation needed]

Logan International Airport with an Air Canada Jazzaircraft taking off over the harbor

Opposition to the construction of 14-32 had been fierce even among residents of nearby communities such as Winthrop and Revere, two areas which were supposed to benefit from a reduction in noise levels once the new runway opened. With construction now having been completed, more wrangling has erupted over guidelines governing use of the new airstrip. Local communities are aggressively pushing for a minimum runway-use threshold of 11.5-knot northwest winds, slightly higher than the 10-knot threshold espoused by Massport. There has also been heated debateWikipedia:Avoid weasel words over a recent FAA proposal to lower the decision height for pilots.

The new runway reduces the need for the existing Runway 15L-33R, which, at only 2557 feet (779 m) is among the shortest hard-surface runways at major airports in the United States. In 1988, Massport had proposed an 800-foot (240 m) extension to this airstrip (a project which would have required additional filling-in of land along an important Wikipedia:Avoid weasel words clam bed), but was thwarted by a court injunction.[citation needed]

Boston's Hyatt Harborside Hotel, which sits only a few hundred yards from the runway threshold, was built primarily [citation needed] to prevent Massport from ever extending 14-32 or using it for takeoffs or landings over the city. Massachusetts lawmakers carefully chose the location of the hotel—directly in the runway centerline—prior to its construction in 1992.

According to Massport records, the very first aircraft to use the new airstrip was a Continental Express ERJ-145 regional jet landing on Runway 32, on the morning of December 2, 2006.

FBOs

The airport is served by several Fixed Base Operators (FBO), which handle fueling, ground handling, aircraft cleaning, cargo service, and aircraft maintenance. They include Swissport USA and Penauille Servisair. General aviation, which is adjacent to the North Cargo area, is handled by Signature Flight Support.

Public safety

Police services are provided by the Massachusetts State Police Troop F. Fire protection is the responsibility of Massport Fire Rescue. Even though the airport is within city limits, by state law the Boston Police Department does not have jurisdiction on Massport property.

Terminals

Logan International Airport has four terminals, A, B, C, and E, all connected by shuttle buses, as well as between Terminals A, B and E via moving walkways pre-security. Moving walkways also connect the terminals to a central parking garage designed for consolidated service between all 4 terminals and the garage itself. The airport has 103 gate positions total, with all 13 of the Terminal E gates being designated as common-use, meaning the gates may be assigned mostly depending on an operational need. All ticket counters and gates in Terminal E are shared among the international carriers, except for the counters and gates leased by Southwest Airlines.

The International Arrivals Hall located at Terminal E, ground level.

Terminals A, C and E have their own buildings, and Terminal B is split into north and south. With the exception of Terminal E, each terminal's upper level is used for departures, while the lower level is used for arrivals, including terminal roadways. In the case of Terminal E, the third level is used for departures while the ground level is used for arrivals and customs, with the second level being used for passport control. The Federal Inspection Station (FIS) located in Terminal E is capable of processing over 2,000 passengers per hour.

Logan's newly built Terminal A, which replaced a previous building that was once occupied by the now-defunct Eastern Airlines, opened to passengers on March 16, 2005. The building is the first airport terminal in the United States to be LEED certified for environmentally friendly design by the U.S. Green Building Council. Among the building's features are heat-reflecting roof and windows, low-flow faucets and waterless urinals, self-dimming lights, and storm water filtration.

The Terminal D gates (the three gates at the north end of Terminal C) were renumbered and labeled as part of Terminal C on February 28, 2006. The two Terminal C security checkpoints currently providing access to Gates 11 through 21 on the left and Gates 25 to 36 on the right are scheduled to be consolidated by the fall of 2010.

Retail management is provided by BAA, a British company, for Terminals B and E. Westfield Group of Australia provides retail management for Terminals A and C.

The airport's USO Lounge is located in the baggage claim area of Terminal C, lower level. It offers most typical amenities as other markets as major as Greater Boston. Military ID is mandatory.

Animal Relief Areas, of which Massport dubs as "Petports", are located near the lower level outside of every terminal, offering a grassy area for pets to relieve themselves, and owners to clean up.

Terminal A

Terminal B

Terminal C

Terminal E

Airlines and destinations

Passenger service

- **Note**: All international arrivals (except flights with customs preclearance) are handled at Terminal E.

Airlines	Destinations	Terminal
Aer Lingus	Dublin **Seasonal**: Shannon	E
Air Canada	Toronto-Pearson	B
Air Canada Jazz	Halifax, Montréal-Trudeau, Ottawa, Toronto-Pearson	B
Air France	Paris-Charles de Gaulle	E
AirTran Airways	Akron/Canton, Atlanta, Baltimore, Milwaukee, Newport News/Williamsburg **Seasonal**: Fort Myers, Orlando, Sarasota/Bradenton	C
Alaska Airlines	Portland (OR), Seattle/Tacoma	A
Alitalia	Rome-Fiumicino	E
American Airlines	Chicago-O'Hare, Dallas/Fort Worth, London-Heathrow, Los Angeles, Miami, San Francisco [ends November 17], San Juan [ends April 4], Santo Domingo [ends April 2] **Seasonal**: Paris-Charles de Gaulle, St. Thomas	B
American Eagle	New York-JFK, New York-LaGuardia, Toronto-Pearson, Washington-National [ends October 31]	B
British Airways	London-Heathrow	E
Cape Air	Hyannis, Lebanon, Martha's Vineyard, Nantucket, Provincetown, Rockland, Rutland, Saranac Lake	C
Continental Airlines	Cleveland, Houston-Intercontinental, Newark	A
Continental Connection operated by Colgan Air	Newark	A
Continental Express operated by Chautauqua Airlines	Cleveland	A
Continental Express operated by ExpressJet Airlines	Cleveland, Newark	A
Delta Air Lines	Amsterdam, Atlanta, Bermuda, Cincinnati/Northern Kentucky, Detroit, Las Vegas, Memphis, Minneapolis/St. Paul, New York-JFK, New York-LaGuardia, Orlando, Salt Lake City **Seasonal**: Cancún, Fort Myers	A

gan International Airport

Delta Connection operated by Chautauqua Airlines	Columbus (OH)	A
Delta Connection operated by Comair	Cincinnati/Northern Kentucky, New York-JFK, Raleigh/Durham, Washington-National	A
Delta Connection operated by Compass Airlines	Memphis	A
Delta Connection operated by Pinnacle Airlines	Indianapolis, Washington-National	A
Delta Connection operated by Shuttle America	Cincinnati/Northern Kentucky, New York-LaGuardia	A
Frontier Airlines	Milwaukee	B
Frontier Airlines operated by Republic Airlines	Kansas City, Milwaukee [ends November 17]	B
Iberia	Madrid	E
Iceland Express	Reykjavik [begins June 13]	E
Icelandair	Reykjavik	E
JetBlue Airways	Aruba, Austin, Baltimore, Buffalo, Cancun, Charlotte, Chicago O'Hare, Denver, Fort Lauderdale, Fort Myers, Jacksonville (FL), Las Vegas, Long Beach, Los Angeles, Montego Bay, New Orleans, New York-JFK, Orlando, Phoenix, Pittsburgh, Punta Cana, Raleigh/Durham, Richmond, St. Maarten, San Diego, San Francisco, San Jose (CA), San Juan, Santo Domingo, Seattle/Tacoma, Tampa, Washington-Dulles, Washington-National [begins November 1], West Palm Beach **Seasonal**: Bermuda, Providenciales [begins February 19], Sarasota [begins November 18]	C
Lufthansa	Frankfurt, Munich	E
Porter Airlines	Toronto-Billy Bishop	E
SATA International	Lisbon, Terceira, Ponta Delgada	E
Southwest Airlines	Baltimore, Chicago-Midway, Denver, Philadelphia, Phoenix, St. Louis	E
Spirit Airlines	Atlantic City, Fort Lauderdale, Myrtle Beach	B

Sun Country Airlines	**Seasonal**: Minneapolis/St. Paul	C
Swiss International Air Lines	Zürich	E
TACV	Praia	E
United Airlines	Chicago-O'Hare, Denver, Los Angeles, San Francisco, Washington-Dulles	C
United Express operated by Atlantic Southeast Airlines	Washington-Dulles	C
United Express operated by Mesa Airlines	Washington-Dulles	C
United Express operated by Shuttle America	Chicago-O'Hare	C
United Express operated by Trans States Airlines	Washington-Dulles	C
US Airways	Aruba, Cancún, Charlotte, Las Vegas, New York-LaGuardia, Philadelphia, Phoenix, Washington-National	B
US Airways Express operated by Air Wisconsin	Buffalo, Philadelphia, Pittsburgh, Richmond, Rochester (NY)	B
US Airways Express operated by Colgan Air	Albany, Augusta (ME), Bar Harbor, Plattsburgh, Presque Isle, Syracuse	B
US Airways Express operated by Piedmont Airlines	Harrisburg	B
US Airways Express operated by Republic Airlines	Philadelphia, Pittsburgh	B
Virgin America	Los Angeles, San Francisco	B

Virgin Atlantic Airways	London-Heathrow	E

Airline lounges

Since many major domestic and international airlines have a large presence at Logan, there are several airline lounges actively in operation there, all of which are post-security.

- Aer Lingus operates a Gold Circle Lounge in Terminal E.
- Air France operates an Air France Lounge in Terminal E.
- American Airlines operates an Admirals Club in Terminal B.
- British Airways operates a First Lounge and a Terraces Lounge in Terminal E.
- Continental Airlines operates a Presidents Club in Terminal A.
- Delta Air Lines operates a Delta Sky Club in the Satellite Terminal of Terminal A on the 3rd floor, used exclusively for the Sky Club.
- Lufthansa operates a Senator Lounge and a Business Lounge in Terminal E.
- United Airlines operates a Red Carpet Club in Terminal C.
- US Airways operates a US Airways Club in Terminal B.
- Virgin Atlantic operates a Clubhouse Lounge in Terminal E.

Air freight

Logan Airport has two cargo facilities (North Cargo adjacent to Terminal E and South Cargo adjacent to Terminals A and B). The airport is served by the several cargo carriers:

- ABX Air
- AirNet Systems
- Air Transport International
- FedEx Express
- UPS Airlines

Ground transportation

Boston Logan International Airport has the accolade of "Easiest Airport to Get To" in a 2007 article on aviation.com because of the variety of options to/from the airport. These options include cars, taxis, the MBTA Blue and Silver lines, regional bus services, shared ride vans, limousines, and a service offered by few U.S. Airports, Logan Express. Logan is also 3 miles (5 kilometers) northeast of downtown Boston, a very short distance compared to airports in other cities.

The Blue Line station, accessible by Massport shuttle buses.

The MBTA's Silver Line SL1 bus rapid transit service connects South Station, a major MBTA Commuter Rail, Amtrak, Red Line subway and bus transportation hub in the downtown Boston financial district, with all Logan terminals. Silverline bus tickets are sold in every terminal building to the far right of the lower level. There is also an Airport stop on the MBTA's Blue Line subway service. The Blue Line stop is not in the airport terminal itself; free shuttle buses 55, 22, and 33 provided by Massport bring passengers from the train station to the terminal buildings. Massport's Logan Express bus service also serves the areas of Braintree, Framingham, Peabody, and the Anderson Regional Transportation Center in Woburn for an adult fare of $12.00 one-way and $22.00 round-trip per passenger. Logan Express operates on the lower level curb of all terminals.

Preceding station	Ⓣ MBTA	Following station

Exit Express pay stations, allowing expedited exit from the parking garages by reducing lines at the toll plaza.

Limousine pickup is also very common at the airport. Limousine drivers are not allowed to leave their vehicles at the designated pickup areas and pickup locations vary depending on the terminal. For Terminal A, the pickup location is on the arrival level, outside baggage claim, in a small parking lot across the road. At Terminal E, pickup is also on the arrival level in a small parking lot across the outermost curb. For Terminal B (both American Airlines and US Airways sides), pickup is at the curbside on the departure level at the outermost curb area. At Terminal C, pickup is also on the departure level at the second and third islands from the building.

Taxi operations are coordinated at each terminal by Massport. Massport's regulations have reduced the number of taxis allowed to wait in front of the terminal at any one time, and prohibit taxis from picking up fares at any location other than the designated taxi stands located at each terminal on the lower level curbs on the far left outside of baggage claim. A large staging area near the South Cargo complex serves as the waiting area for taxis, before they are called to the taxi stands to replenish the supply. Metered-rates from Logan to the Boston-area hotels range from approximately $25.00 to $50.00. The airport fee for trips leaving the airport is $2.25. Additionally, the city of Boston charges a $2.75 fee for trips to Logan Airport.

Cell Phone Waiting Lot on Harborside Dr.

The MBTA operates a water shuttle connecting Logan with downtown Boston, Quincy, and Hull. On demand service from the airport to various locations on the downtown waterfront is provided by a fleet of water taxis. A free shuttle bus ferries passengers between the airport dock and the various terminals.

On Harborside Dr., Logan International Airport offers a 30-minute cell phone waiting lot area, which is complimentary and five minutes from all terminals by car. This convenience service exists to reduce congestion and pollution problems.

By public roads, the airport is accessible via Exit 26 on I-90 near the eastern terminus of the Massachusetts Turnpike of which I-90 ends at and transitions to Route 1A to Lynn and New Hampshire, which provides easy access from the west via the Ted Williams Tunnel. From the south, travellers on Interstate 93 can connect to the Masspike east, through the Ted Williams Tunnel and take exit 26 to reach the airport. From the north, I-93 traffic to the airport uses the Callahan Tunnel, Route 1A North. From the North Shore, access is via Route 1A South. Additionally, road traffic from most of downtown Boston, Back Bay and Fenway/Boston University should use the Callahan Tunnel. The westbound twin tunnel to the Callahan Tunnel is known as the Sumner Tunnel. Eastbound travel through the tunnels is free, but there is a $3.50 toll for westbound travel, and a $5.25 toll for taxis, which passengers are responsible for.

On July 10, 2006, the connector tunnel leading from the Massachusetts Turnpike to the Ted Williams Tunnel was closed due to a ceiling collapse that killed a woman. This complicated airport access from the south and west. This connector tunnel was part of the Big Dig project which extended the Massachusetts Turnpike to the airport via the Ted Williams Tunnel. Access from I-90 Eastbound was restored in August 2006, and access to I-90 Westbound was restored on December 23, 2006. I-90 access was completely restored the weekend of January 14, 2007.

Notable incidents

- On October 4, 1960, Eastern Air Lines Flight 375 crashed into the sea while attempting to take off from Logan Airport. 62 people died and 9 people survived, incurring serious injuries.

- On November 15, 1961, A Vickers Viscount N6592C of Northeast Airlines was written off when it collided with a Douglas DC-6 N8228H of National Airlines after landing at Logan International Airport. The DC-6 had started to take-off without receiving clearance to do so.

- On July 31, 1973, Delta Air Lines Flight 723, operated on a DC-9 airplane, crashed into a seawall at Logan Airport, causing the deaths of all 83 passengers and 6 crew members on board. One of the passengers initially survived the accident but later died in a hospital.

- On January 23, 1982, World Airways Flight 30 from Newark to Boston made a non-precision instrument approach to runway 15R and touched down 2800 feet past the displaced threshold on an icy runway. When the crew sensed that the DC-10-30-CF couldn't be stopped on the remaining runway, they steered the DC-10 off the side of the runway to avoid the approach light pier, and slid into the shallow water of Boston Harbor. The nose section separated as the DC-10 came to rest 250 feet past the runway end, 110 feet left of the extended centerline. 2 passengers (a father and son) were never found and are presumed to have been swept out to sea.

- On September 11, 2001, two of the aircraft involved in the 9/11 terrorist attacks, American Airlines Flight 11 and United Airlines Flight 175, departed from Logan International Airport, both bound for Los Angeles and slamming into the North and South Tower, respectively, of New York's World Trade Center. United and American Airlines have mounted American flags on Gates B32 and C19, the gates from which the flights departed that day.

- On December 22, 2001, Richard Reid attempted to blow up American Airlines Flight 63 with a bomb in his shoe over the Atlantic Ocean. The flight was diverted to Boston after the passengers and crew overpowered and subdued Reid. One flight attendant received minor injuries after being bitten on the thumb by Reid. The flight departed from Paris-Charles de Gaulle Airport and its intended destination was Miami International Airport.

- On June 15, 2010, Alitalia Flight 615, an Airbus A330 with 258 passengers, from Boston, Massachusetts to Rome was forced to make an emergency landing at Logan Airport after an engine failed shortly after take-off.[33] The incident is still under investigation.

General reliever airports

To address Logan Airport's overcrowding, Massport has designated two out-of-state airports as the second and third airports of Boston: Manchester-Boston Regional Airport in Manchester, New Hampshire, located approximately 44 statute miles (72 kilometers) north-northwest of Logan, which converts to an average drive time of 48 minutes via I-93; and T. F. Green Airport in Providence, Rhode Island, located 63 statute miles (101 kilometers) south-southwest of Logan, averaging a 1 hour, 8 minute drive to Logan via I-95. Massport does not operate these facilities.

For a time, Massport also operated scheduled flights at Hanscom Field in Bedford, Massachusetts, and Worcester Regional Airport in Worcester, each of which are operated by Massport.

See also

- Massachusetts World War II Army Airfields

External links

- Massport: Logan Airport [1]
- Terminal Map of Logan International Airport [2]
- Airport Wayfinder: Boston [3]
- Noise Complaints [4]
- FAA Airport Diagram [5] (PDF), effective 23 Sep 2010
- Resources for this airport:
  - AirNav airport information for KBOS [6]
  - ASN accident history for BOS [7]
  - FlightAware airport information [8] and live flight tracker [9]
  - NOAA/NWS latest weather observations [10]
  - SkyVector aeronautical chart for KBOS [11]
  - FAA current BOS delay information [12]

Massachusetts Route 2A

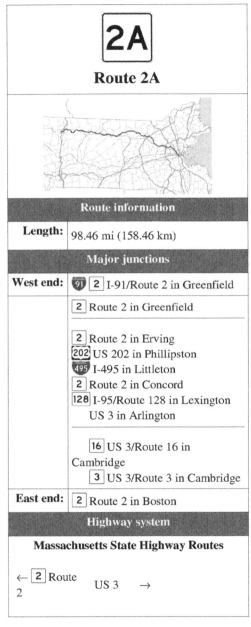

2A

Route 2A

Route information	
Length:	98.46 mi (158.46 km)
Major junctions	
West end:	🛡91 [2] I-91/Route 2 in Greenfield
	[2] Route 2 in Greenfield
	[2] Route 2 in Erving
	[202] US 202 in Phillipston
	🛡495 I-495 in Littleton
	[2] Route 2 in Concord
	[128] I-95/Route 128 in Lexington
	US 3 in Arlington
	[16] US 3/Route 16 in Cambridge
	[3] US 3/Route 3 in Cambridge
East end:	[2] Route 2 in Boston
Highway system	
Massachusetts State Highway Routes	
← [2] Route 2 US 3 →	

Route 2A exists in several sections of Massachusetts, mainly as parts of former Route 2 that have been moved or upgraded. Route 2A runs from Greenfield in the west to Boston in the east. Route 2A used to extend all the way to Shelburne Falls in Buckland in the west, but as of 2007, the route now terminates at Interstate 91 in Greenfield.

From Boston to Concord, Route 2A is a separate artery. It also services Hanscom Field and Hanscom Air Force Base. After merging briefly with Route 2 in Concord, Route 2A again separates from Route 2 until Erving. From there, Route 2A runs concurrent with Route 2 until Greenfield, where it separates just north of Turners Falls, runs through downtown Greenfield and terminates when it meets Route 2 again.

Eastbound at the Garden Theater in Greenfield

Towns along the route

- Greenfield (sharing roadway with Route 2)
- Gill (sharing roadway with Route 2)
- Erving (sharing roadway with Route 2)
- Orange
- Athol (sharing roadway with Route 32)
- Phillipston
- Templeton (sharing roadway with US 202 and Route 101)
- Gardner
- Westminster
- Fitchburg (sharing roadway with Route 31 and Route 12)
- Lunenburg (sharing roadway with Route 13)
- Shirley
- Ayer (sharing roadway with Route 111 and Route 110)

- Littleton (sharing roadway with Route 110 and Route 119)
- Acton (sharing roadway with Route 119)
- Concord (sharing roadway with Route 2)
- Lincoln
- Lexington (sharing roadway with Route 4/Route 225)
- Arlington (sharing roadway with US 3)
- Cambridge
- Boston

See also

- Massachusetts Avenue

Massachusetts Route 16

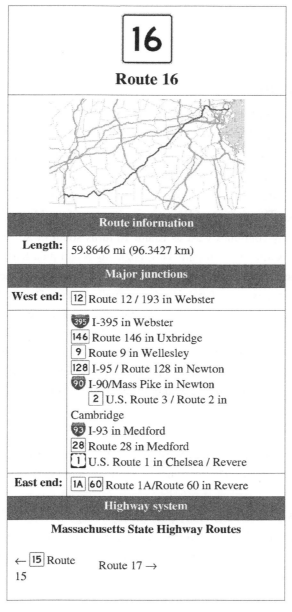

16

Route 16

Route information	
Length:	59.8646 mi (96.3427 km)
Major junctions	
West end:	[12] Route 12 / 193 in Webster
	[395] I-395 in Webster
	[146] Route 146 in Uxbridge
	[9] Route 9 in Wellesley
	[128] I-95 / Route 128 in Newton
	[90] I-90/Mass Pike in Newton
	[2] U.S. Route 3 / Route 2 in Cambridge
	[93] I-93 in Medford
	[28] Route 28 in Medford
	[1] U.S. Route 1 in Chelsea / Revere
East end:	[1A] [60] Route 1A/Route 60 in Revere
Highway system	
Massachusetts State Highway Routes	
← [15] Route 15 Route 17 →	

Route 16 is an east–west state highway in Massachusetts. It begins in the west at an intersection with Route 12 and Route 193 in Webster, just north of the Connecticut state border. It runs in a generally southwest-northeast routing through a number of Boston's suburbs and runs to the west and then north of the city before ending in Revere at an intersection with Route 1A and Route 60.

Much of Route 16 east of the Newton-Wellesley town line, and especially from Cambridge eastward, is a multi-lane parkway, although it is not limited access for any significant length of road. Segments of Route 16 are also known as the Mystic Valley Parkway, the Alewife Brook Parkway, and the Revere Beach Parkway, among other names.

Route description

From the shore to the Pike

Route 16 runs north and west of the City of Boston, beginning at the Atlantic Ocean at Revere Beach, where it intersects with Route 1A and 60 at Timothy J. Mahoney Circle in Revere.

The route proceeds west by a winding path through several mixed-used industrial, commercial, and residential areas in the cities of Everett and Malden until it intersects Interstate 93 in Medford. It then veers north, traveling beside the Mystic River upstream, and passing near Medford Square, the downtown area of that city. This portion of Route 16 is also part of the Mystic Valley Parkway.

The Mystic Valley Parkway continues west as Route 16 turns south in Somerville on Alewife Brook Parkway. This section of Route 16 soon joins U.S. Highway 3 and then Route 2 at the eastern end of the freeway portion of the Concord Turnpike. From there, Route 16 passes the large parking garage at the MBTA Alewife Station, passes by Fresh Pond, eventually leaving Routes 2 and 3 as they continue along Fresh Pond Parkway. It then continues west through Cambridge, passing by Mount Auburn Cemetery before entering Watertown. Route 16 crosses U.S. Highway 20 in Watertown Square, then crosses the Charles River. It enters Newton near the village of Nonantum, and eventually crosses I-90, the Massachusetts Turnpike, in West Newton; Pike Exit 16 here provides access to and from the east only. Still in Newton, Route 16 then crosses Route 30 and Route 128 (Interstate 95).

From Newton to I-495

This area west of Boston, also called MetroWest, that Route 16 now travels through contains several quintessential New England towns. The route now goes by restored antique, colonial homes and town buildings.

From the Pike, Route 16 goes southwesterly past Lasell College in Newton, and through Wellesley, where Wellesley College and Babson College are located. The road then passes the Elm Bank Reservation in Sherborn, through Holliston, by Weston Pond, and shortly thereafter passes beneath I-495.

From I-495 to Lake Chaubunagungamaug

After passing I-495, the route continues to the southwest, going through Milford, Hopedale, Mendon, Uxbridge, the Blackstone River Valley National Heritage Corridor and Douglas with a trip through the Douglas State Forest in the last town.

Route 16 continues to its intersection with I-395 in Webster, along the shore of Lake Chaubunagungamaug, and not far from the Connecticut border. It ends at Route 12 just to the west.

Junction list

County	Location	Mile	Roads intersected	Notes
Worcester	Webster	0.0	12 Route 12 Route 193	Northern terminus of Route 193.
		0.2	395 Interstate 395	I-395 Exit 2.
	Douglas		96 Route 96	Northern terminus of Route 96.
	Uxbridge		146 Route 146	Route 146 Exit 3.
			122 Route 122	Brief concurrency with Route 122. To 146A Route 146A, via Route 122 south.
	Milford		140 Route 140	
			Route 85	Southern terminus of Route 85. To 495 Interstate 495.
			109 Route 109	Western terminus of Route 109. To 495 Interstate 495.
Middlesex	Holliston		SOUTH 126 Route 126 south	Southern terminus of Route 16/126 concurrency.
			126 Route 126 north	Northern terminus of Route 16/126 concurrency.
	Sherborn		SOUTH 27 Route 27 south	No access to Route 27 south from Route 16 east. No access to Route 16 west from Route 27 north. These movements are facilitated via Sawin Street. Southern terminus of Route 16/27 concurrency.
			27 Route 27 north	Northern terminus of Route 16/27 concurrency.

County	Town	Route	Notes
Norfolk	Wellesley	135 Route 135 west	No access to Route 135 west from Route 16 east. No access to Route 16 west from Route 135 east. These movements are facilitated via Weston Road. Western terminus of Route 16/135 concurrency.
		EAST 135 Route 135 east	Eastern terminus of Route 16/135 concurrency.
		9 Route 9	Partial interchange with signals; under construction.
	Newton	Interstate 95 128 Route 128	I-95 Exit 21.
		30 Route 30	Commonwealth Avenue
		90 I-90/Mass Pike	Mass Pike Exit 16; partial interchange. Access to I-90 east only from Route 16. Access to Route 16 from I-90 west only.
Middlesex	Watertown	20 U.S. Route 20	Main Street (west), North Beacon Street (east)
	Cambridge	SOUTH U.S. Route 3 south EAST 2 Route 2 east	Fresh Pond Parkway Southern terminus of US-3/Route 2/16 concurrency.
		2 Route 2 west	Cambridge Turnpike Northern terminus of US-3/Route 2/16 concurrency.
		U.S. Route 3 north 2A Route 2A	Massachusetts Avenue Northern terminus of US-3/Route 16 concurrency.
	Medford	38 Route 38	Brief concurrency with Route 38. To 60 Route 60, via Route 38 north.
		93 Interstate 93	I-93 Exit 31; partial interchange. Access to I-93 (in both directions) from Route 16 east only. Access to Route 16 east only from I-93 south. Access to Route 16 west only from I-93 north. Access to I-93 from Route 16 west can be facilitated via Routes 38 north and 60 east to the Exit 32 interchange.
		28 Route 28	Fellsway
	Everett	99 Route 99	Broadway; dual rotary intersection.

Suffolk	Revere		[1] U.S. Route 1	Northeast Expressway; interchange.
			Route 107	Broadway; interchange. Southern terminus of Route 107.
			[145] Route 145	Continuation of Revere Beach Parkway. Northern terminus of Route 145. To [1A] Route 1A south.
		59.9	[1A] Route 1A [60] Route 60	Eastern terminus of Route 16. Eastern terminus of Route 60. Rotary intersection.

Street names

Route 16 is known by the following street names

Webster

- East Main Street (Route 12/193 to I-395)
- Gore Road
- Douglas Road

Douglas

- Webster Street
- South Street
- Main Street
- Davis Street

Uxbridge

- Douglas Street
- Mendon Street

Mendon

- Uxbridge Road
- Hastings Street
- Milford Street

Milford

- Mendon Street
- Main Street
- East Main Street

Holliston

- Washington Street (partly concurrent with Route 126)

Sherborn

- Washington Street
- North Main Street (concurrency with Route 27)
- Eliot Street

Natick

- Eliot Street

Wellesley

- Washington Street (partly concurrent with Route 135)

Newton

- Washington Street
- Watertown Street
- Galen Street (Charles River crossing)

Watertown

- Mount Auburn Street
- Aberdeen Avenue
- Huron Avenue

Cambridge

- Fresh Pond Parkway (concurrency with US-3 and Route 2)
- Alewife Brook Parkway (partly concurrent with US-3 and Route 2)
- Mystic Valley Parkway

Medford

- Mystic Valley Parkway (partly concurrent with Route 38)
- Revere Beach Parkway

Everett

- Revere Beach Parkway

Chelsea

- Revere Beach Parkway

Revere

- Revere Beach Parkway

History

Parts of Route 16 were historically maintained by the Metropolitan District Commission (MDC), and while the MDC no longer exists, the parkway portions of the route are still patrolled by the Massachusetts State Police and maintained by the Massachusetts Department of Conservation and Recreation as a remnant of the former MDC jurisdiction.

Photos

Westbound entering Wellesley

Red Line (MBTA)

MBTA Red Line	
An MBTA Red Line train composed of #3 Red Line stock leaving Charles/MGH station bound for Alewife, going over the Longfellow Bridge.	
Overview	
Type	Rapid transit
Locale	Boston, Massachusetts
Termini	Alewife Ashmont or Braintree
Stations	17 (Alewife-Ashmont) 18 (Alewife-Braintree)
Services	2
Daily ridership	178,657
Operation	
Opened	1912
Owner	MBTA
Operator(s)	MBTA
Character	Subway, Grade-separated ROW
Rolling stock	1. 1, #2, #3 Red Line
Technical	
Track gauge	4 ft 8 $\frac{1}{2}$ in (1435 mm)
Electrification	Third rail

Route
map

Legend

Alewife Yard

Layup tracks

Alewife

Davis

Fitchburg Line

Porter

Fitchburg Line

Harvard

Central

Kendall/MIT

Longfellow Bridge incline

Charles River

Charles/MGH

Park Street

Downtown Crossing

South Station

Broadway

Andrew

Old Colony Lines

JFK/UMass

Old Colony Lines

Savin Hill

Fields Corner

Shawmut

Ashmont

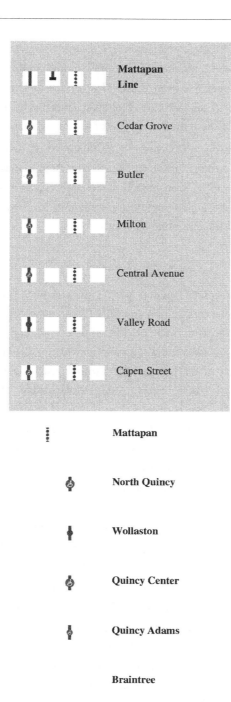

Mattapan
Line

Cedar Grove

Butler

Milton

Central Avenue

Valley Road

Capen Street

Mattapan

North Quincy

Wollaston

Quincy Center

Quincy Adams

Braintree

The **Red Line** is a rapid transit line operated by the MBTA running roughly north-south through Boston, Massachusetts into neighboring communities. The line begins west of Boston, in Cambridge, Massachusetts at Alewife station, near the intersection of Alewife Brook Parkway and Route 2. The line passes through downtown Boston, with transfers to the Green Line at Park Street station, the Orange Line at Downtown Crossing, and the Silver Line at South Station. South of downtown, the line splits at JFK/UMass station, where one branch provides service to Braintree station and the other to Ashmont station. A connection to the Ashmont-Mattapan High Speed Line extends the reach of the Ashmont branch to Mattapan station in the lower right of the city to the west.

Regular fare is $1.70 when using a CharlieCard or $2.00 when using cash or a Charlie Ticket, regardless of point of boarding or departure. Exit fares on the Braintree extension were discontinued in 2007. Approximate travel times to or from Park Street station are as follows: northbound to Harvard station, 11 minutes; Alewife station, 20 minutes; southbound to JFK/UMass, 8 minutes; Ashmont station, 17 minutes; Braintree station, 28 minutes.

History

The Red Line was the last of the four original Boston subway lines (Green, Orange, Blue) to begin construction. The section from Harvard station and Eliot Yard connecting to Park Street station and the Tremont Street Subway opened on March 23, 1912. At Harvard, a prepayment station was provided for easy transfer to streetcar routes operating in a separate tunnel (now the Harvard Bus Tunnel). Opening of the line required construction of the **Cambridge Tunnel** just beneath Massachusetts Avenue and Main Street from Harvard onto the (now historic) Longfellow Bridge. The line occupied a previously constructed rail right-of-way in the center of the bridge.[citation needed] On the Boston side of the bridge, the line briefly transformed into an elevated railway, rising over Charles Circle and connecting to another tunnel dug through Beacon Hill to Park Street. Further extensions (built as the **Dorchester Tunnel**) to Washington Street and South Station opened on April 4, 1915 and December 3, 1916, with transfers to the Washington Street Tunnel and Atlantic Avenue Elevated respectively. Further extensions opened to Broadway on December 15, 1917 and Andrew on June 29, 1918, both prepayment stations for streetcar transfer. The Broadway station included an upper level with its own tunnel for streetcars, which was abandoned in 1919 due to most lines being truncated to Andrew. The upper level has since been incorporated into the mezzanine.

Next came the **Dorchester Extension**, now known as the **Ashmont Branch**. The branch followed a rail right-of-way created in 1870 by the **Shawmut Branch Railroad**. In 1872, the right-of-way was acquired by the Old Colony Railroad to connect the main line at Harrison Square with the Dorchester and Milton Branch Railroad, running from the Old Colony at Neponset, west to what is now Mattapan station. The New York, New Haven and Hartford Railroad succeeded Old Colony in operating the branch and rail passenger service ceased in anticipation of the Boston Elevated Railway expansion on September 4, 1926,

The Boston Elevated opened the first phase of the Dorchester Extension to Field's Corner station on November 5, 1927. Service ran south from Andrew station, turned southeast to the surface, and ran along the west side of the Old Colony mainline in a depressed right-of-way. Columbia station and

Savin Hill station were built on the surface at the sites of former Old Colony stations. The remainder of the extension opened to Ashmont station and Codman Yard on September 1, 1928, and included a station - Shawmut - where there had been no Old Colony station due to the relatively close proximity to Fields Corner. The first phase of the Ashmont-Mattapan High Speed Line opened on August 26, 1929, using the rest of the Shawmut Branch right-of-way, including Cedar Grove station, and part of the old Dorchester and Milton Branch.

The color red was assigned on August 26, 1965 to what had been called the **Cambridge-Dorchester Tunnel** and marked on maps as route 1. The color was chosen because the line ended at Harvard University, whose school color is crimson, a shade of red.

The first section of the **South Shore Line** opened on September 1, 1971. This line branched from the original line at a flying junction north of Columbia and ran along the west side of the Old Colony right-of-way (since reduced to one track), crossing to the east side north of Savin Hill. Its northernmost station was North Quincy, with two others at Wollaston and Quincy Center. The rest of the line, the **Braintree Extension** (first planned by the Boston Transportation Planning Review) to Braintree station, opened March 22, 1980, and the intermediate station at Quincy Adams station opened on September 10, 1983.

The first part of the **Northwest Extension**, the relocation of Harvard station, was finished on September 6, 1983. During construction, several temporary stations were built at Harvard Square. The old Eliot Yard was demolished; Harvard's Kennedy School of Government now sits inside the retaining walls built for the railyard. Subsequent extensions to Porter station, Davis station on December 8, 1984, and Alewife station on March 30, 1985 brought the Red Line to its current terminus. This extension was scaled back from the original plan to extend the Red Line from Harvard to Route 128 in Lexington-Bedford via the former Bedford Branch rail right-of-way. That plan had been supported by the Town of Lexington but was scuttled by fierce anti-urban sentiment in parts of Arlington. A platform on the South Shore Line opened at JFK/UMass (formerly Columbia) on December 14, 1988.

Platforms on older stations were lengthened in the late 1980s to allow six-car trains, which first ran January 21, 1988. During the expansion, the MBTA invested in an *Arts on the line* public art program.

In 1968, letters were assigned to the south branches - "A" for Quincy (planned to extend to South Braintree) and "C" for Ashmont. "B" was probably reserved for a planned branch from Braintree to Brockton. As new rollsigns were made, this lettering was phased out. In 1994, new electronic signs included a different labeling - "A" for Ashmont, "B" for Braintree and "C" for Alewife. [1]

Operations and signalling

The line used trip-stop wayside signalling for the Ashmont and Harvard branches until the mid-1980s, while the Braintree Branch was one of the earliest examples of Automatic Train Control (ATC). The Alewife Branch was built with ATC, at which point the remainder of the line was upgraded to ATC as well. The line was under local control at towers until 1985 when an electromechanical panel was completed at 45 High St. This was replaced in the late 1990s with a software-controlled Automatic Train Supervision, using a product by Union Switch & Signal, subcontracted to Syseca Inc. (now ARINC), at a new theater at 45 High St. Subsequent revisions to the system were made internally at the MBTA.

The shortest scheduled headway ever run on the Red Line is most likely the $1 \frac{3}{4}$ minute interval in the schedule published in 1928. Ridership peaked on the line around 1947, when passenger counters logged over 850 people per four car train during peak periods. The newer ATC signalling was designed to higher safety standards, but the particular design of the block layout in the downtown area reduced the capacity by 50% over the previous wayside signalling system. The net loss of capacity measured in cars per hour has not been rectified, although at the same time the platforms were lengthened to run 6-car trains which are now operated on a longer headway. Additionally, the shifting between speed codes that is inherent in an ATC system near capacity caused peak period energy consumption to skyrocket, and accelerated the decline of the 01400 series fleet.[citation needed]

Accessibility

Most, but not all, Red Line stations are wheelchair accessible. See also MBTA accessibility.

Equipment

The Red Line is standard gauge heavy rail. Trains consist of mated pairs of Electrical Multiple Unit cars powered from a 600 VDC third rail. Trains run either in 4-car or 6-car sets.

Rolling stock is stored and maintained at the Cabot Yard, near the Broadway station in South Boston. The connection to this yard is at the junction where the two branches split, near JFK/UMass station.

1912 Cambridge Subway Cars

The so-called Cambridge Subway began service in 1912 with 40 all-steel motor cars built by Standard Steel Car Co. They featured a novel design as a result of studies about Boston's existing lines. The cars had an extraordinary length of 69 ft. 2½ in. over buffers and large standees capacity, weighed only 85,900 lb. and featured an all-new door arrangement. There were three single sliding doors per side that were evenly distributed along the car's length so that the maximum distance from any location inside the car to a door was around 9 ft. The idea was later taken over by the BMT Standards and Philadelphia's Frankford Elevated Line cars. Moreover about 20 ft of the car was separated by a bulkhead and used as a smoking compartment. In contrast to the elevated lines passenger flow was not intended here, so every door was used as entrance and exit as well.

Two basic types of cars are in use today:

Aluminum-bodied cars

Aluminium-bodied Red Line train at Braintree.

Aluminium-bodied Red Line cars at Harvard.

Three series of older aluminum-bodied cars built by Pullman-Standard and UTDC. The older two series of this batch, the 01500 and 01600 series, were built by Pullman in 1969–1970. The 1700 series was built by UTDC in 1988. These cars seat 62 to 64 customers and approximately 132 cars are in active service. All cars in these series are painted white with red trim and use manually-operated exterior roll signs. Before their overhauls, the 1500 and 1600 series had a brushed aluminum livery with a thin red stripes.

All three groups of these older cars (units 1500 through 1757) use traditional DC traction motors with electromechanical controls manufactured by Westinghouse and can inter-operate among the three series. The 1500 and 1700 series cars could operate as singletons, but in practice, are always operated as mated pairs. The 1600 series could only operate as married pairs. Originally, the 1500s were double-ended and had two cabs, but were converted to single ended during its midlife overhaul. Headlights are still present on the non-cab ends on the 1500s. The 1700s also have headlights on their non-cab end, however they were built with only one cab.

Stainless steel-bodied cars

One series of newer stainless steel-bodied cars built by Bombardier from components manufactured in Canada and assembled in Barre, Vermont. These cars seat 50 passengers and 86 cars are in active service. An automated stop announcement system provides station announcements synchronized with visual announcements displayed on red LED signs located in each car. These cars are stainless steel with red trim and use yellow LCD exterior signs. Unlike the previous series, these train cars originally had red cloth seats (in contrast to the black leather seats of other models), but in the early 21st century, the cloth seats were replaced with black leather seats. Recently the black leather seats were replaced with vandalism-proof cloth seats containing multi-colored patterns, as did the other Red Line rolling stock still in use.

A Bombardier car at Harvard.

Known as the 1800 series, they were built in 1993–1994. These newer cars (units 1800 through 1885) use modern AC traction motors with solid state controls manufactured by General Electric, can only operate as mated pairs, and can not interoperate with the older three series of cars.

A Bombardier car's cab at Braintree.

Increasing capacity

As of December 2008, the MBTA began running a set of modified 1800 series cars without seats in order to increase train capacity and accommodate more passengers during on-peak hours. This makes the MBTA the first transit operator in the United States with heavy rail operations to run cars modified for this purpose. These cars have been designated as 'Big Red' cars, denoted by large stickers applied adjacent to the side loading doors of each car. New automated service announcements have been recorded for playback at station platforms in order to alert passengers to the arrival of these 'Big Red' high capacity trains. So far, the MBTA only has one pair of the modified rolling stock and the cars operate in a consist that runs only once during the morning rush hour toward Alewife and once during the evening rush hour toward Braintree, departing Alewife at the top of the evening rush.

Replacement of 1500, 1600 series cars

The MBTA is starting to design the next generation trains for the Red Line, which will replace the 1500 and 1600 series, which are approaching 40 years old. The new Red Line train will probably use elements from the new Orange Line equipment.[citation needed] The new cars will mechanically but not electrically couple with the older two series of cars (1700 and 1800).

Art and architecture

Newer aboveground stations (particularly Alewife, Braintree, and Quincy Adams) are excellent examples of brutalist architecture.

The Kendall station features an interactive public art installation by Paul Matisse called the Kendall Band, which allows the public to activate three sound-producing machines utilizing cranks on the wall of the station. Above the tracks at Alewife hangs a series of red neon tubes called "End of Red Line". Several other stations feature public art.

Advertising

Between South Station and Broadway, and also between Harvard station and Central Square, there is an advertisement in the form of a zoetrope. Each frame of the ad flashes as the train goes by, to create an animation effect. There are similar advertisements in parts of the New York City Subway, the Washington Metro, Bay Area Rapid Transit (BART), and the Singapore MRT.

Station listing

Main line

Outbound train approaching South Station.

Station	Location	Opened	Transfers and notes
♿ Alewife	Alewife Brook Parkway, Cambridge	March 30, 1985	bus terminal, park and ride garage, Minuteman Bikeway
♿ Davis	Davis Square, Somerville	December 8, 1984	Somerville Community Path
♿ Porter	Porter Square, Cambridge	December 8, 1984	MBTA Commuter Rail, Fitchburg Line
Stadium	Harvard Square, Cambridge	October 26, 1912	Across Charles River from Harvard Stadium. Only used during Harvard football games, last known use November 18, 1967
Harvard/Brattle	Harvard Square, Cambridge	March 24, 1979	Closed September 1, 1983, supplemented Harvard during construction of the Alewife extension
♿ Harvard	Harvard Square, Cambridge	September 6, 1983	Original station opened March 23, 1912 and closed January 30, 1981, Harvard/Holyoke opened January 31, 1981 and closed September 1, 1983
♿ Central	Central Square, Cambridge	March 23, 1912	
♿ Kendall/MIT	Kendall Square, Cambridge	March 23, 1912	originally Kendall until August 6, 1978, named Cambridge Center/MIT between December 2, 1982 and June 25, 1985
♿ Charles/MGH	Cambridge and Charles Streets, Boston	February 27, 1932	originally Charles until December 1973
♿ Park Street	Park, Tremont, and Winter Streets, Boston	March 23, 1912	Green Line originally Park Street Under
♿ Downtown Crossing	Summer, Washington, and Winter Streets, Boston	April 4, 1915	Orange Line and Silver Line Phase I originally Washington until May 3, 1987
♿ South Station	Dewey Square, Boston	December 3, 1916	Silver Line Phase II and MBTA Commuter Rail south side lines Had a transfer to the Atlantic Avenue Elevated
♿ Broadway	Broadway and Dorchester Avenue, South Boston	December 15, 1917	
♿ Andrew	Andrew Square, South Boston	June 29, 1918	

North of JFK/UMass, the Red Line surfaces and separates into two branches which operate on separate platforms at JFK/UMass. Just south of the station, the two branches divide as described below.

♿ JFK/UMass	Columbia Road and Morrissey Boulevard, Dorchester	November 5, 1927	MBTA Commuter Rail, Plymouth/Kingston Line and Middleborough/Lakeville Line originally Columbia until December 1, 1982, Braintree platform opened December 14, 1988 was called Crescent Avenue as an Old Colony Railroad station

Ashmont Branch

Diverging from JFK/UMass:

Station	Location	Opened	Transfers and notes
♿ Savin Hill	Savin Hill Avenue and Sydney Street	November 5, 1927	was an Old Colony Railroad station
Harrison Square			former split and transfer station between the Old Colony Railroad mainline and the Shawmut Branch Railroad, never a rapid transit station
♿ Fields Corner	Charles Street and Dorchester Avenue	November 5, 1927	was a Shawmut Branch Railroad station
♿ Shawmut	Dayton Street	September 1, 1928	
♿ Ashmont	Ashmont Street and Dorchester Avenue	September 1, 1928	Continuing service to Mattapan via the 10-minute Ashmont-Mattapan High Speed Line (opened December 21, 1929) was a Shawmut Branch Railroad station Cedar Grove station on the Shawmut Branch Railroad is now a station on the Mattapan Line, after which the line merges with the former Dorchester and Milton Branch Railroad right-of-way

Braintree Branch

Diverging from JFK/UMass:

Station	Location	Opened	Transfers and notes
♿ North Quincy	East Squantum and Hancock Streets, Quincy	September 1, 1971	
Wollaston	Newport Avenue and Beale Street, Quincy	September 1, 1971	
♿ Quincy Center	Hancock and Washington Streets, Quincy	September 1, 1971	MBTA Commuter Rail, Plymouth/Kingston Line and Middleborough/Lakeville Line
♿ Quincy Adams	Burgin Parkway and Centre Street, Quincy	September 10, 1983	Park and ride
♿ Braintree	Ivory and Union Streets, Braintree	March 22, 1980	MBTA Commuter Rail, Plymouth/Kingston Line and Middleborough/Lakeville Line Park and ride

External links

- MBTA - Red Line [2]
- nycsubway.org - MBTA Red Line [3]

References

- Changes to Transit Service in the MBTA district [4] (PDF)
- Railroad History Database [5]

Alewife (MBTA station)

Alewife Station	
"T" sign and top of glass pyramid from roof-level parking deck of Alewife Station	
Station statistics	
Address	11 Cambridgepark West, Cambridge, MA 02140
Coordinates	42°23′47″N 71°08′31″W
Lines	Red Line
Platforms	1 center island
Parking	2,733 space garage
Bicycle facilities	~500 spaces total, 300 in two secured cages
Other information	
Opened	March 30, 1985
Accessible	♿
Owned by	Massachusetts Bay Transportation Authority
Services	
Preceding station	Ⓣ MBTA	**Following station**

Alewife Station, located at the intersection of Alewife Brook Parkway and Cambridgepark West in Cambridge, Massachusetts, is a local intermodal transportation hub. It is the northern terminus of the MBTA's Red Line, and a bus terminal for several local routes. It opened on March 30, 1985. [citation needed]

The station is named after Alewife Brook, a nearby tributary of the Mystic River. The alewife is a species of fish which inhabits the Mystic River system.

The station is unusual among MBTA stations for using Eurostile as a typeface for signage instead of Helvetica.

Its facilities include:

- A 2733-space multi-level "park and ride" garage, with a direct connection to Route 2
- Bicycle parking for approximately 500 bicycles. Two gated bike parking cages were added in 2008. Access is controlled by special Bike CharlieCards
- a Zipcar location in the employee parking area
- Connections to the Minuteman Bikeway, the Cambridge Linear Park and the Fitchburg Cutoff Path
- Pedestrian access to East Arlington, via the Minuteman Bikeway and Thorndike Street in Arlington
- A retail area with food and services
- Several works of public art commissioned for the station, including carved benches in the passenger pickup area.

Terminating bus routes

- 62 Bedford V.A. Hospital via Lexington Center and Arlington Heights
- 67 Turkey Hill via Arlington Center
- 76 Hanscom/Lincoln Lab via Lexington Center
- 79 Arlington Heights
- 83 Central Square Cambridge via Inman Square (terminates nearby at Russell Field)
- 84 Arlmont Village
- 350 North Burlington
- 351 Oak Park/Bedford Woods
- The Route 128 Business Council provides daily shuttle bus services from Alewife traveling to many companies along the Route 2 and Route 128 corridor.

History

Boston transportation planners expected to build an Inner Belt within the Route 128 corridor in the 1970s. MA Route 2 was designed with eight lanes to carry large volumes of radial traffic, east from Alewife Brook Parkway, through Cambridge and Somerville to the Inner Belt at the border of eastern Somerville and eastern Cambridge. When the Inner Belt was canceled, Route 2 became an overbuilt highway that terminated at what was little more than major city streets. When the westward extension of the Red Line was being designed, building a station near the end of Route 2 with a large parking garage seemed like a way to capitalize on the original Route 2 investment.

There was little near the site of the Alewife station besides a largely abandoned industrial park, a chemical factory and a protected wetlands. Following principles that came to be known as transit-oriented development, the City of Cambridge zoned the area immediately near the station for high rise buildings. Over the next 20 years, a mini-city developed with office and research and development buildings, along with high rise housing.

A state law required planning the Red Line Extension so it could later be brought out to Route 128 to Bedford, via Arlington and Lexington, along the route of the former Lexington and West Cambridge Railroad. The Red line tracks extend past the station, under Route 2, and terminate in a small underground storage yard.

When the adjacent chemical plant eventually closed and was replaced by an office and hotel development, the rail spur to the plant (along a short remaining portion of the Fitchburg Cutoff) was no longer needed and its underpass was converted to an access ramp from the station to Route 2.[citation needed]

Expansion

On September 18, 2008, two bike parking cages opened at the Alewife station. The cages can hold up to 150 bikes each. To use these cages, one must obtain a free plastic **Bike CharlieCard**, similar to the CharlieCard used to board the trains. Cards can be obtained from the MBTA customer service agents at Alewife station, or at the MBTA customer service center at Downtown Crossing station. Though the cages are covered, enclosed with security fences, and watched by security cameras, the MBTA advises riders to lock their bikes.

As of April 2008, the MBTA has said that they do not have funds to add two levels to the parking garage to add capacity, which would cost $30 million to $35 million and add about 1300 spaces. The structure was originally designed to have two more levels, but whether the condition of the structure and building codes would allow that today is not clear.

Gallery

High-density development at
Alewife

Looking
down to the
concourse
from the
escalator

Bicycle parking

The MBTA's "T"
logo on the side of
the station.

The metal T
sculpture
outside the
station

Attractions

- Alewife Brook Reservation, a wetlands conservation area with walking trails, adjacent to the station on the north side. The station is named after the fish in the reservation's Little River.
- Fresh Pond reservation
- Fresh Pond Shopping Center and cinema
- The Rindge Avenue Extension office park
- Russell Field and Danehy Park
- The Minuteman Trail

External links

- Alewife Station website [1]
- Google map [2]

Porter (MBTA station)

Porter Station	
Red Line inbound platform, January 2005	
Station statistics	
Address	Somerville and Massachusetts Avenue intersection Cambridge, MA
Coordinates	42°23′18.0″N 71°07′08.5″W
Lines	Fitchburg Line Red Line
Platforms	on separate levels
Parking	no spaces
Bicycle facilities	34 spaces
Other information	
Opened	December 8, 1984
Accessible	♿
Owned by	Massachusetts Bay Transportation Authority
Fare zone	1A
Services	

Preceding station	Ⓣ MBTA	Following station

Porter is a train station in Cambridge, Massachusetts. It is located at the intersection of Massachusetts Avenue and Somerville Avenue (Porter Square). It also serves portions of Somerville. The station was designed by Cambridge Seven Associates and opened on December 8, 1984. At 105 feet below ground, it is the deepest station in the Boston area. Its facilities include:

- A stop on the Boston subway's Red Line
- A stop on the MBTA Commuter Rail Fitchburg Line
- Bus and trolleybus connections at street level, including the Number 77 Massachusetts Avenue bus.
- Bicycle parking
- An unusually deep set of escalators (143 feet long) descending three levels, with fixed stairs next to them (steps, descending: 60+117+22 = 199 total).

- Public art includes *Glove Cycle* [1] by Mags Harries, an installation of bronze castings of lost gloves flowing down the escalator and scattered throughout the station, and Susumu Shingu's "Gift of the Wind" at street level.

Porter station's unusual depth is due to the MBTA's decision to build the station in rock rather than soft clay, saving time and money in the construction process.

The Porter Square article describes nearby attractions.

The station has no automobile parking. It is inadvisable to park in the nearby shopping center and take the train; they will tow. Somerville residents with permits may be able to park on Somerville Avenue near the station.

Porter Square Station is wheelchair accessible, with a short high platform at the commuter rail tracks. See MBTA accessibility.

Fitchburg Line commuter railroad platform

External links

- MBTA Commuter Rail [2] and Red Line [3]

Lechmere (MBTA station)

<table>
<tr><td colspan="2" align="center">Lechmere</td></tr>
<tr><td colspan="2" align="center">
Lechmere Station</td></tr>
<tr><td colspan="2" align="center">Station statistics</td></tr>
<tr><td>Address</td><td>Cambridge Street at O'Brien Highway
East Cambridge, Massachusetts</td></tr>
<tr><td>Coordinates</td><td>42°22′14.93″N 71°4′36.94″W</td></tr>
<tr><td>Lines</td><td>Green Line "E" Branch</td></tr>
<tr><td>Platforms</td><td>1 balloon loop</td></tr>
<tr><td>Tracks</td><td>1 (in effect 2)</td></tr>
<tr><td>Parking</td><td>347 spaces</td></tr>
<tr><td colspan="2" align="center">Other information</td></tr>
<tr><td>Opened</td><td>July 10, 1922</td></tr>
<tr><td>Rebuilt</td><td>2010</td></tr>
<tr><td>Accessible</td><td align="center">♿</td></tr>
<tr><td>Owned by</td><td>MBTA</td></tr>
<tr><td colspan="2" align="center">Traffic</td></tr>
<tr><td>Passengers (1997)</td><td>1.409 million ▬ 0%</td></tr>
<tr><td colspan="2" align="center">Services</td></tr>
<tr><td>Preceding station</td><td>Ⓣ MBTA</td></tr>
</table>

Preceding station	Ⓣ MBTA	Following station

Lechmere is the northern terminus of the MBTA Green Line. It is located in Lechmere Square in East Cambridge, Massachusetts, near the intersection of Cambridge Street and Monsignor O'Brien Highway (Route 28). The tracks make a loop at Lechmere, with a small yard. The station will be replaced in 2010 by a new facility located on the east side of the O'Brien Highway, with a direct connection to the Somerville Community Path.

Lechmere station is near the former site of a well known Lechmere Department Store by the same name. The store has been replaced by a large shopping mall, the CambridgeSide Galleria. The MBTA is working on a proposal to extend the Green Line northwest through Somerville, Massachusetts and into Medford, Massachusetts, called the "Green Line Extension Project", next to the Lowell and Fitchburg Lines of the Commuter Rail.

History

The concrete Lechmere Viaduct leading up to the station opened on June 1, 1912. At the Lechmere end, there was no station, but track connections to existing streetcar lines on Cambridge Street and Bridge Street (now O'Brien Highway), which had continued downtown via the Charles River Dam Bridge. Due to schedule problems caused by delays on the surface propagating into the subway, a new prepayment station opened on July 10, 1922, and the existing loop was built to turn subway cars, while surface cars also looped on a separate track. As most if not all existing subway service from the south and west looped at Park Street, a new service was inaugurated between Lechmere and the Pleasant Street Incline. Beginning January 2, 1923, this was changed to loop at Kenmore (a surface station at the time), and some trips were extended along the Beacon Street Line to loop at Washington Square. On February 7, 1931, Commonwealth Avenue and Beacon Street service was extended from Park Street to Lechmere, and this separate service was removed.

On February 11, 1983, a Lechmere-Government Center shuttle was brought back during rush hours and middays, due to the "E" Branch, which had been the only service to Lechmere at those times, being closed by a snowstorm. This shuttle stayed even once the "E" Branch reopened, last running over 14 years later, on June 21, 1997. From December 28, 1985 to July 25, 1986, additional shuttle service ran between Lechmere and Kenmore.

Lechmere was planned for closure June 18, 2004, but fire alarm systems at North Station had to be tested more. Lechmere closed one week later, in the evening of June 25, and the Green Line Bus Shuttle to Government Center began operating. The "D" Branch was cut back to Government Center at that time, but "E" trains continued operating to Lechmere, with additional shuttle service added to Government Center. The new alignment opened November 12, 2005, returning streetcar service to Lechmere.

The 77 (renumbered 69 ca. 1967) streetcar to Harvard became the first trackless trolley in the Boston area on April 11, 1936. The 87 and 88 streetcar routes were replaced with trackless trolleys on November 8, 1941, and with buses March 30, 1963; the 77 became a bus route on March 31. The 80 ran to Sullivan Square as a streetcar, and was replaced with a bus to Lechmere on July 9, 1932. It later too became a trackless trolley route before reverting back to bus on March 29, 1963.

Future plans

The MBTA has broken ground on construction of a new Lechmere station, located on the opposite side of McGrath/O'Brien Highway, in the NorthPoint project [1] and part of North Point Park (Cambridge, Massachusetts). Planned to open in 2010, the station relocation will enable the Green Line Extension into Somerville and Medford, and the connection of the associated Somerville Community Path bicycle and pedestrian route.

The moved Lechmere station is a proposed stop on the MBTA's planned Urban Ring Project. The Urban Ring will be a Bus Rapid Transit (BRT) Line designed to connect the current MBTA Lines to reduce strain on the downtown stations.

Timeline

This timeline shows which services extended through to Lechmere at which times (before 1922, surface routes simply entered the viaduct at Lechmere).

Bus connections

- 69 Harvard/Holyoke Gate via Cambridge St.
- 80 Arlington Center via Medford Hillside
- 87 Arlington Center or Clarendon Hill via Somerville Ave.
- 88 Clarendon Hill via Highland Avenue
- EZRide Cambridge - North Station

Accessibility

The station is accessible when served by the MBTA's newer low-floor light rail vehicles. It is an alternative to the non-accessible Science Park stop for visiting the Museum of Science, Boston. See MBTA accessibility.

References

- Changes to Transit Service in the MBTA district [4] (PDF)

External links

- MBTA Green Line -- Lechmere Station [1]

Massachusetts Route 2

WARNING: Article could not be rendered - ouputting plain text.

Potential causes of the problem are: (a) a bug in the pdf-writer software (b) problematic Mediawiki markup (c) table is too wide

Route 2Route informationLength: 142.29 miExecutive Office of Transportation (Massachusetts)Executive Office of Transportation, Office of Transportation Planning - 2005 Road Inventory (228.99 km)Existed: 1927, 1971 (current alignment) – presentMajor junctionsWest end: NY Route 2 in Petersburgh, New YorkPetersburgh, NY I-91 (MA)I-91 in Greenfield (MA)Greenfield U.S. Route 202US 202 in Athol, MassachusettsAthol Interstate 190 (Massachusetts)I-190 in Leominster, MassachusettsLeominster I-495 (MA)I-495 in Littleton, MassachusettsLittleton I-95 (MA)I-95/Route 128 (Massachusetts)Route 128 in Lexington (MA)Lexington US 3 (MA)US 3/Route 16 (Massachusetts)Route 16 in Cambridge (MA)Cambridge U.S. Route 20US 20 in BostonEast end: Route 28 (Massachusetts)Route 28 in BostonHighway systemList of numbered routes in MassachusettsMassachusetts State Highway Routes← Massachusetts Route 1ARoute 1AMassachusetts Route 2ARoute 2A →← Route 6B (New England)Route 6BNew England road marking systemN.E.Route 8 (New England)Route 8 → Route 2 is a major east–west state highway in Massachusetts, parts of which are sometimes known as the Cambridge and Concord Turnpike. Along with Route 9 (Massachusetts)Route 9 and U.S. Route 20 to the South, these highways are the main alternatives to the Massachusetts Turnpike/Interstate 90 in MassachusettsI-90 toll highway. Route 2 runs the entire length of the northern tier of Massachusetts, beginning at the New York border, where it connects with New York State Route 2, and ending near Boston Common (park)Boston Common in Boston.Route description Route 2 proceeds east from the New York state line on a winding, scenic path in Williamstown, MassachusettsWilliamstown. It serves the Williams College area and North Adams, MassachusettsNorth Adams. East of North Adams, Route 2 ascends via a hairpin turn into the Berkshire Mountains along the old Mohawk Trail. It then goes from Berkshire County into Franklin County, Massachusetts, running into Interstate 91 at an road junction#Interchangesinterchange in Greenfield, MassachusettsGreenfield and briefly runs concurrent with the interstate highway. At this point the old Route 2 becomes Route 2A (Massachusetts)Route 2A and goes through downtown

Greenfield. Route 2, however, exits off I-91, becoming a freeway briefly before becoming a two-lane freeway. Outside of Greenfield, Route 2A temporarily ends and merges with Route 2. Route 2 then becomes a regular two-lane surface road in Gill, MassachusettsGill and through Erving though it has some grade-separated interchanges in Millers Falls, MassachusettsMillers Falls at its intersection with Route 63 (Massachusetts)Route 63. There is another gap in the two-lane freeway in the Erving, MassachusettsErving area. Recently, the road in Erving was routed to the north and straightened to avoid the paper mill next to the river. This rerouting led to the road being shortened by less than a tenth of a mile. Once the road enters the Orange, MassachusettsTown of Orange, Route 2A resumes and breaks off Route 2. At this point Route 2 again becomes a two-lane freeway. In Orange, Route 2 runs concurrent with U.S. Route 202. The road at this point enters the town of Athol in Worcester County, Massachusetts. After its eastern interchange in Phillipston, MassachusettsPhillipston when US 202 breaks off to the north, Route 2 becomes a full four-lane freeway, though not to Interstate standards in most points. It continues through Gardner, MassachusettsGardner and Leominster, MassachusettsLeominster, where Interstate 190 (Massachusetts)Interstate 190 begins, heading south to Worcester, MassachusettsWorcester. In Leominster, Route 2 has several at-grade intersections with Oak Hill Road, Palmer Road, Mt. Elam Road, and Abbott Avenue. At the intersection with Mt. Elam Road, a traffic light remains in use on the eastbound side. Route 2 continues east to Middlesex County, Massachusetts. At this point it enters Boston's outer loop at the interchange with Interstate 495 (Massachusetts)Interstate 495 in Littleton. It continues as a freeway until it goes into Acton, MassachusettsActon, where it runs into Piper Road and Taylor Road at a traffic light (Exit 44). At this point the freeway ends and Route 2 becomes a regular divided highway at most points and just a four-lane highway at other points. At the Concord, MassachusettsConcord roundaboutRotary, a major traffic choke point, Route 2 intersects with Route 2A and the beginning of Route 119 (Massachusetts)Route 119 (which is overlapped with 2A at that point). After the rotary the road loses its dividing wall as it passes past the State Police (who have an emergency-only traffic light) and over the Assabet River. Route 2A used to then break away from Route 2 at the next traffic light to go left into Concord but is now overlaid with Route 2. At Crosby's Corner, the sixth intersection after the rotary, Route 2A goes straight while Route 2 veers right (but still heads east). The highway loses its dividing wall until the Bedford St intersection in Lincoln where it becomes divided again. MassHighway currently expects to rebuild the Crosby Corner intersection and create a dividing wall from there to Bedford St in 2011-2013.Massachusetts Department of Transportation, Project InformationAt this point Route 2 enters Lexington, MassachusettsLexington and still is a divided 4-lane road with surface intersections. It then heads to Boston's inner belt, crossing Interstate 95 in MassachusettsInterstate 95/Route 128 (Massachusetts)Route 128. From there, Route 2 is a six-lane and then eight-lane limited access highway until Exit 60, where it narrows with little warning to six lanes and then to four lanes. This section of freeway actually meets the standards of an interstate highway. The final off-ramp leads directly to the large parking garage at the Massachusetts Bay Transportation AuthorityMBTA Alewife Station (Massachusetts Bay Transportation Authority)Alewife Station. At this point the road heads into Cambridge, Massachusetts. Convergence of Routes 2, 3, and 16 at Alewife. The limited access freeway portion ends at a signalized intersection, where it merges with U.S. Route 3 south and Route 16 (Massachusetts)Route 16 west in Cambridge, MassachusettsCambridge and continues as a four-lane surface road to the Boston Public Garden. Route 2 follows Alewife Brook Parkway, Fresh Pond Parkway, Gerry's Landing Road, and Memorial Drive (Cambridge)Memorial Drive (all parkways maintained by the Department of Conservation and Recreation) through Cambridge. It crosses into Boston on the Boston University Bridge. After crossing Commonwealth Avenue (U.S. Route 20), it follows Montfort Street and Beacon Street into Kenmore Square which is the eastern terminus of US Route 20. From Kenmore Square, Route 2 follows Commonwealth Avenue to Arlington Street. It circles the Public Garden in Boston, using Arlington Street to Boylston Street to Charles Street. Route 2 ends at Route 28 (Massachusetts)Route 28 at the intersection of Charles Street and Beacon Street between Boston Common and the Boston Public Garden. History In the early 1920s, Route 2 was known as New England road marking systemNew England Interstate Route 7 (NE-7), a major road connecting Boston with Troy, New York. NE-7 ran roughly where Route 2A (Massachusetts)Route 2A (the original surface alignment of Route 2) does now except near the New York state line. NE-7 used current Route 43 (Massachusetts), New York State Route 43 and New York State Route 66 to reach Troy. Current Route 2 from Williamstown, MassachusettsWilliamstown to Petersburgh, New YorkPetersburgh was previously numbered as Route 96.Route 2 connected as a highway in its current right-of-way at Alewife Brook Parkway at some point before 1937.http://www.schlichtman.org/mahighways/bosmap37.gifAn upgraded Route 2 was originally planned to continue as Boston's Northwest Expressway (Boston)Northwest Expressway (merging with a re-routed U.S. Route 3 at the Arlington-Lexington or Arlington-Cambridge border) to a junction with Interstate 695 (Massachusetts)Interstate 695, the Inner Beltway, but this, along with the Inner Beltway itself, was cancelled in 1970, accounting for the abrupt narrowing at Alewife.http://www.brorson.com/maps/BostonHighwayPlan_1965_Detail/BostonHPDetailLevel1.jpg In place of the highway project, the MBTA Red Line (MBTA)Red Line was extended from Harvard (MBTA station)Harvard to Alewife (MBTA station)Alewife in the 1980s. Highway Improvements2002In 2002 a $1.5 million project constructed a new concrete median barrier on Route 2 in Lincoln. 2004A $4.3 million project completed in 2004 replaced the bridge that carried Route 2 over the Minuteman Bikeway in Arlington. 2006In 2006 a $6.7 million project that reconstructed 1.1 miles of Route 2 through Concord was completed. 2008In 2008 a $925,160 project was completed that cleaned and painted the Spring Street overpass in Lexington. 2009In 2009 a $3.7 million project that resurfaced Route 2 through Lexington was completed. A $1.5 million stimulus project completed in Fall 2009 resurfaced Route 2 in Lincoln from the Lexington line to Bedford Street in Lincoln. In 2009 a $2.1 million project was completed that replaced traffic signs from the Concord Rotary to Exit 38 in Harvard. 2010 and futureA $2 million project expected for completion in 2010 is replacing traffic signs on Route 2 from Route 16 in Cambridge to Bedford Road in Lincoln. A $422,758 project expected to begin in Fall 2010 is Installing a cable barriercable median barrier on Route 2 in Lexington. The new cable barrier will prevent traffic from crossing the median. A $4 million stimulus project planned for completion in November 2010 is resurfacing two sections of Route 2 in Concord. A $4.4 million project expected for completion in December 2010 is resurfacing 3 miles of Route 2 Cambridge to Belmont. The Route 2 bridge over the Charles River in Boston (Boston University Bridge) is undergoing a $19.6 million bridge deck replacement project. The project funded by the Accelerated Bridge Program is expected for completion in November 2011. In 2011 a $1.9 million project will rebuild the intersection of Route 16 and Route 2 in Cambridge. In 2015 a $24 million project will replace the 2 bridges over I-95 in Lexington. In 2015 a $9.8 million project will replace the existing Route 2 bridge over the Sudbury River in Concord. The existing bridge was built in 1934. Crosbys Corner Improvement Project This major project has been in planning since 1999. The intersection sees an average of 90 accidents a year. The project will solve the traffic and safety problems at the very dangerous Crosby's Corner intersection (junction of Route 2 and 2A) in Concord. The project, expected to cost $71.9 million, will widen Route 2 from Bedford Road in Lincoln to 300FT west of Sandy Pond Road in Concord. The project will eliminate the at grade intersection and realign it and construct new on & off ramps along with constructing new service roads next to Route 2. The project is expected to begin in 2011. The state has recently spent between $25 & $35 million for property takings in the path of the new alignent of Route 2. In January 2010 a speeding tanker truck carrying liquid asphalt flipped over on Route 2 and crushed three cars. The truck driver was med-flighted to a Boston hospital with serious injuries. The highway was shutdown for five hours causing traffic delays for the 46,000 commuters daily. The accident put the spotlight back on the Crosby Corner project. Further information: Freeway and expressway revoltsExit listCounty Location Mile Exit Destinations Notes Berkshire_County,_MassachusettsBerkshireWilliamstown,_MassachusettsWilliamstown0.00   New York State Route 2NY 2 westEastern terminus of NY Route 2; western terminus of MA Route 2 U.S. Route 7 in MassachusettsUS 7 southSouthern end of US 7 concurrency U.S. Route 7 in MassachusettsUS 7 northNorthern end of US 7 concurrency Route 43 (Massachusetts)Route 43 southNorthern terminus of Route 43North Adams,_MassachusettsNorth Adams Route 8 (Massachusetts)Route 8 westWestern end of Route 8 concurrency Route 8 (Massachusetts)Route 8 eastEastern   end   of   Route   8 concurrencyFranklin_County,_MassachusettsFranklinCharlemont,_MassachusettsCharlemont   Route 8A (Massachusetts)Route 8A westWestern end of Route 8A concurrency Route 8A (Massachusetts)Route 8A eastEastern end of Route 8A concurrencyShelburne Falls,_MassachusettsShelburne   Falls   Route   112   (Massachusetts)Route 112Greenfield,_MassachusettsGreenfield26 Interstate 91 (Massachusetts)I-91 south / Route 2A (Massachusetts)Route 2A eastSouthern end of I-91 concurrency; western terminus of Route 2A27 Interstate 91 (Massachusetts)I-91 northNorthern end of I-91 concurrency U.S. Route 5 in MassachusettsUS 5 / Route 10 (Massachusetts)Route 10InterchangeFreeway endsTurners Falls,_MassachusettsTurners Falls Route 2A (Massachusetts)Route 2AWestern terminus of Route 2A concurrencyMillers Falls,_MassachusettsMillers Falls Route 63 (Massachusetts)Route

63InterchangeOrange,_MassachusettsOrange Route 2A (Massachusetts)Route 2A eastEastern terminus of Route 2A concurrency; Super-2 freeway begins14West River Street – Orange Center15 Route 122 (Massachusetts)Route 122 – Orange, MassachusettsOrange, Worcester, MassachusettsWorcester16 U.S. Route 202 in MassachusettsUS 202 south – Belchertown, MassachusettsBelchertownDaniel Shays Highway – Athol, MassachusettsAtholWestern end of US 202 concurrencyWorcester_County,_MassachusettsWorcesterAthol,_MassachusettsAthol17 Route 32 (Massachusetts)Route 32 – Athol, MassachusettsAthol, Petersham, MassachusettsPetershamPhillipston,_MassachusettsPhillipston18 Route 2A (Massachusetts)Route 2A – Athol, MassachusettsAthol, Phillipston, MassachusettsPhillipston19 U.S. Route 202 in MassachusettsUS 202 north / Route 2A (Massachusetts)Route 2A – Phillipston, MassachusettsPhillipston, Winchendon, MassachusettsWinchendonEastern end of US 202 concurrencyTempleton,_MassachusettsTempleton20Baldwinville Road – Templeton, MassachusettsTempleton, Baldwinville, MassachusettsBaldwinville21 Route 2A (Massachusetts)Route 2A / Route 101 (Massachusetts)Route 101 – Templeton, MassachusettsTempleton, Ashburnham, MassachusettsAshburnhamGardner,_MassachusettsGardner22 Route 68 (Massachusetts)Route 68 – Gardner, MassachusettsGardner, Hubbardston, MassachusettsHubbardston23Gardner, South GardnerWestminster,_MassachusettsWestminster24 Route 140 (Massachusetts)Route 140 north / West Main Street – Ashburnham, MassachusettsAshburnham, Winchendon, MassachusettsWinchendonWestern end of Route 140 concurrency; signed as exits 24B-A westbound25 Route 2A (Massachusetts)Route 2A / Route 140 (Massachusetts)Route 140 south – Fitchburg, MassachusettsFitchburg, Princeton, MassachusettsPrincetonEastern end of Route 140 concurrency26Willard Road, Village Inn RoadEastbound exit only27Narrows Road, Depot RoadFitchburg,_MassachusettsFitchburg28 Route 31 (Massachusetts)Route 31 – Fitchburg, MassachusettsFitchburg, Princeton, MassachusettsPrinceton(29)Mount Elam RoadAt-grade intersection with barrier in the middle of the road and flashing lightLeominster,_MassachusettsLeominster30Merriam Avenue, South Street – Leominster, MassachusettsLeominster, Fitchburg, MassachusettsFitchburg31 Route 12 (Massachusetts)Route 12 – Leominster, MassachusettsLeominster, Fitchburg, MassachusettsFitchburg32 Route 13 (Massachusetts)Route 13 – Leominster, MassachusettsLeominster, Lunenburg, MassachusettsLunenburg33 Interstate 190 (Massachusetts)I-190 south – Leominster, MassachusettsLeominster, Worcester, MassachusettsWorcesterNorthern terminus of I-190Lancaster,_MassachusettsLancaster34Mechanic Street, Harvard Street35 Route 70 (Massachusetts)Route 70 south – Lancaster, MassachusettsLancaster, Lunenburg, MassachusettsLunenburgNorthern terminus of Route 7036Shirley Road – Shirley, MassachusettsShirley37BJackson Road – Devens, MassachusettsDevens Reserve Forces Training AreaNo public access to Exit 37A (westbound)Harvard,_MassachusettsHarvard38 Route 110 (Massachusetts)Route 110 / Route 111 (Massachusetts)Route 111 – Harvard, MassachusettsHarvard, Worcester, MassachusettsWorcester, Ayer, MassachusettsAyer, Groton, MassachusettsGrotonSigned as   exits   34A   and 34BMiddlesex_County,_MassachusettsMiddlesexLittleton,_MassachusettsLittleton39Taylor Street – Littleton, MassachusettsLittleton, Boxboro, MassachusettsBoxboro40= Interstate 495 (Massachusetts)I-495 – Marlboro, MassachusettsMarlboro, Worcester, MassachusettsWorcester, Lowell, MassachusettsLowell, Lawrence, MassachusettsLawrenceSigned as exits 40A and 40BBoxborough,_MassachusettsBoxborough41Newtown Road, Central Street – West Acton, MassachusettsWest Acton, Littleton, MassachusettsLittletonActon,_MassachusettsActon42 Route 27 (Massachusetts)Route 27 – Acton, MassachusettsActon, Maynard, MassachusettsMaynard118.0043 Route 111 (Massachusetts)Route 111 north – West Acton, MassachusettsWest ActonWestbound exit and eastbound entrance only; left exitPiper Road, Taylor RoadFreeway resumes east of traffic lightConcord,_MassachusettsConcord120.60 Route 2A (Massachusetts)Route 2A Route 119 (Massachusetts)Route 119 northWestern terminus of Route 2A concurrency; southern terminus of Route 119121.60 Route 62 (Massachusetts)Route 62124.00 Route 126 (Massachusetts)Route 126 southNorthern terminus of Route 126 Route 2A (Massachusetts)Route 2A eastEastern terminus of Route 2A concurrencyLexington,_MassachusettsLexingtonFreeway resumes just east of Lincoln, MassachusettsLincoln–Lexington, MassachusettsLexington line128.7052Interstate 95 (Massachusetts)I-95 – Attleboro, MassachusettsAttleboro, Peabody, MassachusettsPeabodySigned as exits 52A and 52B53Spring Street – Lexington, MassachusettsLexington, Waltham, MassachusettsWalthamNo westbound exit54Waltham Street – Lexington, MassachusettsLexington, Waltham, MassachusettsWalthamSigned as exits 54A and 54B; westbound exits and eastbound entrances only55Pleasant Street – Lexington, MassachusettsLexington, Waltham, MassachusettsWalthamEastbound exit and westbound entrance only131.6056 Route 4 (Massachusetts)Route 4 north / Route 225 (Massachusetts)Route 225 west – Lexington, MassachusettsLexington, Bedford, MassachusettsBedfordWinter Street – WaverlySouthern terminus of Route 4; eastern terminus of Route 225Arlington,_MassachusettsArlington131.7057Dow Avenue – Arlmont, Arlington, MassachusettsArlington, Belmont, MassachusettsBelmontArlington, MassachusettsArlington–Belmont, MassachusettsBelmont58Park Avenue – Belmont, MassachusettsBelmont, Arlington Heights133.9059 Route 60 (Massachusetts)Route 60 – Arlington Center, Belmont CenterArlington,_MassachusettsArlington135.0060Lake Street – East Arlington, MassachusettsEast Arlington, Belmont, MassachusettsBelmontCambridge,_MassachusettsCambridgeAlewife (MBTA station)Alewife T StationEastbound exit only U.S. Route 3 in MassachusettsUS 3 north / Route 16 (Massachusetts)Route 16 north (Alewife Brook Parkway north)Northern terminus of US 3/Route 16 concurrency; freeway ends Route 16 (Massachusetts)Route 16 south (Huron Avenue)Southern terminus of Route 16 concurrency U.S. Route 3 in MassachusettsUS 3 south (Memorial Drive)Southern terminus of US 3; Route 2 exits Memorial Drive via the Boston University Bridge eastboundSuffolk_County,_MassachusettsSuffolkBoston,_MassachusettsBoston U.S. Route 20 in MassachusettsUS 20 west (Commonwealth Avenue)Eastern terminus of US 20 at Kenmore Square;

Route 2 leaves Beacon Street for Commonwealth Avenue eastbound Route 2A (Massachusetts)Route 2A west (Massachusetts Avenue)Eastern terminus of Route 2AArlington StreetEastern terminus of Route 21.000 mi = 1.609 km; 1.000 km = 0.621 mi   Concurrency (road)Concurrency terminus • Closed   •   Incomplete   access   •   UnopenedPhotosWestbound   in   Shelburne, MassachusettsShelburneEastbound at Whitcomb Summit in Florida, MassachusettsFlorida

Article Sources and Contributors

Cambridge, Massachusetts *Source*: http://en.wikipedia.org/?oldid=390359080 *Contributors*: Hertz1888

Kendall Square *Source*: http://en.wikipedia.org/?oldid=380455220 *Contributors*: Beland

Central Square (Cambridge) *Source*: http://en.wikipedia.org/?oldid=386785595 *Contributors*: Xeno

Harvard Square *Source*: http://en.wikipedia.org/?oldid=388625598 *Contributors*: Hertz1888

Inman Square *Source*: http://en.wikipedia.org/?oldid=389595208 *Contributors*:

Lechmere Square *Source*: http://en.wikipedia.org/?oldid=387853192 *Contributors*: Hmains

Porter Square *Source*: http://en.wikipedia.org/?oldid=389491905 *Contributors*: Woohookitty

Cambridgeport *Source*: http://en.wikipedia.org/?oldid=383533012 *Contributors*: Bmclaughlin9

Cambridge Common *Source*: http://en.wikipedia.org/?oldid=389499730 *Contributors*: Jllm06

Wellington-Harrington *Source*: http://en.wikipedia.org/?oldid=367851162 *Contributors*: Faolin42

Mid-Cambridge *Source*: http://en.wikipedia.org/?oldid=336149106 *Contributors*: Swampyank

Area 4, Cambridge *Source*: http://en.wikipedia.org/?oldid=367845467 *Contributors*: Faolin42

East Cambridge, Massachusetts *Source*: http://en.wikipedia.org/?oldid=375479962 *Contributors*: Hertz1888

Riverside, Cambridge *Source*: http://en.wikipedia.org/?oldid=367846146 *Contributors*: Faolin42

Agassiz, Cambridge, Massachusetts *Source*: http://en.wikipedia.org/?oldid=333840917 *Contributors*: Diplomacy Guy

North Cambridge, Massachusetts *Source*: http://en.wikipedia.org/?oldid=383164979 *Contributors*: Hertz1888

West Cambridge (neighborhood) *Source*: http://en.wikipedia.org/?oldid=369831774 *Contributors*: Faolin42

Peabody, Cambridge, Massachusetts *Source*: http://en.wikipedia.org/?oldid=369832000 *Contributors*: Faolin42

Cambridge Highlands *Source*: http://en.wikipedia.org/?oldid=386020286 *Contributors*: Hertz1888

Strawberry Hill, Cambridge *Source*: http://en.wikipedia.org/?oldid=367850762 *Contributors*: Faolin42

Asa Gray House *Source*: http://en.wikipedia.org/?oldid=366655291 *Contributors*:

Elmwood (Cambridge, Massachusetts) *Source*: http://en.wikipedia.org/?oldid=387955497 *Contributors*: Midnightdreary

Hooper-Lee-Nichols House *Source*: http://en.wikipedia.org/?oldid=352576813 *Contributors*: Hmains

Cooper-Frost-Austin House *Source*: http://en.wikipedia.org/?oldid=351904960 *Contributors*: Hmains

Cambridge Public Library *Source*: http://en.wikipedia.org/?oldid=389510403 *Contributors*: Jllm06

Middlesex County Courthouse (Massachusetts) *Source*: http://en.wikipedia.org/?oldid=365051572 *Contributors*: Hmains

Cambridge, Massachusetts City Hall *Source*: http://en.wikipedia.org/?oldid=380775942 *Contributors*: Vegaswikian

Austin Hall (Harvard University) *Source*: http://en.wikipedia.org/?oldid=365732896 *Contributors*: Ale jrb

Memorial Hall (Harvard University) *Source*: http://en.wikipedia.org/?oldid=379808394 *Contributors*: Chris the speller

Kresge Auditorium *Source*: http://en.wikipedia.org/?oldid=390614562 *Contributors*: Look2See1

Stata Center *Source*: http://en.wikipedia.org/?oldid=390616353 *Contributors*: Look2See1

Massachusetts Institute of Technology *Source*: http://en.wikipedia.org/?oldid=390466722 *Contributors*: 1 anonymous edits

Traditions and student activities at MIT *Source*: http://en.wikipedia.org/?oldid=389556285 *Contributors*:

Longfellow Bridge *Source*: http://en.wikipedia.org/?oldid=389569857 *Contributors*: Jllm06

Charles River *Source*: http://en.wikipedia.org/?oldid=390665111 *Contributors*: Ospalh

MIT Museum *Source*: http://en.wikipedia.org/?oldid=363773237 *Contributors*: 1 anonymous edits

Harvard Art Museums *Source*: http://en.wikipedia.org/?oldid=373206987 *Contributors*: Cjs2111

Harvard Museum of Natural History *Source*: http://en.wikipedia.org/?oldid=359116381 *Contributors*: Hmnh2010

Harvard University Herbaria *Source*: http://en.wikipedia.org/?oldid=387645578 *Contributors*: 1 anonymous edits

Harvard Mineralogical Museum *Source*: http://en.wikipedia.org/?oldid=306927113 *Contributors*: Dmadeo

Museum of Comparative Zoology *Source*: http://en.wikipedia.org/?oldid=372350195 *Contributors*:

Busch–Reisinger Museum *Source*: http://en.wikipedia.org/?oldid=373207144 *Contributors*: Cjs2111

Fogg Museum *Source*: http://en.wikipedia.org/?oldid=373206603 *Contributors*: Cjs2111

Arthur M. Sackler Museum *Source*: http://en.wikipedia.org/?oldid=373206731 *Contributors*: Cjs2111

Glass Flowers *Source*: http://en.wikipedia.org/?oldid=385732687 *Contributors*:

Peabody Museum of Archaeology and Ethnology *Source*: http://en.wikipedia.org/?oldid=384341469 *Contributors*:

Semitic Museum *Source*: http://en.wikipedia.org/?oldid=388763029 *Contributors*: Wikiklrsc

MIT Chapel *Source*: http://en.wikipedia.org/?oldid=390615886 *Contributors*: Look2See1

St. John's Roman Catholic Church *Source*: http://en.wikipedia.org/?oldid=390554874 *Contributors*: 1 anonymous edits

Christ Church (Cambridge, Massachusetts) *Source*: http://en.wikipedia.org/?oldid=389698518 *Contributors*: Jllm06

First Church of Christ, Scientist (Cambridge, Massachusetts) *Source*: http://en.wikipedia.org/?oldid=328647280 *Contributors*:

The First Parish in Cambridge *Source*: http://en.wikipedia.org/?oldid=389708210 *Contributors*: Jllm06

Memorial Church of Harvard University *Source*: http://en.wikipedia.org/?oldid=389698726 *Contributors*: Jllm06

Harvard-Epworth United Methodist Church *Source*: http://en.wikipedia.org/?oldid=389706675 *Contributors*: Jllm06

Longfellow National Historic Site *Source*: http://en.wikipedia.org/?oldid=389536010 *Contributors*: Midnightdreary

List Visual Arts Center *Source*: http://en.wikipedia.org/?oldid=382140460 *Contributors*: Leszek Jańczuk

Carpenter Center for the Visual Arts *Source*: http://en.wikipedia.org/?oldid=390615702 *Contributors*: Look2See1

Walden Street Cattle Pass *Source*: http://en.wikipedia.org/?oldid=356908753 *Contributors*: Hertz1888

Lexington and West Cambridge Railroad *Source*: http://en.wikipedia.org/?oldid=387645127 *Contributors*: Hertz1888

Alewife Linear Park *Source*: http://en.wikipedia.org/?oldid=351212420 *Contributors*: Hmains

Harvard Bridge *Source*: http://en.wikipedia.org/?oldid=389553080 *Contributors*: Jllm06

Harvard Yard *Source*: http://en.wikipedia.org/?oldid=386858947 *Contributors*: Ucucha

Mount Auburn Cemetery *Source*: http://en.wikipedia.org/?oldid=390049786 *Contributors*: M2545

Alewife Brook Reservation *Source*: http://en.wikipedia.org/?oldid=383385930 *Contributors*:

Fresh Pond (Cambridge, Massachusetts) *Source*: http://en.wikipedia.org/?oldid=378221535 *Contributors*: 1 anonymous edits

Minuteman Bikeway *Source*: http://en.wikipedia.org/?oldid=385853995 *Contributors*: Twp

Harvard Lampoon *Source*: http://en.wikipedia.org/?oldid=390493737 *Contributors*: Navalmoney

Harvard Lampoon Building *Source*: http://en.wikipedia.org/?oldid=362493940 *Contributors*: Kenilworth Terrace

Logan International Airport *Source*: http://en.wikipedia.org/?oldid=390642283 *Contributors*: Pentawing

Massachusetts Route 2A *Source*: http://en.wikipedia.org/?oldid=369380170 *Contributors*: TwinsMetsFan

Massachusetts Route 16 *Source*: http://en.wikipedia.org/?oldid=375675269 *Contributors*: Breffni Whelan

Red Line (MBTA) *Source*: http://en.wikipedia.org/?oldid=389629112 *Contributors*: Grk1011

Alewife (MBTA station) *Source*: http://en.wikipedia.org/?oldid=386147123 *Contributors*: ArnoldReinhold

Porter (MBTA station) *Source*: http://en.wikipedia.org/?oldid=386941867 *Contributors*: Mackensen

Lechmere (MBTA station) *Source*: http://en.wikipedia.org/?oldid=351181355 *Contributors*: Dogru144

Massachusetts Route 2 *Source*: http://en.wikipedia.org/?oldid=390531088 *Contributors*: 1 anonymous edits

Image Sources, Licenses and Contributors

File:CambridgeMACityHall2.jpg *Source*: http://bibliocm.bibliolabs.com/mwAnon/index.php?title=File:CambridgeMACityHall2.jpg *License*: unknown *Contributors*: -

File:Cambridge_ma_highlight.png *Source*: http://bibliocm.bibliolabs.com/mwAnon/index.php?title=File:Cambridge_ma_highlight.png *License*: unknown *Contributors*: -

Image:Middlesex Canal (Massachusetts) map, 1852.jpg *Source*: http://bibliocm.bibliolabs.com/mwAnon/index.php?title=File:Middlesex_Canal_(Massachusetts)_map,_1852.jpg *License*: unknown *Contributors*: -

Image:Charles River Cambridge USA.jpg *Source*: http://bibliocm.bibliolabs.com/mwAnon/index.php?title=File:Charles_River_Cambridge_USA.jpg *License*: unknown *Contributors*: -

File:Centralsquarecambridgemass.jpg *Source*: http://bibliocm.bibliolabs.com/mwAnon/index.php?title=File:Centralsquarecambridgemass.jpg *License*: unknown *Contributors*: Vrysxy

File:Harvard square 2009j.JPG *Source*: http://bibliocm.bibliolabs.com/mwAnon/index.php?title=File:Harvard_square_2009j.JPG *License*: GNU Free Documentation License *Contributors*: chensiyuan

File:Cambridge MA Inman Square.jpg *Source*: http://bibliocm.bibliolabs.com/mwAnon/index.php?title=File:Cambridge_MA_Inman_Square.jpg *License*: unknown *Contributors*: -

File:Alewife Brook Reservation.jpg *Source*: http://bibliocm.bibliolabs.com/mwAnon/index.php?title=File:Alewife_Brook_Reservation.jpg *License*: unknown *Contributors*: -

File:MIT Main Campus Aerial.jpg *Source*: http://bibliocm.bibliolabs.com/mwAnon/index.php?title=File:MIT_Main_Campus_Aerial.jpg *License*: unknown *Contributors*: -

File:Dunster House.jpg *Source*: http://bibliocm.bibliolabs.com/mwAnon/index.php?title=File:Dunster_House.jpg *License*: unknown *Contributors*: -

Image:Cambridge Public Library, Cambridge, Massachusetts.JPG *Source*: http://bibliocm.bibliolabs.com/mwAnon/index.php?title=File:Cambridge_Public_Library,_Cambridge,_Massachusetts.JPG *License*: unknown *Contributors*: -

File:Cambridge Skyline.jpg *Source*: http://bibliocm.bibliolabs.com/mwAnon/index.php?title=File:Cambridge_Skyline.jpg *License*: unknown *Contributors*: -

File:Harvard Square at Peabody Street and Mass Avenue.jpg *Source*: http://bibliocm.bibliolabs.com/mwAnon/index.php?title=File:Harvard_Square_at_Peabody_Street_and_Mass_Avenue.jpg *License*: unknown *Contributors*: -

File:Central MBTA station.jpg *Source*: http://bibliocm.bibliolabs.com/mwAnon/index.php?title=File:Central_MBTA_station.jpg *License*: unknown *Contributors*: -

File:Weeks Footbridge Cambridge, MA.jpg *Source*: http://bibliocm.bibliolabs.com/mwAnon/index.php?title=File:Weeks_Footbridge_Cambridge,_MA.jpg *License*: unknown *Contributors*: -

File:Fogg.jpg *Source*: http://bibliocm.bibliolabs.com/mwAnon/index.php?title=File:Fogg.jpg *License*: unknown *Contributors*: -

Image:Longfellow National Historic Site, Cambridge, Massachusetts.JPG *Source*: http://bibliocm.bibliolabs.com/mwAnon/index.php?title=File:Longfellow_National_Historic_Site,_Cambridge,_Massachusetts.JPG *License*: GNU Free Documentation License *Contributors*: Daderot at en.wikipedia

File:Wfm stata center.jpg *Source*: http://bibliocm.bibliolabs.com/mwAnon/index.php?title=File:Wfm_stata_center.jpg *License*: unknown *Contributors*: -

File:Simmons Hall, MIT, Cambridge, Massachusetts.JPG *Source*: http://bibliocm.bibliolabs.com/mwAnon/index.php?title=File:Simmons_Hall,_MIT,_Cambridge,_Massachusetts.JPG *License*: unknown *Contributors*: -

File:Flag of the United Kingdom.svg *Source*: http://bibliocm.bibliolabs.com/mwAnon/index.php?title=File:Flag_of_the_United_Kingdom.svg *License*: unknown *Contributors*: -

File:Flag of Portugal.svg *Source*: http://bibliocm.bibliolabs.com/mwAnon/index.php?title=File:Flag_of_Portugal.svg *License*: unknown *Contributors*: -

File:Flag of Cuba.svg *Source*: http://bibliocm.bibliolabs.com/mwAnon/index.php?title=File:Flag_of_Cuba.svg *License*: unknown *Contributors*: -

File:Flag of Italy.svg *Source*: http://bibliocm.bibliolabs.com/mwAnon/index.php?title=File:Flag_of_Italy.svg *License*: unknown *Contributors*: -

File:Flag of Ireland.svg *Source*: http://bibliocm.bibliolabs.com/mwAnon/index.php?title=File:Flag_of_Ireland.svg *License*: unknown *Contributors*: -

File:Flag of Armenia.svg *Source*: http://bibliocm.bibliolabs.com/mwAnon/index.php?title=File:Flag_of_Armenia.svg *License*: unknown *Contributors*: -

File:Flag of El Salvador.svg *Source*: http://bibliocm.bibliolabs.com/mwAnon/index.php?title=File:Flag_of_El_Salvador.svg *License*: unknown *Contributors*: -

File:Flag of Japan.svg *Source*: http://bibliocm.bibliolabs.com/mwAnon/index.php?title=File:Flag_of_Japan.svg *License*: unknown *Contributors*: -

File:Flag of Poland.svg *Source*: http://bibliocm.bibliolabs.com/mwAnon/index.php?title=File:Flag_of_Poland.svg *License*: unknown *Contributors*: -

File:Flag of Indonesia.svg *Source*: http://bibliocm.bibliolabs.com/mwAnon/index.php?title=File:Flag_of_Indonesia.svg *License*: unknown *Contributors*: -

Image:Galaxy_Cambridge.jpg *Source*: http://bibliocm.bibliolabs.com/mwAnon/index.php?title=File:Galaxy_Cambridge.jpg *License*: unknown *Contributors*: -

Image:Kendall Square.jpg *Source*: http://bibliocm.bibliolabs.com/mwAnon/index.php?title=File:Kendall_Square.jpg *License*: unknown *Contributors*: -

File:Cambridge_biotech.jpg *Source*: http://bibliocm.bibliolabs.com/mwAnon/index.php?title=File:Cambridge_biotech.jpg *License*: unknown *Contributors*: -

File:Akamai Technologies.jpg *Source*: http://bibliocm.bibliolabs.com/mwAnon/index.php?title=File:Akamai_Technologies.jpg *License*: unknown *Contributors*: -

File:USA Massachusetts location map.svg *Source*: http://bibliocm.bibliolabs.com/mwAnon/index.php?title=File:USA_Massachusetts_location_map.svg *License*: unknown *Contributors*: -

File:Red pog.svg *Source*: http://bibliocm.bibliolabs.com/mwAnon/index.php?title=File:Red_pog.svg *License*: unknown *Contributors*: -

File:harvard square 2009j.JPG *Source*: http://bibliocm.bibliolabs.com/mwAnon/index.php?title=File:Harvard_square_2009j.JPG *License*: GNU Free Documentation License *Contributors*: chensiyuan

File:Car Talk Plaza.jpg *Source*: http://bibliocm.bibliolabs.com/mwAnon/index.php?title=File:Car_Talk_Plaza.jpg *License*: Creative Commons Attribution 2.0 *Contributors*: Patricia Drury

Image:Harvard Square, view in 1869.jpg *Source*: http://bibliocm.bibliolabs.com/mwAnon/index.php?title=File:Harvard_Square,_view_in_1869.jpg *License*: Public Domain *Contributors*: Photographer unnamed.

Contributors: -

File:Minuteman Bikeway Sonik art.jpg *Source*: http://bibliocm.bibliolabs.com/mwAnon/index.php?title=File:Minuteman_Bikeway_Sonik_art.jpg *License*: unknown *Contributors*: -

Image:KBOS Aerial NGS.jpg *Source*: http://bibliocm.bibliolabs.com/mwAnon/index.php?title=File:KBOS_Aerial_NGS.jpg *License*: unknown *Contributors*: -

File:Airplane_silhouette.svg *Source*: http://bibliocm.bibliolabs.com/mwAnon/index.php?title=File:Airplane_silhouette.svg *License*: unknown *Contributors*: -

File:BOS Airport New.png *Source*: http://bibliocm.bibliolabs.com/mwAnon/index.php?title=File:BOS_Airport_New.png *License*: unknown *Contributors*: -

Image:Boston Logan Airport from Terminal E.JPG *Source*: http://bibliocm.bibliolabs.com/mwAnon/index.php?title=File:Boston_Logan_Airport_from_Terminal_E.JPG *License*: unknown *Contributors*: -

Image:USA Boston airport loading MA.jpg *Source*: http://bibliocm.bibliolabs.com/mwAnon/index.php?title=File:USA_Boston_airport_loading_MA.jpg *License*: unknown *Contributors*: -

Image:Boston Logan Interntional Airport control tower (2009).jpg *Source*: http://bibliocm.bibliolabs.com/mwAnon/index.php?title=File:Boston_Logan_Interntional_Airport_control_tower_(2009).jpg *License*: unknown *Contributors*: -

Image:Loganairportwithplane.JPG *Source*: http://bibliocm.bibliolabs.com/mwAnon/index.php?title=File:Loganairportwithplane.JPG *License*: unknown *Contributors*: -

Image:Logan Airport International Arrivals Hall.jpg *Source*: http://bibliocm.bibliolabs.com/mwAnon/index.php?title=File:Logan_Airport_International_Arrivals_Hall.jpg *License*: unknown *Contributors*: -

File:Terminal A, Logan International Airport, Boston.jpg *Source*: http://bibliocm.bibliolabs.com/mwAnon/index.php?title=File:Terminal_A,_Logan_International_Airport,_Boston.jpg *License*: unknown *Contributors*: -

File:Terminal B, Logan International Airport, Boston.jpg *Source*: http://bibliocm.bibliolabs.com/mwAnon/index.php?title=File:Terminal_B,_Logan_International_Airport,_Boston.jpg *License*: unknown *Contributors*: -

File:Terminal C, Logan International Airport, Boston.jpg *Source*: http://bibliocm.bibliolabs.com/mwAnon/index.php?title=File:Terminal_C,_Logan_International_Airport,_Boston.jpg *License*: unknown *Contributors*: -

File:Terminal E, Logan International Airport, Boston.jpg *Source*: http://bibliocm.bibliolabs.com/mwAnon/index.php?title=File:Terminal_E,_Logan_International_Airport,_Boston.jpg *License*: unknown *Contributors*: -

File:MBTA Blue Line Airport Subway Station.jpg *Source*: http://bibliocm.bibliolabs.com/mwAnon/index.php?title=File:MBTA_Blue_Line_Airport_Subway_Station.jpg *License*: unknown *Contributors*: -

File:MBTA.svg *Source*: http://bibliocm.bibliolabs.com/mwAnon/index.php?title=File:MBTA.svg *License*: unknown *Contributors*: -

Image:Boston Logan International Airport Exit Express.jpg *Source*: http://bibliocm.bibliolabs.com/mwAnon/index.php?title=File:Boston_Logan_International_Airport_Exit_Express.jpg *License*: unknown *Contributors*: -

Image:Boston Logan International Airport Cell Phone Waiting Lot.jpg *Source*: http://bibliocm.bibliolabs.com/mwAnon/index.php?title=File:Boston_Logan_International_Airport_Cell_Phone_Waiting_Lot.jpg *License*: unknown *Contributors*: -

File:MA Route 2A.svg *Source*: http://bibliocm.bibliolabs.com/mwAnon/index.php?title=File:MA_Route_2A.svg *License*: unknown *Contributors*: -

File:Massachusetts Route 2A.png *Source*: http://bibliocm.bibliolabs.com/mwAnon/index.php?title=File:Massachusetts_Route_2A.png *License*: unknown *Contributors*: -

Image:I-91.svg *Source*: http://bibliocm.bibliolabs.com/mwAnon/index.php?title=File:I-91.svg *License*: unknown *Contributors*: -

Image:MA Route 2.svg *Source*: http://bibliocm.bibliolabs.com/mwAnon/index.php?title=File:MA_Route_2.svg *License*: unknown *Contributors*: -

Image:US 202.svg *Source*: http://bibliocm.bibliolabs.com/mwAnon/index.php?title=File:US_202.svg *License*: unknown *Contributors*: -

Image:I-495.svg *Source*: http://bibliocm.bibliolabs.com/mwAnon/index.php?title=File:I-495.svg *License*: unknown *Contributors*: -

Image:MA Route 128.svg *Source*: http://bibliocm.bibliolabs.com/mwAnon/index.php?title=File:MA_Route_128.svg *License*: unknown *Contributors*: -

Image:US 3.svg *Source*: http://bibliocm.bibliolabs.com/mwAnon/index.php?title=File:US_3.svg *License*: unknown *Contributors*: -

Image:MA Route 16.svg *Source*: http://bibliocm.bibliolabs.com/mwAnon/index.php?title=File:MA_Route_16.svg *License*: unknown *Contributors*: -

Image:MA Route 3.svg *Source*: http://bibliocm.bibliolabs.com/mwAnon/index.php?title=File:MA_Route_3.svg *License*: unknown *Contributors*: -

File:MA Route 2.svg *Source*: http://bibliocm.bibliolabs.com/mwAnon/index.php?title=File:MA_Route_2.svg *License*: unknown *Contributors*: -

File:US 3.svg *Source*: http://bibliocm.bibliolabs.com/mwAnon/index.php?title=File:US_3.svg *License*: unknown *Contributors*: -

Image:Eastbound MA Route 2A at the Garden Theater, Greenfield MA.jpg *Source*: http://bibliocm.bibliolabs.com/mwAnon/index.php?title=File:Eastbound_MA_Route_2A_at_the_Garden_Theater,_Greenfield_MA.jpg *License*: unknown *Contributors*: -

File:MA Route 16.svg *Source*: http://bibliocm.bibliolabs.com/mwAnon/index.php?title=File:MA_Route_16.svg *License*: unknown *Contributors*: -

File:Massachusetts_Route_16.png *Source*: http://bibliocm.bibliolabs.com/mwAnon/index.php?title=File:Massachusetts_Route_16.png *License*: unknown *Contributors*: -

Image:MA Route 12.svg *Source*: http://bibliocm.bibliolabs.com/mwAnon/index.php?title=File:MA_Route_12.svg *License*: unknown *Contributors*: -

Image:I-395.svg *Source*: http://bibliocm.bibliolabs.com/mwAnon/index.php?title=File:I-395.svg *License*: unknown *Contributors*: -

Image:MA Route 146.svg *Source*: http://bibliocm.bibliolabs.com/mwAnon/index.php?title=File:MA_Route_146.svg *License*: unknown *Contributors*: -

Image:MA Route 9.svg *Source*: http://bibliocm.bibliolabs.com/mwAnon/index.php?title=File:MA_Route_9.svg *License*: unknown *Contributors*: -

Image:I-90.svg *Source*: http://bibliocm.bibliolabs.com/mwAnon/index.php?title=File:I-90.svg *License*: unknown *Contributors*: -

Image:I-93.svg *Source*: http://bibliocm.bibliolabs.com/mwAnon/index.php?title=File:I-93.svg *License*: unknown *Contributors*: -

Image:MA Route 28.svg *Source*: http://bibliocm.bibliolabs.com/mwAnon/index.php?title=File:MA_Route_28.svg *License*: Public Domain *Contributors*: SPUI, TwinsMetsFan

Image:US 1.svg *Source*: http://bibliocm.bibliolabs.com/mwAnon/index.php?title=File:US_1.svg *License*: unknown *Contributors*: -

Image:MA Route 1A.svg *Source*: http://bibliocm.bibliolabs.com/mwAnon/index.php?title=File:MA_Route_1A.svg *License*: unknown *Contributors*: -

Image:MA Route 60.svg *Source*: http://bibliocm.bibliolabs.com/mwAnon/index.php?title=File:MA_Route_60.svg *License*: unknown *Contributors*: -

File:MA Route 15.svg *Source*: http://bibliocm.bibliolabs.com/mwAnon/index.php?title=File:MA_Route_15.svg *License*: unknown *Contributors*: -

Image:MA Route 96.svg *Source*: http://bibliocm.bibliolabs.com/mwAnon/index.php?title=File:MA_Route_96.svg *License*: unknown *Contributors*: -

Lightning Source UK Ltd.
Milton Keynes UK
UKOW06f1838300713

214644UK00007B/457/P